AF752974

Transactional Perspectives on Occupation

Malcolm P. Cutchin • Virginia A. Dickie
Editors

Transactional Perspectives on Occupation

Springer

Editors
Malcolm P. Cutchin
Department of Allied Health Sciences
Division of Occupational Science
and Occupational Therapy
University of North Carolina at Chapel Hill
Chapel Hill, NC, USA

Virginia A. Dickie
Department of Allied Health Sciences
Division of Occupational Science
and Occupational Therapy
University of North Carolina at Chapel Hill
Chapel Hill, NC, USA

ISBN 978-94-007-4428-8 ISBN 978-94-007-4429-5 (eBook)
DOI 10.1007/978-94-007-4429-5
Springer Dordrecht Heidelberg New York London

Library of Congress Control Number: 2012943051

© Springer Science+Business Media B.V. 2013
This work is subject to copyright. All rights are reserved by the Publisher, whether the whole or part of the material is concerned, specifically the rights of translation, reprinting, reuse of illustrations, recitation, broadcasting, reproduction on microfilms or in any other physical way, and transmission or information storage and retrieval, electronic adaptation, computer software, or by similar or dissimilar methodology now known or hereafter developed. Exempted from this legal reservation are brief excerpts in connection with reviews or scholarly analysis or material supplied specifically for the purpose of being entered and executed on a computer system, for exclusive use by the purchaser of the work. Duplication of this publication or parts thereof is permitted only under the provisions of the Copyright Law of the Publisher's location, in its current version, and permission for use must always be obtained from Springer. Permissions for use may be obtained through RightsLink at the Copyright Clearance Center. Violations are liable to prosecution under the respective Copyright Law.
The use of general descriptive names, registered names, trademarks, service marks, etc. in this publication does not imply, even in the absence of a specific statement, that such names are exempt from the relevant protective laws and regulations and therefore free for general use.
While the advice and information in this book are believed to be true and accurate at the date of publication, neither the authors nor the editors nor the publisher can accept any legal responsibility for any errors or omissions that may be made. The publisher makes no warranty, express or implied, with respect to the material contained herein.

Printed on acid-free paper

Springer is part of Springer Science+Business Media (www.springer.com)

Contents

Chapter 1
Transactional Perspectives on Occupation: An Introduction and Rationale

Malcolm P. Cutchin and Virginia A. Dickie

1.1 Introduction and Invitation

The editors and the contributors to this book have varied histories that have led them to their subject matter. While some of us hold degrees in the social and behavioral sciences with no clinical background, others have at least some of their training in professional and/or doctoral programs directly related to the profession of occupational therapy. Indeed, the state of the emerging discipline of occupational science reflects that dual connection to the clinical concerns of therapists as well as to the sciences and humanities that make up much of academia. The quest for a more solid understanding of the core concept of the new discipline and the profession—occupation—has drawn on various theories and philosophies since the beginning (e.g., Yerxa et al. 1989). While that quest continues, the relatively recent emergence of transactional perspectives on occupation has been notable in that the perspectives challenge some fundamental ways that we have come to think about occupation. Yet those involved in the formation of transactional perspectives have hastened to point out the need for additional development (e.g., Cutchin and Dickie 2012). We believe this book illustrates progress in that development and presents a lively, provocative, and multifaceted dialogue on the topic of transactional perspectives on occupation.

This book invites readers who are already interested in transactional perspectives on occupation, those from occupational therapy or science who want to learn what the perspectives are about, and those from other disciplines who work either on subjects related to the study of occupation or in fields where a transactional perspective may be beneficial. Although defined in numerous ways in the literature, occupations are, most simply put, activities we participate in that engage (occupy) our attention, interests, and/or expectations. Occupations encompass a wide range of

M.P. Cutchin (✉) • V.A. Dickie
Department of Allied Health Sciences, Division of Occupational Science and Occupational Therapy, University of North Carolina at Chapel Hill, Chapel Hill, NC, USA
e-mail: mcutchin@med.unc.edu

M.P. Cutchin and V.A. Dickie (eds.), *Transactional Perspectives on Occupation*,
DOI 10.1007/978-94-007-4429-5_1, © Springer Science+Business Media B.V. 2013

activities, from reading a story to playing a game with others to flying an airplane. We believe that scholars from fields other than occupational therapy and occupational science should be interested in the subject matter of this book. Humans are by nature an active and social species, and occupations cut across all domains of experience and inquiry. The fact that other disciplines do not focus on occupations in this sense might be related to the largely taken-for-granted status of such activity. Why should a scholar or researcher care, for example, about the way a grandmother takes daily strolls around her neighborhood? Our particular view on the things that we do—through the transactional perspectives articulated in various ways in this book—both implicitly and explicitly suggests that occupations are forms of activity that create and re-create a multitude of our relationships with the worlds we experience. The precursors, internal dynamics, and outcomes of occupations are thus central to understanding experience, social development, and human well-being (and to a large extent the well-being of our ecosystem). Indeed, the possible connections between transactional perspectives on occupation and other disciplines are many.

1.2 Development of Transactional Perspectives on Occupation

The primary basis for transactional perspectives on occupation is the philosophical movement known as pragmatism. More specifically, the work of American philosopher John Dewey, the most well-known and influential pragmatist of the twentieth century, has been the well-spring of most transactional thinking in occupational science. And, as several authors within this text note, the concept of occupation as used here also comes from Dewey. We have elsewhere traced much of the development of the transactional perspective (Cutchin and Dickie 2012). Moreover, many of the following chapters do a splendid job of laying out the perspective. Therefore, we will provide a relatively selective and succinct summary here.

Dewey's career was one dedicated to the unification and extension of key arguments and themes developed by the major pragmatists who had preceded him, Peirce and James (Margolis 2009a). Among those themes are a holistic form of naturalism; an account of the continuity of humans and their environments as well as between past, present, and future in experience; the flux, contingency, and uncertainty of experience; the avoidance of conceptual dualisms; and recognition of the fallibility of knowledge and its implications (Alexander 2009; Cutchin 2008; Margolis 2009a). Particularly important for Dewey's later unification of many of these themes was his conception of the "indeterminate situation" which becomes the energizing force in human thought/action (Margolis 2009a). These themes are fully a part of the transactional perspective on occupation.

Dewey's theory of action, which is fully integrated into this philosophical worldview and especially pertinent to the concept of occupation, is an important part of his philosophy. While this has become known as *transaction* within the occupational science literature, the term itself was not commonly used by Dewey until late in his career (e.g., Dewey and Bentley 1949). Dewey had provided an account of action that was consistent with transaction as early as 1896. Alexander explains the core of Dewey's concept of transaction as it was argued in Dewey's 1896 article:

> In place of the "reflex arc" that James himself had used, in which the older dualism of body and soul is replaced by the "dualism of stimulus and response," Dewey proposes a model of a "circuit of coordination" in which both stimulus and response emerge as phases of "divisions of labor" in the ongoing adjustment of a living creature with its environment. For example, by the reflex arc model, a child receives the "stimulus" of the light of a candle and has the "response" of reaching for it. This is followed by the "stimulus" of being burned and then by the "response" of withdrawal of the hand. Dewey regarded this as "a patchwork of disjointed parts." Instead, by the model of the circuit of coordination, the child is an organism already dynamically engaged with her environment; she is a center of activity, who *focuses* on the candle as an object of interest and who *reaches* toward it in a gesture of *grasping*. The burn is thus felt as the *outcome* or *meaning* of the act so that an experience of learning takes place. The "seeing" and the "reaching" mutually influence each other in a continuous pattern of sensori-motor coordination and not in a linear relation of cause and effect; an expanding process of learning and refinement of meaning replaces a series of discrete acts (Alexander 2009, pp. 187–188, emphasis in the original).

Dewey's later work wove a much richer conceptual tapestry from these central strands of the transactional argument. In particular, the role of the social, cultural, and moral components of action (especially in the form of habits) came to be seen as an essential part of understanding human experience in an uncertain, fluctuating world (Garrison 2002; Cutchin 2007, 2008). Researchers in occupational science have more frequently utilized the more expansive version of Dewey's transactional theory. And while that is also the case in this volume, we suggest that it is important to understand the original, core elements of Dewey's transactional thinking and how radical it was for its time. From what we see in the sciences related to occupation, it remains a radical and significantly innovative position on action and occupation.

Dewey's influence waned during the mid-twentieth century and then underwent a revival. Not long after the resurgence of interest in Dewey's work in philosophy and the social sciences during the 1980s and 1990s, Cutchin began to utilize Dewey in a series of geographical and gerontological studies (e.g., Cutchin 1997, 1999, 2001, 2003). By 2001, Cutchin was working in an academic department of occupational therapy and began to critique prevailing views of occupation, specifically the understanding of person-environment relationships in theorizations of occupation (Cutchin 2004). During the same period, Dickie's (1996, 1998, 2003a, b, 2004) work on the occupations of craft production and marketing and quilt-making led her to question the dominant view of occupation as an individualized act. The collaboration of Cutchin and Dickie to develop a perspective on occupation that would overcome those fundamental problems was joined by Humphry, who had similar concerns with the notion of children's occupations within the child development literature (Humphry 2005). The result was the first thorough accounting of occupation as a transactional phenomenon from a substantially theorized, Deweyan perspective (Dickie et al. 2006). The primary goal of those initial efforts was to recast thinking about occupation in a way that would overcome the limitations of overly dualistic, individualized (decontextualized), linear, and mechanistic theories.

Since that publication, those authors and others have been working to flesh out the transactional argument regarding occupation by extending the perspective in new directions (Aldrich 2011; Aldrich and Callanan 2011; Hooper 2011; Kuo 2011), connecting and contrasting the viewpoint with other perspectives (Aldrich 2008; Cutchin et al. 2008; Rudman 2010), and using the perspective in empirical work (Brorsson et al. 2011; Dickie 2010; Erikson et al. 2010; Frank 2010; Heatwole Shank and Cutchin 2010; Johansson et al 2009; Rosenberg et al. 2011). More recently, we called for attention to root metaphors of Dewey's pragmatic attitude as a way to achieve more from those efforts (Cutchin and Dickie 2012). Among those metaphors are growth, criticism, inquiry, community, and responsibility. These metaphors help to understand transactive processes of occupation as more than just the action itself. This is consistent with Dewey's work—his publications and social involvement that focused on action as a means to improve individual capabilities as well as broader human affairs. We see those metaphors and the broader pragmatic attitude implemented in various ways in the chapters that follow.

The "transactional perspective" on occupation is probably a better term for this theoretical movement rather than "transactionalism." Rather than codify boundaries of the emerging view with the "ism" suffix, we think this book suggests that the word perspective*s* (plural emphasized) more suitably emphases the acceptable variety of authors' interpretation of Dewey's work and the use of core themes and concepts. In addition to the pragmatic and Deweyan themes noted above, the focus on relations that connect person with context and enable occupation is a notable feature. That part of the perspective is closely related to Dewey's opposition to dualisms, such as subject-object distinctions. Furthermore, occupation is seen as an important form of "functional coordination" (Garrison 2001) of person and world. Functional coordination relies on Dewey's theory of habit. A fundamental part of all action, the ongoing use of a complex array of interpenetrating habits (which are both subconscious and creative in their operation) derives from the socio-cultural and environmental dimensions of humans' experience (Cutchin 2007; Cutchin et al. 2008). The relational, coordinative, and habitual are joined with a view of occupation as an integrated part of ongoing action to understand the way in which people experience and reconstruct situations as centers of action. Meanings, learning, growth, morals and social improvement stem from those dimensions as important parts of occupation in the transactional perspective.

1.3 A Pluralistic Approach

There is a commitment to pluralism in pragmatism, beginning in James and carried on by Dewey (Stuhr 2003; Margolis 2009b). In Dewey's case, his strong sense of the potential in democratic life and the need for reconstruction of social institutions to enhance social experience is perhaps the best example of his commitment to pluralism. Yet Stuhr made an argument for a more thoroughly pluralistic pragmatism that is not only more fully engaged with experience but also engaged with other philosophies, such as postmodern varieties. Others have suggested a need for greater examination of how pragmatism might be usefully informed by particular types of phenomenology (Margolis 1998). Indeed, early in the emergence of the transactional perspective on occupation, Barber (2006) critiqued the perspective from the view of phenomenology and "first-person" accounts of occupation. Cutchin et al. (2006) responded that there was some significant incommensurability between the two views but that possibilities of linking phenomenological and transactional perspectives on occupation existed. Until this volume, however, there has been little done along those lines. Moreover, this volume also begins a dialogue between Deweyan positions on occupation and those of postmodern philosophy, in this case, Foucault.

Other forms of pluralism exist within this book. Among the authors, there are 4 from Canada, 5 from New Zealand, 1 from Australia, 4 from Sweden, 1 from Norway, and 11 from the United States. Such relatively widespread representation of the transactional perspective on occupation is notable for at least two reasons. First, the theoretical traditions and orientations toward occupation are different from region to region—occupational science is not uniform across those countries. Second, pragmatism is native to the United States and has not found nearly as much exposure outside the United States. The fact that some top scholars in the field of occupational science within these varied academic cultures have contributed chapters here speaks well of the ideas' potential to diffuse further and have more impact on how various scholars and practitioners think. We believe this process will enrich the conceptualization of occupation as transaction.

As mentioned at the outset of this introduction, the academic background of the editors and contributors also demonstrates a form of pluralism. Cutchin has a Ph.D. in geography while Dickie's is in anthropology. Several contributors have doctorates in sociology, anthropology, and human development and another is completing a Ph.D. in education. Others have doctorate degrees or are pursing doctorates in degrees in occupational therapy or occupational science. The diversity of training and experience of the authors has provided the basis for a collection of chapters that cover much territory within the purview of transactional perspectives on occupation.

1.4 Structure and Content of the Book

We have organized the tour through this intellectual territory with a logic in mind. To us, the contributions fall into four groups that we have organized into the following parts: (I) Theoretical Extensions, (II) Case Studies, (III) Methodological Implications, and (IV) Applications. We see this as a logical sequence for reading the book because the first part contains what are relatively more in-depth theoretical discussions of larger themes within the general transactional perspective. That is a good foundation from which to read about case studies in which authors have used more specific guiding concepts or taken up particular issues well-suited to the transactional perspective. Methodological implications, which are applicable across a range of research contexts, provide a different set of arguments for what the transactional perspective means for conducting inquiry. And the final part on applications introduces a set of chapters about the more real-world meaning of transactional perspectives in the realms of education and practice. The last two parts are particularly innovative in the context of the transactional occupation literature. To date, most publications on the topic have been theoretical or case studies of some type. Very little work on methods, education, or practice has been produced. The primary organizational logic is that educational scaffolding can be achieved if one reads the book in this order. Of course, individual chapters may stand out for their particular interest based on the reader's familiarity with the topic or intellectual needs.

In Part I, Theoretical Extensions, there are five chapters that extend previous theoretical efforts on transactional perspectives on occupation. While there are significant theoretical contributions in chapters in each of the other parts, the chapters included in the first part make more focused and substantive theoretical arguments. Aldrich and Cutchin (Chap. 2) begin the part by digging deeper into the work of Dewey to create additional utilities of his transactional perspective for theorizing occupation. The focus is on Dewey's sense of embodiment as well as his concept of growth. The authors trace Dewey's concept of occupation and its significance when considered in light of the other two concepts. The next two chapters provide comparative analyses of Heideggerian and Deweyan perspectives on occupation. Wright-St Clair and Smythe (Chap. 3) take a fresh look through a Deweyan perspective at an interpretive phenomenological analysis of the everyday occupations of older people in New Zealand. They compare and contrast Heidegger's and Dewey's theoretical analyses of the habitual, the relational (temporal and social/physical), and the precarious. In doing so, they note how each view complements the other and that a transactional perspective adds important insights to a phenomenological perspective. Reed and Hocking (Chap. 4) focus on the meanings of everyday occupation, and compare and contrast Heideggerian and Deweyan theorizations. Using empirical data to exemplify differences, they note how a Heideggarian focus on the horizon of meaning (where the past and present meet) whereas a Deweyan view of meaning is oriented toward the imagination of future outcomes from action. They note that both views extend previous research by putting the understanding of meaning fully with the contexts in which it arises, but they also suggest that the transactional perspective helps to bring the complexity of meaning into greater relief. Rudman and Huot (Chap. 5) attend to a need for a better analysis of power relations at the heart of situations and offer two theoretical approaches that are compatible with transactional perspectives. One is critical discourse theory and more specifically the governmentality literature's use of them. The other is the theory of practice developed by Bourdieu. Alsaker and Josephsson (Chap. 6) complete the part by complimenting and extending the transactional perspective with the use of Ricoeur's theory of narrative-in-action. Based on an analysis of women with chronic conditions, the authors examine the fluidity and emergence of everyday occupations. Because the authors view occupations as taking place in local cultures, they suggest that Ricoeur's theory is a useful way to access complex transactions of everyday occupations.

The second part of the book, Case Studies, collects chapters that take on more specific issues or concepts relevant to occupation and use particular case studies to do so. While also utilizing theory to make sense of their subject matter, these chapters more clearly emphasize the use of transactional perspectives for particular scholarly problems. Nayar and Hocking (Chap. 7) begin the part with an analysis of the immigration, settlement, and acculturation process and the role occupation plays within it. Based on a case study of South Asian immigrants to New Zealand, they find that a transactional perspective using the concepts of habit and situation improves the understanding provided by more traditional approaches. Their analysis leads to recommendations for policy to make settlement and acculturation processes easier for immigrants. Stone (Chap. 8) takes up the problem of how scholars have understood disability. In her assessment, based on several case studies, she asserts that a transactional perspective on the person-situation relationship is an important enhancement to understanding disability. Moreover, Stone illustrates that the transactional perspective is compatible with symbolic interactionist, critical disability studies, and social model understandings of disability. Johansson, Cutchin and Lilja (Chap. 9) use a case study of older adults receiving home modifications in Sweden to illustrate the utility of transactional perspectives. Using the concepts of problematic situation and place integration, the authors unpack the complex, dynamic, and ongoing process of negotiating home modifications. They conclude that the place integration perspective can inform intervention design and implementation. Wicks (Chap. 10) develops a case study of the Berry Men's Shed in Australia. Shedding, a relatively new occupation that is growing across Australia, is shown as a transactional and transformational occupation. Wicks illustrates the holistic and dynamic character of shedding and how it links and affects individuals and community in positive ways. Holahan, Ray and Dickie (Chap. 11) conclude the part with an analysis of the consultant role of two therapists working within an academic setting and a state educational system. Using the concept of functional coordination as a primary mode of understanding the consultants work, the authors show the ongoing challenges of having to coordinate the various elements and dynamics of emerging work situations. They also display the power in managing situational relations well and how the transactional view makes that power more readily apparent.

Part III presents four chapters that provide insights into methodological implications of transactional perspectives. These contributions are innovative in the sense that little work has been done on the methodological implications of transactional perspectives. We have argued that a transactional perspective builds a rich *understanding* of occupation but few if any have examined how the perspective might inform the process of discovery itself. Rosenberg and Johansson (Chap. 12) provide an argument that the Deweyan situation offers a unit of analysis for research on occupational topics. They draw from research studies on adaptive technology and home modifications for older people to show how a situational focus can be advantageous. Moreover, they suggest particular strategies along with this focus for such research. Bailliard, Aldrich and Dickie (Chap. 13) also employ the concept of situation, but they focus on the ability of ethnography to understand occupational situations. The authors use a study of discouraged workers in a rural community and a study of the occupations of Latino immigrants in a small town to support their contention that ethnography is a natural fit with transactional thinking. The authors discuss the advantages of ethnography to understand such situations as well as the transactional character of doing ethnography. Rudman (Chap. 14) also focuses on situational knowledge production, but she presents critical discourse analysis as a preferred approach. Particularly useful for analyzing the political and power dimensions of situations and occupations, Rudman explains the theory and practice of critical discourse analysis. Along the way, she argues that the method can enhance transactional perspectives by allowing analysts to see how power is implemented in the construction of occupational possibilities within situations and how the outcomes vary for those within the situation. Heatwole Shank (Chap. 15) presents a nuanced argument about the relationship of Deweyan philosophy and mixed methods designs. She reviews the major arguments for and against the relationship between pragmatism and mixed methods. Her conclusion is that we can move beyond those arguments by realizing that some fundamental tenants of Dewey's pragmatism provide a rationale for, not just a justification of, mixed methods research. She suggests how this might work in studies of occupation and community.

The final part presents four chapters on applications of transactional perspectives to education and practice. In the first chapter in this part, Coppola (Chap. 16) offers an in-depth view of Dewey's philosophy and educational theory and reveals the transactional basis of his pedagogical ideas. Tying together Dewey's emphasis on the social basis of learning, habits, and the conditions (situation) of classroom learning, Coppola then provides examples from her own pedagogic experience. Her argument concludes with an assessment of what this means for education about occupation. Humphry and Wakeford (Chap. 17) take on the challenge of how to educate students for professions like occupational therapy so that they can engage with transactional processes in their practice. They use the problem of practice with young children and illustrate a series of steps used to enable new practitioners to accomplish that goal. Their approach gives primacy to encouraging critical analysis of existing views, explicating transactional concepts, and scaffolding to build on new knowledge. In her contribution, Frank (Chap. 18) focuses on the issue of occupations in Latin America and efforts intended to engender them. She suggests how the process of globalization and its ills create problematic situations for occupation in places like Guatemala. Marshaling the pragmatist concern for (and history of) progressive reform, she illustrates the parallels and promise in three NGOs in Guatemala. Finally, Thibeault (Chap. 19), with the support of years of experience in developing countries, presents a more cautious assessment of working to improve the occupational situation of those who are less advantaged than the people who have come to help them. Underlining how belief in one's (an outsider's) ability to solve problems can cause more harm than good, Thibeault argues that, consistent with Dewey's vision for criticism and responsibility, a focus on community empowerment and inclusion in occupational justice efforts is a better approach. Suggesting principles for such encounters, Thibeault concludes that there is great potential for occupational therapists engaged in community development work if approached properly.

1.5 Our Hopes

Dewey's pragmatism and the transactional perspective are optimistic points of view. Although they do not solve social problems theoretically or practically, they give us a method of inquiry—through the concepts and analysis they enable—to act in order to make a better world. And while not critical enough in orientation for some, Dewey (1929) argued that critical analysis of our situations was an obligation of scholars. We have suggested that the transactional perspective was introduced into occupational science through the desire to find a better course to understand occupation. Yet it is only through ongoing critical dialogue among adherents and critics that we will continue to develop this viewpoint on occupation. This book intends to stimulate more of that type of dialogue and inquiry. We hope that you will find some aspect of the text that makes you want to join in the shared transactional process.

References

Aldrich, R. M. (2008). From complexity theory to transactionalism: Moving occupational science forward in theorizing the complexities of behavior. *Journal of Occupational Science, 15*, 147–156.

Aldrich, R. M. (2011). A review and critique of well-being in occupational therapy and occupational science. *Scandinavia Journal of Occupational Therapy, 18*, 93–100.

Aldrich, R. M., & Callanan, Y. (2011). Insights about researching discouraged workers. *Journal of Occupational Science, 18*, 153–166.

Alexander, T. M. (2009). Dewey, dualism, and naturalism. In J. R. Shook & J. Margolis (Eds.), *A companion to pragmatism* (pp. 184–192). Chichester: Blackwell.

Barber, M. (2006). Occupational science and the first-person perspective. *Journal of Occupational Science, 13*, 94–96.

Brorsson, A., Öhman, A., Lundberg, S., & Nygård, L. (2011). Accessibility in public space as perceived by people with Alzheimer's disease. *Dementia*. doi:10.1177/1471301211415314.

Cutchin, M. P. (1997). Physician retention in rural communities: The perspective of experiential place integration. *Health & Place, 3*, 25–41.

Cutchin, M. P. (1999). Qualitative explorations in health geography: Using pragmatism and related concepts as guides. *The Professional Geographer, 51*, 265–274.

Cutchin, M. P. (2001). Deweyan integration: Moving beyond place attachment in elderly migration theory. *International Journal of Aging & Human Development, 52*, 29–44.

Cutchin, M. P. (2003). The process of mediated aging-in-place: A theoretically and empirically-based model. *Social Science & Medicine, 57*, 1077–1090.

Cutchin, M. P. (2004). Using Deweyan philosophy to rename and reframe adaptation-to-environment. *American Journal of Occupational Therapy, 58*, 303–312.

Cutchin, M. P. (2007). From society to self (and back) through place: Habit in transactional context. *OTJR: Occupation, Participation, and Health, 27*, 50S–59S.

Cutchin, M. P. (2008). John Dewey's metaphysical ground-map and its implications for geographical inquiry. *Geoforum, 39*, 1555–1565.

Cutchin, M. P., & Dickie, V. (2012). Transactionalism: Occupational science and the pragmatic attitude. In G. Whiteford & C. Hocking (Eds.), *Critical perspectives on occupational science: Society, inclusion, participation* (pp. 23–37). London: Wiley.

Cutchin, M. P., Dickie, V., & Humphry, R. (2006). Transaction versus interpretation, or transaction and interpretation? A response to Michael Barber. *Journal of Occupational Science, 13*(1), 97–99.

Cutchin, M. P., Aldrich, R. M., Bailliard, A., & Coppola, S. (2008). Action theories for occupational science: The contributions of Dewey and Bourdieu. *Journal of Occupational Science, 15*, 157–165.
Dewey, J. (1896). The reflex arc concept in psychology. *Psychological Review, 3*, 357–370.
Dewey, J. (1929). *Experience and nature*. La Salle: Open Court.
Dewey, J., & Bentley, A. (1949). *Knowing and the known*. Boston: Beacon.
Dickie, V. (1996). Craft production in Detroit: Spatial, temporal, and social relations of work in the home. *Journal of Occupational Science: Australia, 3*, 65–71.
Dickie, V. (1998). Households, multiple livelihoods, and the informal economy: A study of American crafters. *Scandinavian Journal of Occupational Therapy, 5*, 109–118.
Dickie, V. (2003a). Establishing worker identity: A study of people in craftwork. *American Journal of Occupational Therapy, 57*, 250–261.
Dickie, V. (2003b). The role of learning in quilt making. *Journal of Occupational Science, 10*, 120–129.
Dickie, V. (2004). From drunkard's path to Kansas cyclones: Discovering creativity inside the blocks. *Journal of Occupational Science, 11*, 51–57.
Dickie, V. A. (2010). Are occupations 'processes too complicated to explain'? What we can learn by trying. *Journal of Occupational Science, 17*, 195–203.
Dickie, V., Cutchin, M. P., & Humphry, R. (2006). Occupation as transactional experience: A critique of individualism in occupational science. *Journal of Occupational Science, 13*, 83–93.
Erikson, A., Park, M., & Tham, K. (2010). Place integration through daily activities 1 year after stroke. *OTJR: Occupation, Participation & Health, 30*, 68–77.
Frank, G. (2010). The transactional relationship between occupation and place: Indigenous cultures in the American Southwest. *Journal of Occupational Science, 18*, 3–20.
Garrison, J. (2001). An introduction to Dewey's theory of functional "trans-action": An alternative paradigm for activity theory. *Mind, Culture, and Activity, 8*, 275–296.
Garrison, J. (2002). Habits as social tools in context. *Occupational Therapy Journal of Research, 22*, 11S–17S.
Heatwole Shank, K., & Cutchin, M. P. (2010). Transactional occupations of older women aging in place: Negotiating change and meaning. *Journal of Occupational Science, 17*, 4–13.
Hooper, B. (2011). The occupation of teaching: Elements of meaning portrayed through educators' teaching diagrams. *Journal of Occupational Science, 18*, 167–181.
Humphry, R. (2005). Model of processes transforming occupations: Exploring societal and social influences. *Journal of Occupational Science, 12*, 27–35.
Johansson, K., Josephsson, S., & Lilja, M. (2009). Creating possibilities for action in the presence of environmental barriers in the process of ageing in place. *Ageing and Society, 29*, 49–70.
Kuo, A. (2011). A transactional view: Occupation as a means to create experiences that matter. *Journal of Occupational Science, 18*, 131–138.
Margolis, J. (1998). Dewey in dialogue with continental philosophy. In L. Hickman (Ed.), *Reading Dewey: Interpretations for a postmodern generation* (pp. 231–256). Bloomington: Indiana University Press.
Margolis, J. (2009a). Introduction: Pragmatism, retrospective and prospective. In J. R. Shook & J. Margolis (Eds.), *A companion to pragmatism* (pp. 1–10). Chichester: Blackwell.
Margolis, J. (2009b). Pluralism, relativism, and historicism. In J. R. Shook & J. Margolis (Eds.), *A companion to pragmatism* (pp. 239–248). Chichester: Blackwell.
Rosenberg, L., Kottorp, A., & Nygård, L. (2011). Readiness for technology use with people with dementia: The perspectives of significant others. *Journal of Applied Gerontology*. doi:10.1177/0733464810396873.
Rudman, D. (2010). Occupational possibilities. *Journal of Occupational Science, 17*(1), 55–59.
Stuhr, J. J. (2003). *Pragmatism, postmodernism, and the future of philosophy*. New York: Routledge.
Yerxa, E., Clark, F., Frank, G., Jackson, J., Parham, D., Pierce, D., et al. (1989). An introduction to occupational science, a foundation for occupational therapy in the 21st century. In J. A. Johnson & E. J. Yerxa (Eds.), *Occupational science: The foundation for new models of practice* (pp. 1–17). Binghamton: Haworth Press.

Part I
Theoretical Extensions

Chapter 2
Dewey's Concepts of Embodiment, Growth, and Occupation: Extended Bases for a Transactional Perspective

Rebecca M. Aldrich and Malcolm P. Cutchin

2.1 Introduction

The transactional view of occupation is derived mainly from the philosophical work of John Dewey and those who interpret and translate him. While much of the early work by transaction-oriented occupational scientists focused on Dewey's metaphysics of action (i.e., transactionalism), scholars (such as the editors of this book) have outlined more detailed theorizations of occupation that draw from other key ideas in Dewey's oeuvre (Cutchin and Dickie 2012). Because Dewey wrote broadly about many types of problems—ones in academic thought as well as those concerning the world in which he lived—he generated many concepts that are ripe for more detailed analysis. In this chapter, we take up Dewey's concepts of embodiment and growth as key notions for understanding occupation. Our use of these two ideas is necessarily extended to other dimensions of Dewey's philosophy, such as democracy, freedom, and the situation. Yet, in our view, his positions on embodiment and growth add especially important conceptual bases for theorizing occupation: theories built on these bases concurrently place people in the natural and social world as well as in a constant process of becoming something new and improved.

A narrative about Dewey's view of embodiment and growth by itself would be a sufficient contribution to the literature. The story we present includes a twist, however, that helps make the case for embodiment and growth more relevant. Rarely, if ever, have theorists of "occupation" used Dewey's own work on that concept to inform occupational science and therapy. This is a noteworthy gap in the literature,

R.M. Aldrich (✉)
Department of Occupational Science and Occupational Therapy, St. Louis University, St. Louis, MO, USA
e-mail: raldrich@slu.edu

M.P. Cutchin
Department of Allied Health Sciences, Division of Occupational Science and Occupational Therapy, University of North Carolina at Chapel Hill, Chapel Hill, NC, USA

M.P. Cutchin and V.A. Dickie (eds.), *Transactional Perspectives on Occupation*,
DOI 10.1007/978-94-007-4429-5_2, © Springer Science+Business Media B.V. 2013

including the emerging literature on transactional occupation. Therefore, after our discussion of embodiment and growth, we take up Dewey's portrayal of occupation and weave it into the narrative in order to compose a stronger case for the relevance of the aforementioned concepts. The inclusion of Dewey's notion of occupation allows us to build a stronger tie between the central concern of occupational scientists and therapists and the Deweyan philosophical position. With this triad of concepts—embodiment, growth, and occupation—we begin to highlight additional layers of significance within the transactional perspective on occupation.

2.2 Embodiment

To speak of the body in the health sciences is to speak of a physical form: a corporeal, fixed object encapsulating organs, bones, and the mind. Implicit in this idea of the body is the idea of separation, of an individual figure whose shape and contents are restricted and apart from the rest of the world. The body is an object or thing that can be understood through mechanics and biochemistry. While this tack is not surprising given the aims of health sciences (remediation of ills through a focus on bodily problems), it is not always helpful in developing understandings about humans as active, social beings. When the body is viewed only as a physical container for the human being, it becomes challenging to deal with the non-physical features of human life. For example, the question of how culture and environment affect the body arises only when the body's separation from the world is taken as a starting point.

As we explain in the following sections, a transactional view of the body replaces a focus on separate form with one on the *process of embodying*, and this focus has direct links to Dewey's ideas about the democratic nature of associated living. Dewey's views of individuality, function, uncertainty, and growth coalesce to form a processual conception of embodiment, making the human a "live creature" who lives *through* (and by virtue of) non-bodily aspects of the world (Campbell 1995; Dewey 1980; Kestenbaum 1977). This further implies that human occupation, as a function of the process of embodiment, ultimately turns on the democratic conditions fostered by associated living.

2.2.1 *Live Creatures*

The usage of "live creature" by Dewey was not just metaphorical. His philosophy, including his argument for transaction, was part of his broader argument for a holistic sense of "experience" in any investigation of human life and its problems (Cutchin 1997). More than that, however, Dewey wanted to stress *experience and nature*, and he titled what is perhaps his most important book exactly that (Dewey 2000). For Dewey, naturalism was the bedrock for thinking about human experience. As live creatures, nature is our origin and our medium for experience. Indeed, in his late work with Bentley (Dewey and Bentley 1949), Dewey suggested the term "organism-in-the-environment-as-a-whole" as a way to indicate the interpenetration of organism and environment as well as their ongoing coordination in an unstable world. Dewey also wrote

> Life denotes a function, a comprehensive activity, in which organism and environment are included. Only upon reflective analysis does it break up into external conditions—air breathed, food taken, ground walked upon—and internal structures—lungs respiring, stomach digesting, legs walking (Dewey 1989, p. 11).

As we shall see, this organic and ecological perspective includes much more than what some have suggested is an argument for the equivalence of humans and lower order animals (Barber 2006; Cutchin et al. 2006).

Organisms of any type are embodied entities. Humans act because they must coordinate with their environment to survive and thrive, like any other live creatures. This coordination, of which we will say more below, is the basis of both experience and Dewey's understanding of action as transaction. In other words, experiences happen because of the ongoing need to coordinate with environments, and at the heart of those experiences and coordination is action that stems from interpenetrating, co-constituted entities (Sullivan 2001). Commenting on the stimulus–response "arc" concept in psychology, Dewey (1998) argued that even though we are embodied organisms "the so-called response [of the organism] is not merely *to* the stimulus, it is *into* it…the 'stimulus' emerges out of this co-ordination" (p. 4). Dewey's point is that the relationship of environment and embodied organism is a continuous one based in the active relationship maintained by the necessity of coordination. Shannon Sullivan (2001) offered an even more fluid interpretation of this coordination by suggesting that bodies are activities [or parts of them] that we live through.

Bodies are products of their environmental transactions from the beginning of life. An important distinction between human bodies and those of other organisms, however, is that human transactions are based on relations with environmental aspects that are particular to human existence. The environment with which a human body transacts is not only comprised by nature as we tend to think of it: the social and cultural dimensions of environments also have particularly powerful roles in the process of embodiment. In this view, bodies become inscribed by their communities in particular ways. We are individuals by the collective set of circumstances—and thus experiences—that shape our process of embodiment. In effect, we come to *embody our communities* through their social and cultural character (Cutchin 2007). As we explain shortly, for humans, the role of the social and the cultural on the body are firmly established through habits. Such habits give us the ability to act not only in response to environmental challenges but also in order to prepare for the future or to modify the environment.

2.2.2 Embodying the Social

A primary thrust of Dewey's overall philosophy involved discrediting false dualisms like the opposition of the individual and society (Alexander 2009). Rather than reify this distinction in his conception of the individual, Dewey (1962) characterized individuality as a product of the associated living that characterizes human experience. For Dewey (1927), "there is no sense in asking how individuals come to be associated" (p. 23). Humans are born into social experience: to speak of a human as if he or she lives in isolation does not make sense because human life begins with the parent-offspring association (Boisvert 1998). Dewey took the associated nature of human life as an undeniable fact, but he did not discard the notion of the individual in doing so. Instead of asserting human individuality as a product of bodily separation, Dewey (1927) defined the individual as "a distinctive way of behaving in conjunction and connection with other distinctive ways of acting" (p. 188). He argued that humans both start and become social via action: humans learn to act based on others' actions, yet they also learn that actions have consequences by watching the effects of action in society. This ability to reflect upon the consequences of action occurs through language, which enables humans to assign and transmit meanings about the outcomes of action. Thus, although humans appear to be individuals because they exist in separate forms, humans are only individuals insofar as they are associated, for the acts that individuate and define humans are only distinct in comparison to other human acts.

Making sense of Dewey's approach to the individual as a process of embodiment requires delving into certain aspects of his theory of action. Cutchin et al. (2008) discussed in detail the relationship of habit and context in Dewey's action theory. For Dewey (2008), habits are mental and physical "ways of using and incorporating the environment" (p. 15), and society, as part of the environment, is both a source and function of habit. Associated living provides the "objective conditions" of individual habit formation and "determines the channels within which [habit] operates" (Dewey 1927, p. 160), but associated living is also sustained through the maintenance of shared habits across society. The relationship of habit and context is characterized in terms of function and is foundational to the idea of transaction: "humans *functionally coordinate* their habit configurations to foster harmonious, balanced transactions with the environment" (emphasis in original) (Cutchin et al. 2008, p. 159). In other words, humans transact with the conditions of associated living (Campbell 1995; Kestenbaum 1977), negotiating their use and adoption of habits to promote a harmonious, functional experience. Dewey (2000) wrote that "the issue of living depends upon the art with which these things are adjusted to each other" (p. 76), and he argued that reflection upon action provided the means for such adjustment.

The need to reflect upon the functional coordination of habits arises in response to the inherent uncertainty in the world. The idea of uncertainty enjoys a celebrated place in Dewey's philosophy: rather than explaining away uncertainty because of the problem it poses for predicting human behavior, Dewey embraced uncertainty as a part of experience that yielded possibilities for human growth. For Dewey (2000), the dynamic uncertainty of experience creates problematic situations in which humans' habits cease to functionally coordinate with the environment. To resume function, humans must engage in a process of inquiry about their habits using "dramatic rehearsal" in the imagination, testing and eventually selecting possible solutions (Fesmire 2003). The process of inquiry that humans apply in response to problematic situations is itself a habit generated via associated living (Boisvert 1998) and is key to the survival of human beings. Because processes, relations, and change are universal to human life (Dewey 1957), humans need a means for addressing the uncertainty that accompanies changing, processual experience. The ultimate goal of inquiry—the resolution of problematic situations—leads to growth (Dewey 2000), which Dewey posits as the primary goal in experience.

2.3 Growth

To fully understand the importance of growth and its relation to embodiment and occupation, it is important to define Dewey's conceptions of freedom and equality. As with Dewey's position on individuality, these conceptions differ slightly from more mainstream understandings of the terms. Dewey rejected the idea that people exist as free and equal individuals prior to their involvement in associated living (Boisvert 1998). Based on his ideas about the relationship of individuals and society, he defined freedom as a person's power to act within the conduits outlined by his or her habits. Rather than constituting an escape from external constraints, this position equates freedom to "that secure release and fulfillment of personal potentialities which takes places only in rich and manifold association with others: the power to be an individualized self making a distinctive contribution and enjoying in its own way the fruits of association" (Dewey 1927, p. 150). Specifically, Dewey (2008) described freedom as

> ...efficiency in action, ability to carry out plans, the absence of cramping and thwarting obstacles; capacity to vary plans, to change the course of action, to experience novelties; and signif[ying] the power of desire and choice to be factors in events (p. 203).

Thus, freedom enables people to use their particular embodied habits to functionally coordinate with situations, and association becomes the "very condition" of freedom because we "appreciate others as individuals who have grown out of unique conditions and transactions, and also hav[e] unique possibilities for future growth and development" (Pappas 2008, p. 225).

Intimately connected to this concept of freedom is Dewey's (1927) idea of equality as "effective regard for whatever is distinctive and unique in each" (p. 151). Rather than implying identity or sameness, this conceptualization holds that all people have equal potential to realize their individual capacities through associated living. People develop different capacities based on their embodied habits and the situations with which they transact, all of which occurs as a result of associated living. Therefore, associated living is also a condition of equality because living with others reveals the need for multiple values to accommodate the variety of peoples' capacities (Boisvert 1998; Pappas 2008). Equality "denotes the unhampered share which each individual member of the community has in the consequences of associated action" (Dewey 1927, p. 150) and "implies both the recognition and encouragement of uniqueness" (Boisvert 1998, p. 7) in individual occupation. Freedom, viewed as the potential to realize one's best possible relationship with the world, cannot exist without an idea of equality that supports people's distinct development of their habit-funded capacities.

With these understandings of freedom and equality in mind, Dewey's notion of growth connects directly to the way people embody habits and function. In writing that "freedom for an individual means growth" (Dewey 1957, p. 207), Dewey characterized growth as "the continual flowering and actualizing of possibilities" and "genuine contingency and contextuality" in experience (Boisvert 1998, pp. 59–60). In contrast to more common understandings of growth as an increase in some capacity or feature, Dewey defines growth as unending opportunities to freely embody and function in concert with an always changing and uncertain situation. In other words, growth results from the process of freely and equally embodying habits, skills, and knowledge based on transactional experiences in the world. Such experiences are part of being a "live creature" trying to survive and thrive. Those powers of embodying include imagination—which is fueled by the moral and the aesthetic modes of thinking.

What does this have to do with understandings about the body? A Deweyan perspective views the body as the locus of these processes of habit formation, reflection, and function. It is the place where the conditions of associated living are experienced and taken on, where different ways of acting are reflected upon, tried out, and executed. It is the vehicle through which growth occurs in uncertain experiences, provided that conditions of freedom and equality exist. Taken together, these concepts suggest an emphasis on the social foundations and functions of the body that is largely absent in the health sciences. Sullivan (2002) underscored the problematic nature of views in which

> …one half of the transactional circle between me and my world, the half in which I direct myself outward into the world, [overshadows] the other half in which the being that I am is constituted in and through the world's impact on me (p. 209).

Focusing on the actions of the body as products of a separate intentional form (rather than a socially funded set of processes) creates a space for dualisms that divide the body and society. Such a partition only complicates attempts to understand humans as both individual and social beings. Approaching the body from a Deweyan point of view escapes this complication by providing a framework for the relationship between bodily and non-bodily elements of transactions. When "the activity of cultivating oneself as an individual cannot be done apart from the world with which one transacts" (Sullivan 2001, p. 19), the body is understood as an active process of "bodying" in which the "live creature" itself constitutes "the activity of engagement with the world" (Sullivan 2002, p. 209).

A transactional perspective hence views the body not as a static capsule of physical, individually possessed elements, but as a dynamic process of a "live creature" *in*habiting the world. To view the body in this way not only accounts for its roots in social experience but also offers a new perspective for health sciences. Dickie et al. (2006) noted that an individualistic focus on the activities of the body creates too narrow a scope for understanding the complexities of bodies' functioning via occupation. However, if we view occupation as the means for accessing and experiencing associated living, then the occupations of individual bodies become potential processes of continual growth that are never without reference to the social aspects of experience. Boisvert (1998) wrote that "the kind of growth, its direction and quality, all depend on the sort of associated activities within which we participate" (p. 60).

2.4 Occupation

Dewey was first and foremost a philosopher, but he was an engaged philosopher who was concerned with how to address social problems. Yet Dewey also was a psychologist as well as a professor of pedagogy who was highly influential as a theorist of education. Dewey applied his theories in his Laboratory School of the University of Chicago (Jackson 2009). It was during his time at Chicago that Dewey worked most intensively on educational issues and developed his ideas about occupation as a central part of his work. Moreover, it is important to foreground the fact that Dewey's work on education stemmed directly from his work in psychology and philosophy as well as informing that work in later years.

Dewey's influence on the concept of occupation has been underexplored in the literature to date. Instead, Adolf Meyer's (1922) famous lecture about occupational therapy has been stressed as an exemplar of pragmatist thinking about occupation (e.g., Hooper and Wood 2002). Dewey influenced Meyer, but Meyer's version of pragmatism was underdeveloped in that he did not utilize Dewey's work on occupation to a significant degree or synthesize relations between it and other key concepts (Cutchin 2004; Cutchin and Dickie 2012). The net effect of this inattention to the more fecund ideas of Dewey was to starve greater theoretical development along the lines we are trying to establish here.

2.4.1 Dewey on Occupation

With that backdrop we can now assess what Dewey meant by occupation and how it relates to processes of embodiment and growth. Some of Dewey's most important statements about occupation come from his text *The School and Society.* It is noteworthy that Dewey's publication of these conceptual developments took place 23 years before Adolph Meyer lectured to the American Occupational Therapy Association. We reproduce several statements below at length in order to capture some of the complexity and meaning of what Dewey was trying to address with his concept.

> By occupation is not meant any kind of "busy work" or exercises that may be given to a child in order to keep him out of mischief or idleness when seated at his desk. By occupation I mean a mode of activity on the part of the child which reproduces, or runs parallel to, some form of work carried on in social life. In the University Elementary School these occupations are represented by the shop-work with wood and tools; by cooking, sewing, and by the textile work. The fundamental point in the psychology of an occupation is that it

maintains a balance between the intellectual and the practical phases of experience. As an occupation it is active or motor; it finds expression through the physical organs—the eyes, hands, etc. But it also involves continual observation of materials, and continual planning and reflection, in order that the practical or executive side may be successfully carried on. Occupation as thus conceived must, therefore, be carefully distinguished from work which educates primarily for a trade. It differs because its end is in itself; in the growth that comes from the continual interplay of ideas and their embodiment in action, not in external utility (Dewey 1976, p. 92).

He [the student] continually sees his elders engaged in such pursuits. He daily has to do with things which are the results of just such occupations. He comes in contact with facts that have no meaning, except in reference to them. Take these things out of the present social life and see how little would remain—and this not only on the material side, but as regards intellectual, aesthetic, and moral activities, for these are largely and necessarily bound up with occupations (Dewey 1976, p. 95).

Boisvert (1998) portrays Dewey's thinking about occupation as being rooted in his position on embodiedness and bodily activity as well as in his focus on the social or communal basis of existence. The fact that Dewey viewed students as integrated creatures in which body and mind are merged through ongoing action makes his position on occupations a logical extension to the classroom. In Dewey's argument for occupations, we see his emphasis on socially relevant activity that mimics other types of experiences, but the objective is to work with others and learn from that type of setting because it is the way we live our lives. The engagement in occupations by students is the "end" or goal in and of itself because that process empowers students through their embodiment of ideas. It is that embodiment that provides the basis of learning and later growth.

2.4.2 *Occupation, Embodiment, and Growth*

It is not difficult to take Dewey's formulation of occupations for young students in school settings and expand it as significant for thinking about occupations in the broader sphere of life. If we take Dewey's version of occupation and realize that it is very much like those of concern to occupational scientists and therapists, we can begin to develop some useful new propositions about what occupations entail and what they have the potential to do for those who engage in them. The general purpose of occupations for any person might be something similar to what we call life-long learning, with the caveat that the ends included in that process of learning are enhanced embodiment of positive experiences and the ability to be able to grow better and contribute to social life better in the future.

When people perform occupations, they are engaging in a natural and practiced way of embodying experience and enhancing their potential through growth. Because occupations force one to balance the intellectual and practical phases of experience, they foster maximal embodying and growth. Dewey implied, however, that occupations operate in even more complex ways. Based on his work at his Laboratory School, Dewey suggested that facts develop meaning for children when they are put in the context of the shared, situated occupation. It is only a small, logical step to suggest that any occupation helps to develop meaning for those involved. Those meanings, as Dewey points out, are intellectual, aesthetic, and moral—but instead of being universal, they are situated meanings. For Dewey, such limited meaning from occupation is not a concern because we recognize similarities across contexts and occupations and are able to transfer and utilize meanings as needed—as long as they have been embodied and we have developed the powers to employ them when needed. Perhaps more interesting and important is that occupations have aesthetic and moral dimensions that have been long overlooked in occupational science. Occupations are therefore important in developing people who can foresee and construct situations in more positive ways than otherwise. Such accomplishment through growth is what Fesmire (2003) has called the ideal "moral artist" that Dewey promotes through his philosophy.

While Dewey viewed occupations as a mode of activity to promote growth, we should similarly view the large collection of occupations that are the foci of our study and interventions as chances to enhance similar growth in any person. In the end, growth through occupation in the Deweyan sense should be central to any understanding of well-being. For it is without the type of growth that Dewey suggested that we fail to thrive in our daily affairs. In this way, occupation is an important mode for assuring well-being in people across the life course.

2.5 Conclusion

A transactional view of the body suggests interesting avenues of exploration for scholars of occupation. As we have tried to explain here, those avenues reach far beyond traditional understandings of embodiment. Dewey's entire philosophy was laced with a political bent. He believed that knowledge and philosophy were only useful insofar as they addressed the problems of the day, and his definition of democracy reflected this belief. Dewey construed democracy as a "product of associated living" rather than a mere political theory (Boisvert 1998), and he suggested that the "problem of the public" lay in people's methods of inquiry and the conditions of habit formation (Dewey 1927). Dewey argued that honing the conditions of habit formation and helping people develop methods of inquiry would fix many of the ills faced by society. In this vein, scholars of occupation can study occupation as one space where the habits and inquiries of the body are or may be shaped, paying particular attention to the ways in which people's occupations connect to elements of their wider situations (cf. Aldrich and Callanan 2011).

This approach to the study of occupation draws in ideas about democracy and justice in light of the fact that some occupations occur in response to problematic situations. One by-product of the process of embodiment is that active engagement with the world also requires active engagement with the world's problems. It is by virtue of encountering the problems of associated living that humans grow through inquiry and reflection about their habits. Accordingly, a transactional perspective of the body necessarily focuses on the real-world problems that foster and affect the performance of various occupations. To understand how humans inhabit experience through occupation, scholars must view these actions of the body as products, processes, and responses to sometimes uncertain and problematic situations in associated life.

Associated living is the wellspring through which humans are exposed to the habits that comprise occupations, and humans need freedom to cultivate those habits with equality so they can functionally coordinate with society via occupation. The acts of embodying that constitute occupations are therefore complex phenomena that may lead to new knowledge about the individual and social development of human beings. By studying occupation through a transactional perspective, scientists can explore a range of phenomena without being mired by the problematic dualisms that often attend more dichotomous views of the body.

We conclude with a final thought about the significance of embodiment, growth, and occupation. Embodiment is always a type of collective process because of the communal and social aspects involved. The more integrated into communal life one becomes, the better the potential for growth. In turn, enhanced individuals promote enhancements in the community. Thus occupations should not be considered solo acts. As Dewey suggested, we learn better by cooperating with others because most of life is spent in cooperation. We think this leads to the conclusion that occupational therapy and science must begin to focus more intently on the community and social aspects of occupation as well as how those aspects might be understood and improved to promote positive embodiment and growth.

References

Aldrich, R. M., & Callanan, Y. (2011). "I just want to store what I have, get in my car, and run away": Researching and understanding disappearance in discouraged workers' situations. *Journal of Occupational Science, 18*, 153–166.

Alexander, T. M. (2009). Dewey, dualism, and naturalism. In J. R. Shook & J. Margolis (Eds.), *A companion to pragmatism* (pp. 184–192). Chichester: Blackwell.

Barber, M. (2006). Occupational science and the first-person perspective. *Journal of Occupational Science, 13*, 94–96.

Boisvert, R. D. (1998). *John Dewey: Rethinking our time*. Albany: State University of New York Press.

Campbell, J. (1995). *Understanding John Dewey: Nature and cooperative intelligence*. Chicago: Open Court.

Cutchin, M. P. (1997). Physician retention in rural communities: The perspective of experiential place integration. *Health & Place, 3*, 25–41.

Cutchin, M. (2004). Using Deweyan philosophy to rename and reframe adaptation-to-environment. *American Journal of Occupational Therapy, 58*, 303–312.

Cutchin, M. P. (2007). From society to self (and back) through place: Habit in transactional context. *OTJR: Occupation, Participation, and Health, 27*, 50S–59S.

Cutchin, M. P., & Dickie, V. A. (2012). Transactionalism: Occupational science and the pragmatic attitude. In G. Whiteford & C. Hocking (Eds.), *Critical perspectives on occupational science: Society, inclusion, participation* (pp. 23–37). London: Wiley.

Cutchin, M. P., Dickie, V., & Humphry, R. (2006). Transaction versus interpretation, or transaction and interpretation? A response to Michael Barber. *Journal of Occupational Science, 13*, 97–99.

Cutchin, M. P., Aldrich, R. M., Bailliard, A., & Coppola, S. (2008). Action theories for occupational science: The contributions of Dewey and Bourdieu. *Journal of Occupational Science, 15*, 157–165.

Dewey, J. (1927). *The public and its problems*. New York: Henry Holt and Company.

Dewey, J. (1957). *Reconstruction in philosophy*. Boston: Beacon (Original work published in 1920).

Dewey, J. (1962). *Individualism old and new*. New York: Capricorn Books (Original work published in 1930).

Dewey, J. (1976). The school and society. In J. A. Boydston (Ed.), *The middle works of John Dewey, 1899–1924. Volume 1: 1899–1901* (pp. 1–109). Carbondale: Southern Illinois University Press (Original work published in 1899).

Dewey, J. (1980). *Art as experience*. New York: Perigree (Original work published in 1934).

Dewey, J. (1989). *Experience and nature* (2nd ed.). La Salle: Open Court (Original work published in 1929).

Dewey, J. (1998). The reflex arc concept in psychology. In L. Hickman & T. Alexander (Eds.), *The essential Dewey* (Vol. 2, pp. 3–18). Bloomington: Indiana University Press (Original work published in 1896).

Dewey, J. (2000). *Experience and nature* (1st ed.). New York: Dover Publications, Inc (Original work published in 1925).

Dewey, J. (2008). *Human nature and conduct*. New York: Barnes and Noble (Original work published in 1922).

Dewey, J., & Bentley, A. (1949). *Knowing and the known*. Boston: Beacon.

Dickie, V., Cutchin, M. P., & Humphry, R. (2006). Occupation as transactional experience: A critique of individualism in occupational science. *Journal of Occupational Science, 13*, 83–93.

Fesmire, S. (2003). *John Dewey and moral imagination: Pragmatism in ethics*. Bloomington: Indiana University Press.

Hooper, B., & Wood, W. (2002). Pragmatism and structuralism in occupational therapy: The long conversation. *American Journal of Occupational Therapy, 56*, 40–50.

Jackson, P. W. (2009). John Dewey. In J. R. Shook & J. Margolis (Eds.), *A companion to pragmatism* (pp. 54–66). Chichester: Blackwell.

Kestenbaum, V. (1977). *The phenomenological sense of John Dewey: Habit and meaning*. Atlantic Highlands: Humanities Press.

Meyer, A. (1922). The philosophy of occupation therapy. *Archives of Occupational Therapy, 1*, 1–10.

Pappas, G. F. (2008). *John Dewey: Democracy as experience*. Bloomington: Indiana University Press.

Sullivan, S. (2001). *Living across and through skins: Transactional bodies, pragmatism, and feminism*. Bloomington: Indiana University Press.

Sullivan, S. (2002). Pragmatist feminism as ecological ontology: Reflections on living across and through skins. *Hypatia, 17*(4), 201–217.

Chapter 3
Being Occupied in the Everyday

Valerie A. Wright-St Clair and Elizabeth A. Smythe

3.1 Introduction

This chapter is designed around the findings from an interpretive phenomenological study which explored how fifteen community-dwelling elder New Zealand Māori and Pākehā[1] aged 71–97 experienced aging in their everyday lives. Philosophically, the research aimed to uncover the ontology, or the lived experience, of being aged within the realm of going about the ordinary day. While the research methodology and methods were guided by Gadamerian hermeneutics and Heideggerian phenomenology, a fresh look is taken through a Deweyan lens to illustrate how a transactional way of thinking can throw new light on the understandings gained. Rather than simply approaching the thinking in a theoretical way, this chapter illustrates the philosophical similarities and differences in an empirical way. It does this by anchoring the discussion within and around the elders' stories of their everyday occupational experiences. Three notions congruent with Heidegger and Dewey are chosen as a means of structuring the interpretations; the habitual, the relational, and the precarious. For each, an illustrative story from the research is presented, followed by a brief hermeneutic analysis of the text. A Heideggerian phenomenological interpretation is offered, followed by a Deweyan transactional perspective. While the three notions discussed in this chapter are presented separately, existentially and pragmatically they co-exist. They are inseparable in the context of being in the everyday and of experiencing the situations of everyday life.

Congruencies between Gadamer, Heidegger and Dewey have already been drawn (Koschmann et al. 1998; Garrison 1999; Polkinghorne 2000; Vessey 2009). Vessey

[1] Pākehā is the Maori term for people of European descent or non-Māori peoples (Kawharu 1994).

V.A. Wright-St Clair (✉) • E.A. Smythe
Department of Occupational Science and Therapy, Auckland University of Technology, Auckland, New Zealand
e-mail: valerie.wright-stclair@aut.ac.nz

M.P. Cutchin and V.A. Dickie (eds.), *Transactional Perspectives on Occupation*,
DOI 10.1007/978-94-007-4429-5_3, © Springer Science+Business Media B.V. 2013

(2009) suggests "philosophical hermeneutics is often favorably compared to John Dewey's pragmatism in at least three ways: in embracing the hermeneutic circle, in recognizing the importance of aesthetic experience, and in rejecting separation between theory and practice" (p. 209). Furthermore, the Gadamerian hermeneutic traditions of assuming the past is always in play in the present, and that interpretation is always on the way to understanding, clearly align with Dewey's portrayal of the interplay between the means and the ends of interpretation (Vessey 2009). Looking more closely, both Dewey and Heidegger were concerned with exploring, in a deep way, philosophies of experience in order to articulate the complexity of ordinary human existence (Dewey 2005b). Yet rather than richly describing the meaning of "being" through an ontological lens as Heidegger did, Dewey sought to elucidate the "original material" of existence (Boisvert 1998). That is, he aimed to elucidate real, everyday situations, like playing a game of cards, in a way that pragmatic solutions might be found for everyday problems (Dewey 2005b). The threads of humanism and social responsibility are evident in Dewey's transactionalism but not in Heiddeger's work. Dewey's philosophy is seen as fundamentally moral in its intentions toward guiding a thoughtful way of living (Boisvert 1998; Jackson 2006). In accord, challenges arise in the attempt to integrate the two philosophical views (Margolis 1998). In spite of such challenges, this chapter sets out to show how the philosophical continuities and differences can reveal deeper interpretations of peoples' engagement in everyday occupations.

3.2 The Habitual

The habitual is, by its very nature, taken-for-granted. Habits underpin the unthinking manner of people going about their day. The participants who tell their stories in this chapter had most of their lives behind them. As such, they came into each day having already experienced innumerable other days and events throughout their life course. In conversation, they spoke of doing the mundane, always-there things in their days, of responding to things which unexpectedly appeared and of making time to do things which particularly interested them. Talk about "yesterday" revealed remarkable similarities in the daily patterns, yet each story was uniquely personal, revealing a personal rhythm and flow of occupations. Curly's story stands out. He said:

> Yesterday, Monday, was just another one of those days as far as I was concerned. I usually rise about 7, 7:30, make myself a cup of tea, and listen to the 8 o'clock news. Then I have my breakfast, wash the dishes, and do whatever is necessary. If I have no odd jobs to do around the place then I will start reading. Or I play patience. I played a game or two of patience yesterday; I always find it interesting. Then I read the paper and I made lunch. I always have a nap every afternoon for an hour and a half, or a couple of hours, which I think is very beneficial. So yesterday, after my nap I made a cup of tea and started preparation for my evening meal. Then I played some music. I play a lot of music. I am very fond of music. I have a whole lot of CDs, tapes and records; some old records; plenty of them.

> At five o'clock I had a glass of sherry, which is another thing that I think is good for me, and at six o'clock I listened to the news on the television. I am never at a loss; I can always turn to do something.

As Curly, at age 97, described his Monday as "just another one of those days", his recounting of occurrences yesterday naturally blended with those that occur every day. Much like other days, yesterday he simply attended to his ordinary, daily concerns. And in saying he did "whatever is necessary", Curly hinted at doing the things which enable him to be, and to remain, where he is; living alone at home. Doing the necessary sustains his mode of going about his life in comfortable ways. Additionally, Curly mentioned doing the necessary first. Then, only "if" he has no "odd jobs" to do, he does other things. The indispensable things which are always there bring a temporal structure to his day. That is, in getting his "breakfast, lunch and evening meal" as well as having his "nap" and his "glass of sherry" at regular times, Curly's day already holds something to do at the beginning, the middle and the end. Being in a routine is a compelling and necessary way of going about his day. His routine evokes a sense of order and certainty in keeping on. Thus, the things Curly concerns himself with seem to speak to who he is as well as how he goes about his days in living alone as a 97-year-old. Being in a daily routine is an embodied experience of being in and knowing how to go about the day, rather than a conceptual activity.

Turning first to Heidegger (1927/1962), the notion of "being-in" speaks to the interpretation of routineness as a mode of being engaged with one's ordinary concerns. Essentially, the ontological nature of "being-in" is the fundamental human state of being-in-the-world. The "in" refers not to a spatial relationship but draws its meaning from the archaic German word "*innan*" (Heidegger 1927/1962, p. 80) meaning "to reside" or "to dwell". It signifies being accustomed to, familiar with, or looking after something. In this way, being-in-the-world is already understood as having the character of everyday familiarity. As Curly said Monday was "just another one of those days", he communicated a contextual understanding of his being "there", in yesterday, "in an everyday manner" (Heidegger 1927/1962, p. 171). Explained ontologically, the essential nature of being human is therefore not in our ability to think but in "our existing in a place with particular things and established ways of doing things" (Wrathall 2005, p. 15). In other words, for Curly, being in a daily routine is a mode of being absorbed or entangled in everyday matters. One day follows much like the others. Yet, Heidegger's (1927/1962) understanding of resoluteness as being a disclosing, allows us to hear Curly's determination to continue doing things in his preferred way. Through his daily routine he is "taking a stand for [himself] as a certain kind of person" (Crowe 2006, p. 189). Curly's everyday routineness is how he is.

Dewey's (1957b) notion of "habit" lines up closely with Heidegger's (1962) understanding of being-in-the-world in an everyday manner. However, Dewey's interpretation of habits as consequences of experience does add contrast to the seemingly similar perspectives. According to Dewey, habits are "acquired predispositions to *ways* or modes of response" (Dewey 1957a, p. 40). Hence, habits underpin a deeply learned way of functioning within everyday occupations

Table 3.1 Summarizing the habitual

Heidegger	Dewey
Being-in-the-world is always about taken-for-granted familiarity and ways	Society shapes us to be how we are, but one also has a moral obligation to shape oneself to be as good as one can
What we are familiar with is enacted in an un-thinking way	The unthinkingness of habits makes learning more challenging
How one goes about things is how one is	One reflects on habits and learns what is good or bad about them when the situation suggests doing so
For Heidegger:	*For Dewey*:
It is about uncovering the habits that "are"	It is about understanding our habits so we can improve the quality of life
i.e. an ontological perspective	*i.e. a pragmatic perspective*

(Cutchin and Dickie 2012). Interpretively, we hear this in Curly saying his daily after-lunch nap and glass of sherry "are very beneficial" for him. His words disclose his learning over time. He habitually engages in these two occupations because they contribute to his healthfulness at 97; they help him keep going day after day. Dewey's pragmatism is underpinned by the assumption that humans tend towards regular and repetitious ways of doing or responding; habits are laid down by previous ways of doing things. In other words, "habit-forming wears grooves…. [making] subsequent learning more difficult" (Dewey 1958, p. 280). In this way, we hear Curly describing the things that are "always" in his day, in the order they are always done. Yet, instead of the habitual grooves being fixed or static, Dewey understands habit-forming tendencies as a function of being highly sensitive, and responsive, to environmental complexity. "Each habit demands appropriate conditions for its exercise and when habits are numerous and complex, as with the human organism, to find these conditions involves search and experimentation" (Dewey 1958, p. 281). Habitual ways, even when seemingly familiar, are always particular to the moment and context. Going further, Dewey's emphasis on morality and social responsibility means he understood habits as being "social or cultural phenomena that entail social relations, social classes, institutions, and customs" (Cutchin 2007, p. 51S). In this way, Curly's daily routine can be seen to align with his socio-cultural context. His story lights up his valuing autonomy and self-determination. His everyday morality exists, not in a moral theory of goods, but in how the theory plays out in the "existential conditions and consequences" (Dewey 1958, p. 433) of his everyday life. From a Deweyan perspective, Curly's "uniquely" individual day is paradoxically situated within entrenched, historical ways of living in New Zealand society (Cutchin 2007).

In summary, the habitual is, to Heidegger, an ontological mode of "being-in", of dwelling in, the familiar; and to Dewey, it is a consequence of doing things as they have previously been done (Table 3.1). A main distinction is the way Dewey's pragmatism calls for seeing the social and moral dimensions of everyday situations, and the learning that reinforces a habit as beneficial.

3.3 The Relational

Just as Heidegger richly describes experiences as always occurring within a context, Dewey speaks to the dynamic nature of person-environment experiences, rejecting dualistic thinking about persons as somehow separate from the environments they inhabit (James 2005; Heatwole Shank and Cutchin 2010). Thinking about how time and relationships play out in a contextual way offers an alternative to habits of thinking in dualisms such as the separation of the past, the present and the future. This opens the way for understanding how the past plays out in current situations (Alexander 2006). In other words, continuities of time and relating exist. Events are continuously constructed and reconstructed over time (James 2005).

3.3.1 Continuity of Time: Past-Present-Future

While having routines in the day may mean that tomorrow is much like today or yesterday, routineness can bring a sense of certainty into everyday occupations. Rather than time being a measurable, linear phenomenon, the stories of older peoples' everyday lives illuminate the complex temporal nature of experiences as they are lived. The following story was told by Ferguson in his 98th year. He had already mentioned there was a lot he could not do now. When offered the opportunity of having a photograph taken doing something he enjoyed, he chose having a whiskey. He went on to say:

> I still like a drink but not as much as I used to. I don't suppose the day will come when that stops. I had a good port there and that's finished. This is the last of my Teacher's whiskey. They haven't made that whiskey for I don't know how long. I got a case when it was going off the market and that's the last bottle of it there. They were supposed to see me out. It looks like I will still be alive to see that finished. I like a scotch. I never was much fond of beer. The only time I drank a lot of beer was when I was younger. We used to come from Auckland on the truck and the first stop was the Albany Pub and we used to get a case, always a case of beer. There used to be a lot of pine trees about half way along the road from Albany to Long Bay. We used to stop at the pine trees and drink our beer there. We would go through a case amongst six of us; all in Big Bertha the truck; every weekend.

As his story unfolds we hear a timeless flow in Ferguson's being in the moment, "still liking a drink", to having a drink in the days still to come, and remembering back to buying the case of whiskey that "was supposed to see him out". The words disclose his wonderment. How is it that he is still going while his Teacher's whiskey is almost gone? He always expected he would be the first to go. In the moment, while sitting enjoying a whiskey, Ferguson is suddenly entangled in his memories of having a drink. The events from his distant past, when he and his friends would always "stop at the pine trees" to enjoy their beer, were always, already with him. In this way, having his glass of whiskey connects Ferguson to his past and future. Although his days of drinking beer at the pine trees have long since passed, the experience is still with Ferguson. His enduring experience of enjoying a drink seamlessly connects occurrences distanced by time.

Turning to Heideggerian philosophy, Ferguson's sudden reflection back to times gone by does not mean he is living in the past; rather it shows how the past remains present to him. "'The past' belongs irretrievably to an earlier time; it belonged to the events of that time; and in spite of that, it can still be present-at-hand 'now'" (Heidegger 1962, p. 430). In other words, Ferguson's memories exist as a remnant of events in his history, and thus the memorable moments in bygone times are not entirely "gone". In this sense, history is "that which is past, but which nevertheless is still having effects" (Heidegger 1962, p. 430). Through remembering, the historical is still present-at-hand, within everyday experiences. It shows that memories matter in advanced age because they safeguard the past within the everyday present. Yet Ferguson also thinks about enjoying a whiskey in the days to come. To Heidegger, dwelling always encompasses the past, present and future.

Dewey's transactionalism deepens the interpretation of Ferguson's story in similar, yet different, ways. As it did for Heidegger, time matters in Dewey's way of thinking (Boisvert 1998). Memories of past situations are relived (Dewey 1957b). Yet, while Heidegger's understandings disclose how being-in-the-world is, ontologically, a mode of being in the past, present and future at the same time, acting in the world is merely implied (Cutchin et al. 2008). On the other hand, Dewey's emphasis on people acting in the world opens up a situated understanding of how "the remote and the past are 'in' behavior making it what it is" (Dewey 1958, p. 279). In other words, in the continuity of time, thinking and acting in the present is related to situations separated by time and space (Dewey 1958). Applying this way of thinking to Ferguson's story, we interpret how his choosing to have a whiskey in this situation was already "charged with echoes and reminiscences of what has gone before" (Dewey 1957b, p. 1). It is Dewey's inclusion of human imagination that is revealing. He reasoned that "the past is recalled not because of itself but because of what it adds to the present" (Dewey 1957b, p. 2). That is, memories become stories with dramatic structure that convey emotional importance to the listener. Memories also guide responses to the situation encountered. Ferguson's imagination allows him to consider alternatives to his present situation (Boisvert 1998). He knows that one drink will be his last, but which one? The question of "will I or won't I" is never far from his mind. Rehearsed in his imagination, Ferguson's "dramatic tale" conveys a rethinking of his plan to have a case of whiskey that would outlast him. His deliberation opens up new ways of perceiving this unexpected situation (Fesmire 2003). He will need more whiskey to see him through to the end of his days.

In addition to the relational nature of time, Ferguson's words hint toward his younger days of drinking as more about being with his mates. Having outlived his friends, enjoying a whisky offers a moment of being-alone-with his memories of mates. Continuity of relating exists in everyday experiences.

Drawing this section to a close, Heidegger's notion of being in the world means we are always in a temporal context. Existing is being in time. Distinctively, Dewey brings in a way of understanding how our capacity to imagine alternative futures means we can change our actions in a thoughtful way (Table 3.2).

Table 3.2 Summarizing the relational: continuity of time

Heidegger	Dewey
Being-in-the-world is being in the past, present and future at the same time	The past, present and future are non-dualistic; they co-exist
The past can be present-at-hand in our current experiences	Engaging with memories is a reliving of past situations
Acting in the world is implied through experiences	The past influences how we think and act now
Being is always being-towards possibilities	Human imagination allows us to consider the consequences of alternative actions
For Heidegger:	*For Dewey*:
We are always within time	Temporal dimensions of experience influence action
i.e. an ontological perspective	*i.e. a pragmatic perspective*

3.3.2 Continuity of Relating: Being-with-Others

May's story is offered next to illustrate the transactional nature of relating to others over time. An elder Māori of 77 years, she told of her yesterday, a time of being-with her grandchildren:

> Yesterday, I had a house full of grandchildren. They were at the school because they had a game of rugby and they all came back from there with their grandfather. I was sitting here watching TV when they came in.... there must have been about 24 of them, and they are all my mokos.[2] Oohh, OK I thought, I'll get something together.... Well I just brought out what I had in the cupboard. I got out a big pot and I cooked six of these packet dinners which make up a lot. It didn't take long, only a couple of minutes. And they quite enjoyed it when I set my table up for them and it wasn't long after that they were all sitting down around the table. Some fitted around the table and some were sitting on the couch. There you are, there you are, and they were quite happy.... I felt lovely knowing that all my mokos were all satisfied.... Well, there might be a time when they have got a family of their own and they do the same thing as I did for them yesterday. I gave them a lesson and hopefully that will come through for them in the future. Well on the marae,[3] for the whānau[4] that comes in, the old people always make sure that the family has kai.[5] This is how we were taught.

In this story, May describes her yesterday which suddenly changed from one of restful solitude to having "a house full of grandchildren". Amid the unexpected, May's story reveals a sureness in what was called for. Without hesitating she knew to "get something together". Knowing to provide for her visitors reaches back into

[2] Mokos is an abbreviation of mokopuna; the Māori term for grandchild or grandchildren (Moorfield 1988).

[3] A marae is the meeting place of people who share ancestors and place.

[4] Whānau refers to the extended family.

[5] Kai is the Māori term for food (Moorfield 1988).

her past, to "how she was taught". These teachings were not formal lessons; they came through being on the marae. Rather than teach by telling, May's elders, through enacting the tribal ways, showed her what to do. As such, May's Māori heritage opens the way for her to know how to be with her mokopuna as their elder. Her preparedness is situated in her ancestral past. At the same time, she gave her grandchildren "a lesson" to serve their future by passing on the traditional ways. Thus May's way of being with her grandchildren yesterday was also a mode of having her ancestors "with" her.

The human entity's co-existence in the world is fundamental to Heidegger's (1962) ontological understanding of the meaning of being (Dasein). Accordingly, "the world of Dasein is a *with-world*" (Heidegger 1962, p. 155), meaning we can never be fully alone, even when no-one else is present. As humans, the situated nature of being-in-the-world is always a mode of "being-with-others". That is, our ways of being in the everyday are called out by a sense of "what matters". Interpreting May's story, the moment of knowing to provide food for her visiting grandchildren was disclosed to her through her early times of being with the tribal elders. Even though her elders have long since passed-on, they are still "with" her as she goes about her day. May's deeply held understandings of how to be a Māori elder are disclosed to her and "call" (Heidegger 1962) or appeal to her to provide food. Ontologically, "the call comes *from* [her] and yet *from beyond* [her]" (Heidegger 1962, p. 320).

Whereas Heidegger thought in terms of everyday moments or encounters, Dewey embedded his thinking in everyday "situations". In doing so, Dewey set out to convey the idea that actions are not a consequence of a single event or even a set of events. They occur within situations that are contextually whole (Campbell 1995). As in the hermeneutic circle, understanding particular events adds to the understanding of the whole situation. And understanding more about the situation itself enables a greater understanding of the single events it entails. Interpreting this in the context of May's story reveals how the events of being with and watching her elders, all those years ago, and the call to pass on the tribal ways to her descendants, come together in the situation of providing for her visitors. She only comes to understand the meaning of passing ancestral ways on through the situation she suddenly finds herself in. The meaning of everyday activities is acquired. Here, Dewey's thinking about social customs as being shared habits of solving everyday problems adds further understanding (Campbell 1995). In May's giving her grandchildren a lesson yesterday, she created a determinant for how they will be with extended family through their future actions. She acts to pass on cultural customs. Hence May's actions yesterday can be seen as being "saturated with story and transmitted meaning" (Campbell 1995, p. 125). More than this, Deweyan thinking means her customary beliefs were consolidated through her experience (Capps and Capps 2005). May's interactions reveal a continuity of relating both with those who have gone before and those who are yet to come. The human experience is one of connectedness (Hollis 1977). This continuity is part of who we are in our everyday lives. She also coordinated relationships in the situation in order to create an outcome that she envisioned as good. In this problematic situation, through her imagination and

Table 3.3 Summarizing the relational: continuity of relating

Heidegger	Dewey
Being-in-the-world is always a mode of "being-with" other people	Our past relationships help account for our current, situated actions
Because we co-exist in the world, we can never be fully alone	Social customs and cultural ways are for the group what habits are for the individual
In everyday moments we can still "be with" those who are absent or who have passed on	The human experience is always one of connectedness
For Heidegger:	*For Dewey*:
We are always in a with-world	Relationships/connections inform ongoing action
i.e. an ontological perspective	*i.e. a pragmatic perspective*

intuition, based on deep knowledge of relationships and her storehouse of habits, May conjured up the ideas of what she could cook. Drawing on the convenience of pre-packaged food she was able to provide a traditional meal of welcome.

To summarize, being in the world is, to Heidegger, a mode of being with others regardless of the context one is in. Even when no-one else is present, we are still "with" others in the world through our memories, our feelings, and our experiences. The distinguishing feature that Dewey brings is his account of culture. Our customary ways of doing things are determined through our community and social relationships (Table 3.3).

3.4 The Precarious

There are things done in a usual day that are so deeply familiar they do not call for thinking; they are just done. It is this characteristic of familiarity which is experienced as a loss when the accustomed experience is suddenly not there. Experiencing the unaccustomed is not a thing outside the body, like encountering an unfamiliar object; it is an embodied in-the-world encountering. It is an experience of things simply not being right. Talk of such events tumbled out in the midst of elders' stories of going about the ordinarily mundane everyday events. Christina (93 years old) was telling of her engagement in music:

> I have to present a cup for music at the local College prize giving each year and last year they had a temporary stairway placed in front of the stage. It had 15 steps… and for the first time in my life I felt a bit uneasy going up the steps. My sight has been weak all my life but the hesitation is unusual. So, I didn't go up the steps. The headmaster was quite gallant and came down the stairs to me. I presented the cup at the base of the steps instead of going up. Now I had gone up the steps at the side of the stage for 12 years, but the new temporary stairs with no supports were a bit worrying to me. But that is a bit strange for me because I had never even thought about going up stairs before. The hesitation was most unusual for me because I have 14 stairs here and I used to run up and down them…. This was something where I hesitated, especially with the steps, and that annoys me.

Christina discloses feeling “a bit uneasy” on the stairs as being a first-ever concern for her. Her uneasiness arose in the moment of anticipating being on the stage presenting the music award. We hear her sense of being taken-aback as she had “never thought about” going up steps before. On other occasions the steps were just there and she went up them without a thought. But in this event, Christina encountered the stairs in a way that was unaccustomed and troubling. Her hesitation did not seem right as she compared “these” steps on “this” day with the stairs in her usual day. She ordinarily goes about her day, going up and down stairs without thinking about the going up or the going down. But the stage stairs were suddenly not there for her in the usual way. The hesitating held Christina back from being on the stage to present the music award. She was suddenly attentive to how uncomfortable she felt in the midst of this usually familiar activity.

Ontologically, the stairway’s usual readiness-to-hand can be seen to withdraw (Heidegger 1962). The stairs are not at her disposal in the usual way. Christina experiences the uncomfortableness of the unaccustomed and hesitates. Heidegger talks about the “uncanniness” of experiencing the unfamiliar. He uses the German word “*unheimlich*” which literally translates as “*unhomely*” (King 2001, p. 96). Conversely, canniness is characterized by “just knowing what to do” as occurs in a “without thinking” engagement. In a mode characterized by uncanniness, or anxiety, the person is brought back from his or her absorption in the customary. Heidegger describes the experience as being one in which “everyday familiarity collapses… being-in enters into the existential ‘mode’ of the ‘*not-at-home*’” (Heidegger 1962, p. 233). Just as Christina spoke of finding these “new temporary stairs” as standing between her and being on the stage, not-at-homeness is always situated. Experiencing it is at all times “thisly” (Harman 2007, p.28). It presents while doing this thing, in this place, at this time. As such, not-being-at-home may spring into the light or remain in the shadows in any one moment; it is not predictable.

Returning to view the story through a Deweyan lens offers a different, yet similar, way of thinking about Christina’s experience. Everything is transacted in a context. “The world is a scene of risk; it is uncertain, unstable, uncannily unstable” (Dewey 1958, p. 41). Accordingly, Dewey described stability and instability as existing in a non-dualistic way. Stability and precariousness, then, coexist within all situations. “The stable exists amid and because of the precariousness and vice versa” (Alexander 2006, p. 190). In other words, the shakiness of Christina’s actions (her hesitating) only occurs because she is so used to going up and down stairs in an unthinking way. So, even though a stairway seems solid, unchanging, Dewey’s thinking suggests “no one thing is completely stable or precarious; the question is one of degree, cause, and consequences” (Alexander 2006, p. 190). Hence the precarious can present itself in any situation. For Christina, at 93, her hesitating causes her to rethink being up on the stage. We “hear” her worry, not of the stairs themselves, but of falling, of hurting herself, of the embarrassment in front of such a large audience. Instead she waited. As a consequence, she simply presented the music award from the bottom of the steps. She still did what she went there to do.

In summary, Heidegger speaks of the comfortableness of experiencing things in an accustomed way, and the uncomfortableness in the moment of experiencing the

Table 3.4 Summarizing the precarious

Heidegger	Dewey
An uncomfortable experience of "not-being-at-home" arises in the midst of the unfamiliar	The world is a risky place
We come to experience the familiarity of something when it is gone	Stability and instability exist as non-dualistic characteristics in the world
Not-at-homeness is particular to the context and is not predictable	The precarious can happen, influencing the consequences of what we do
For Heidegger:	*For Dewey*:
Not-at-homeness is part of our human experience	The precarious changes relationships within situations and corresponding actions
i.e. an ontological perspective	*i.e. a pragmatic perspective*

unaccustomed or unfamiliar. An important difference with Dewey's account of the world as being both stable and precarious is how we can learn from such experiences and change how we act (Table 3.4).

3.5 Occupational Practice as Listening

The stories shared in this chapter show how Heidegger's and Dewey's philosophies can deepen understandings of elders' engagement in everyday occupations. By drawing on philosophers such as Heidegger and Dewey we can "hear" what it *is* to be in the everyday in advanced age. To hear beyond the facts, the myths and the common assumptions about aging and the aged, calls for another approach. It calls for "listening" for that which is hidden from the outside; the experience being in the everyday in advanced age. Bringing these ideas forward into the world of practice, it implies researchers and practitioners who listen in different ways, beyond the self-evident and the taken-for-granted, will have richer understandings to call on when making inferences and decisions. Fiumara (1990) referred to "the listening attitude" (p. 145). It is a "way of listening" that influences not only what the practitioner hears but also what the person is drawn to say. Listening is a mode of "inviting." It invites talking openly and reflecting deeply. Listening is also a mode of "showing." It shows that experiences are heard, understood and affirmed. Hence, listening is a way of informing practice through being attuned to what is otherwise merely hinted at. The questions which "need" to be asked in the moment will come in the midst of listening. As such, "practice as listening" is not a turning away from the doing of practice but a turning towards it. Practice as listening invites conversation in the direction of what is ordinarily covered over. Thus, listening also involves silence which opens up the space for that which may be said.

How might listening become a more intentional habit of practice? Fiumara's (1990) listening attitude as a way of informing practice needs to become, in Dewey's terms, an attitude or "habit of mind" (Jackson 2006, p. 60) that aims to deeply understand experiences in order to find solutions to everyday challenges. Dewey's pragmatic approach is deeply moral. It is "a way of employing intelligence for the betterment of humankind in general and of the individual in particular" (Jackson 2006, p. 60). It is suggested that listening is the mode of achieving this.

3.6 Conclusion

Both Heidegger's and Dewey's thinking dwelled in the complex realm of ordinary, everyday human existence. This means there are fundamental points which seem to line up in their philosophies, and those that diverge. In spite of those differences, both Dewey's transactionalism and Heidegger's interpretive phenomenology can inform a way of thinking, a listening attitude, which guides how we come to think about, and understand peoples' occupational experiences.

This chapter has approached the conundrum of understanding how Heideggerian phenomenology and Deweyan transactionalism might inform an occupational understanding of the world through sharing four ordinary stories told by elder New Zealanders, aged 77–97 years. In turn, and collectively, the stories told by Curly, Ferguson, May, and Christina allow the reader to listen for the way notions of the habitual, the relational, and the precarious can play out through doing everyday occupations. Intentionally, the text aimed to light up what bringing in a transactional lens, alongside a phenomenological lens, can add to our understandings of occupational engagement. Both approaches have their place; the Heideggerian perspective illuminates more of the experiences and meanings of understandings of being in the world while the Deweyan perspective reveals more of the understandings of acting thoughtfully in the world of everyday situations.

In bringing the chapter to a close, one question is left; "how might the practitioner or researcher know when to choose a Heideggerian versus a Deweyan perspective?" We suggest it will be when the fundamental notions appeal; that is, when the basic underpinnings feel right. Essentially, Heidegger wanted to know what "is". Heidegger's truth is grounded in a primordial disclosure of things as they exist in the world. In contrast, Dewey wanted to know what works. Dewey's truth is only validated if it solves practical problems in the real world (Blattner 2000). In relation to understanding the world of human occupation more deeply, both have their distinctive place.

References

Alexander, T. M. (2006). Dewey, dualism and naturalism. In J. R. Shook & J. Margolis (Eds.), *A companion to pragmatism* (pp. 184–192). Malden: Blackwell.

Blattner, W. D. (2000). The primacy of practice and assertoric truth: Dewey and Heidegger. In M. Wrathall & J. Malpas (Eds.), *Heidegger, authenticity, and modernity: Essays in honour of Hubert L. Dreyfus* (Vol. 1, pp. 231–250). Cambridge: Massachusettes Institute of Technology.

Boisvert, R. D. (1998). *John Dewey: Rethinking our time*. Albany: State University of New York Press.

Campbell, J. (1995). *Understanding John Dewey: Nature and cooperative intelligence*. Chicago: Open Court.
Capps, J. M., & Capps, D. (Eds.). (2005). *James and Dewey on belief and experience*. Chicago: University of Illinois Press.
Crowe, B. D. (2006). *Heiddeger's religious origins: Destruction and authenticity*. Bloomington: Indiana University Press.
Cutchin, M. P. (2007). From society to self (and back) through place: Habit in transactional context. *OTJR: Occupation, Participation and Health, 27*(supp), 50S–59S.
Cutchin, M. P., & Dickie, V. (2012). Transactionalism: Occupational science and the pragmatic attitude. In G. Whiteford & C. Hocking (Eds.), *Critical perspectives on occupational science: Society, inclusion, participation* (pp. 23–37). London: Wiley.
Cutchin, M. P., Aldrich, R. M., Bailliard, A. L., & Coppola, S. (2008). Action theories for occupational science: The contributions of Dewey and Bordieu. *Journal of Occupational Science, 15*, 157–165.
Dewey, J. (1957a). *Human nature and conduct: An introduction to social psychology*. New York: The Modern Library (Original work published in 1922).
Dewey, J. (1957b). *Reconstruction in philosophy*. Boston: Beacon (Original work published in 1920).
Dewey, J. (1958). *Experience and nature*. New York: Dover Publications.
Dewey, J. (2005a). Art as experience (1934). In J. M. Capps & D. Capps (Eds.), *James and Dewey on belief and experience* (pp. 268–283). Chicago: University of Illinois Press.
Dewey, J. (2005b). The postulate of immediate empiricism. In J. M. Capps & D. Capps (Eds.), *James and Dewey on belief and experience* (pp. 189–195). Chicago: University of Illinois Press (Original work published in 1909).
Fesmire, S. (2003). *John Dewey and moral imagination*. Bloomington: Indiana University Press.
Fiumara, G. C. (1990). *The other side of language: A philosophy of listening* (C. Lambert, Trans.). New York: Routledge.
Garrison, J. (1999). John Dewey, Jacques Derrida, and the metaphysics of presence. *Transactions of the Charles S. Peirce Society, XXXV*(2), 346–372.
Harman, G. (2007). *Heidegger explained: From phenomenon to thing*. Chicago: Open Court.
Heatwole Shank, K., & Cutchin, M. P. (2010). Transactional occupations of older women aging-in-place: Negotiating change and meaning. *Journal of Occupational Science, 17*, 4–13.
Heidegger, M. (1962). *Being and time* (J. Macquarrie & E. Robinson, Trans., 7th ed.). Oxford: Blackwell (Original work published in 1927).
Hollis, M. (1977). The self in action. In R. S. Peters (Ed.), *John Dewey reconsidered* (pp. 56–75). London: Routledge & Kegan Paul.
Jackson, P. W. (2006). John Dewey. In J. R. Shook & J. Margolis (Eds.), *A companion to pragmatism* (pp. 54–66). Malden: Blackwell.
James, W. (2005). The Chicago school. In J. M. Capps & D. Capps (Eds.), *James and Dewey on belief and experience* (pp. 172–178). Chicago: University of Illinois Press (Original work published in 1904).
Kawharu, I. H. (Ed.). (1994). *Waitangi: Māori and Pākehā perspectives of the Treaty of Waitangi*. Auckland: Oxford University Press.
King, M. (2001). *A guide to Heidegger's being and time*. Albany/New York: State University of New York Press.
Koschmann, T., Kuutti, K., & Hickman, L. (1998). The concept of breakdown in Heidegger, Leont'ev, and Dewey and its implications for education. *Mind, Culture, and Activity, 5*(1), 25–41.
Margolis, J. (1998). Dewey in dialogue with continental philosophy. In L. A. Hickman (Ed.), *Reading Dewey: Interpretations for a postmodern generation* (pp. 231–256). Bloomington: Indiana University Press.
Moorfield, J. C. (1988). *Te kakano*. Auckland: Longman Paul.
Polkinghorne, D. E. (2000). Psychological inquiry and the pragmatic and hermeneutic traditions. *Theory & Psychology, 10*(4), 453–479.
Vessey, D. (2009). Philosophical hermeneutics. In J. R. Shook & J. Margolis (Eds.), *A companion to pragmatism* (pp. 209–214). Chichester: Wiley-Blackwell.
Wrathall, J. (2005). *How to read Heidegger*. London: Granta Books.

Chapter 4
Resituating the Meaning of Occupation: A Transactional Perspective

Kirk Reed and Clare Hocking

4.1 Introduction

The focus of this chapter is the transactional nature of the meaning of occupation. The discussion draws on the findings of a hermeneutic phenomenological study (Reed 2008) and is informed by the works of Martin Heidegger and John Dewey. It highlights that the meanings of occupations are situated in the context of people's everyday experience and shaped by others in the world as well as the constellation of concerns that make up people's lives. The chapter will begin by exploring the notion of meaning. It moves on to discuss the meanings uncovered in Reed's study and the transactional nature of occupation's meaning, and concludes by discussing the implications for occupational therapy, occupational science and research. Our intent is to show that the meaning of occupation should be considered from broad perspectives that look beyond the individual.

Our opening proposition is that people engage in occupation every waking moment of their lives. Based on that experience, individuals are likely to have a broad but shared understanding of what the physical doing of an occupation looks like in their own culture and arguably what that occupation means for others. Recent neuroscience findings lend some support to that proposal, demonstrating links between observing others' actions, understanding their experience, and the semantic meaning of language (Liew and Aziz-Zadeh 2011). Yet the meaning of occupation is often unspoken; it is hidden in the everyday doing, and this is what creates its complexity. The taken for granted nature of occupation raises the question of how well people understand the complex and interwoven layers of meaning that exist in occupation, which like a kaleidoscope are "different again" in each situation.

K. Reed (✉) • C. Hocking
Department of Occupational Science and Therapy, Auckland University of Technology, Auckland, New Zealand
e-mail: kirk.reed@aut.ac.nz

M.P. Cutchin and V.A. Dickie (eds.), *Transactional Perspectives on Occupation*,
DOI 10.1007/978-94-007-4429-5_4, © Springer Science+Business Media B.V. 2013

4.2 Meaning Explored

To understand more about the meaning of occupation, it is necessary to discover what is signified by "meaning." The concept itself relates to knowledge of an entity and understanding what is perceived by it, based on its purpose or how it is experienced or intended. Scholars and researchers from a range of fields have explored meaning as expressed through language, arising from personal experience, being situated in the social world, embedded in human occupation, and having deep philosophical roots. The work of some of these scholars and researchers will now be considered.

4.2.1 Social Science Perspectives on Meaning

Meaning is primarily expressed through language. Accordingly, linguistic theories have been advanced to explain how words convey meaning. Putman's (1975) Theory of Meaning, for example, posited that every word has a specific number of components that convey its meaning, including the object to which it refers, the general category to which that object belongs, and its characteristic qualities, such as being wet, ambulant or aggressive. In addition to linguistic concerns about how meaning is communicated, attention has been given to where it resides. From a psychological perspective, Reker and Wong (1988) proposed that meaning is situated in a continuum of contexts. At one end of the continuum there are self-definitions, where a person's sense of meaning depends on his or her personal history, and depth and breadth of experience, while social definitions of meaning are at the other end of the continuum.

At the individualist end, Berman (1993), another psychologist, suggested that the meaning of life originates in the dynamic interplay between individuality and conformity. He proposed that there is a never ending search for uniqueness and selfhood along with a search for community and a sense of belonging. More recently, a group of American psychologists established a strong link between positive affect and experiencing meaning in life, in the subjective sense that one's life has a purpose or coherence, at least amongst undergraduate psychology students. Experiencing meaning was less strongly associated with goal-related activity, and the research did not shed light on meaning-making itself (King et al. 2006). At the social end of Reker and Wong's (1988) continuum, Bruner (1990), also a psychologist, considered meaning to be something that is negotiated with others and passed between them, thus constructed in a person's social world. Similar understandings about the socially mediated nature of meaning are central to Blumer's (1969) theory of symbolic interactionism, which holds that social interaction is both the source of the symbolic meanings held by people, objects, events and so on, and the interpretive process through which individuals understand their experiences. The essence of symbolic interactionism is that people act towards things on the basis of the symbolic meanings they hold, that the meaning arises out of social interaction with others, and that the meaning is modified through an interpretative process in dealing with the things that a person encounters.

4.2.2 Occupational Perspectives on Meaning

Occupational therapists and occupational scientists have also paid attention to the meaning of occupation; however, this is an area that continues to be relatively unexplored, particularly from the perspective of lived experience. This is somewhat surprising given that Kielhofner asserted in 1995 that "it is a long standing adage that, to be effective occupational therapy must be meaningful to the patient" (p. 265). Support for the idea that meaning is one of the key features of occupation comes from Hasselkus' (2002) assertion that "meaning and everyday occupation are the essentials for life" (p. xi), and Jackson and her colleagues' (1998) suggestion that "the ability to find meaning through occupation is a central consideration in people's lives" (p. 328). Therefore, to understand the true nature of occupation it is essential to understand meaning. Nelson's (1987) work in defining occupational forms identified a critical aspect of meaning in relation to occupation, in recognizing that while the purpose of engaging in occupation can be a source of meaning, the purpose might equally evolve from meaning. The meaning of occupation is also believed to arise from a range of other sources, in particular through social organizations. For instance, Persson et al. (2001) identified that one way of establishing the meaning held by particular occupations is through social organizations, which determine the value placed on an occupation and embed that meaning in position descriptions, organizational structures and codes of conduct.

Another way of assigning occupational meaning is through identification with a group, which creates a sense of belonging and self-identity. For instance, Magnus (2001) described meaning as being connected to how occupations are seen in the culture in which a person belongs, and frequently, as allowing others to create and associate the identity of a person with a particular set of occupations. It also seems that when a person experiences an occupational loss, the meaning associated with that occupation becomes more apparent and no longer being able to perform the occupation changes one's self concept. That suggestion arises from Laliberte Rudman et al. (1996) finding that when healthy people talk about occupation, basic occupations such as cooking or grooming are identified as automatic and having diminished meaning that people are no longer able to articulate. The results of that study are in sharp contrast to a study of older Thai and New Zealand women, which found that when they engaged in cooking and recipe work for culturally significant events, Songkran and Christmas, these occupations held rich meanings. For the Thai women this included bringing people together in a social network through food and for the New Zealand women the meaning of the occupation lay in the preparation of food and its connection to past, present and future (Hocking et al. 2002).

4.2.3 Philosophical Perspectives on Meaning: Heidegger and Dewey

The works of Martin Heidegger [1889–1976], a German phenomenological philosopher, and John Dewey [1859–1952], an American pragmatist philosopher, are brought together to inform this discussion. Heidegger and Dewey were writing at about the same time in history, and their works have been influential in how the everydayness of being is understood. Heidegger's (1962) life work rested on the fundamental question, what is the "meaning of Being"[1] (p. 24). From his perspective, meaning is that "from which something is understandable as the thing it is" (King 2001, p. 6). Meaning enables us to understand a thing from a world of human existence. In attempting to find meaning, Heidegger's notion of horizon is fundamental. It is from the horizon of Being-in-the-World that we primarily understand things. Everyday experiences are interpreted through this horizon—the eye of background meaning—which includes past experience, knowledge, and attitudes. This notion is more clearly articulated by King (2001) who told us that "the world of our own existence is the horizon in which our everyday understanding moves" (p. 6).

Like others, Heidegger's view is that our understandings are passed down through language and the culture we are born into; these pre-understandings are subject to change over time, however we are never free from our own pre-understandings and it is from these pre-understandings that understanding moves. It is the horizon of our world that is primarily "meaning giving". From our reading of Dewey it seems that his notion of "habits" is akin to Heidegger's notion of pre-understandings. Dewey (1922) conceives habits as essentially social customs that individuals take up, and which then enable or constrain their behavior. Heidegger's pre-understanding is more personal in its origins, and acts as a pre-reflective understanding of Being that helps constitute experience, in that we always start that experience from somewhere. These notions have some alignment but they are involved in different ways that seem too complex to discuss here.

Dewey (2008) also offered a complimentary perspective, suggesting that "the meaning of anything (or better, of any event) lies in its future, in that which succeeds it" (p. 403). Thus meaning is acquired when a person is able to take and use things as a means to achieve the remote consequences which may coordinate his or her actions in the present. What Dewey seems to be saying is that we choose an action after imagining a range of actions and their potential consequences. The potential meaning is imagined in the context and future situation, in the ongoing and shifting transactions that occur between others and objects in the world. An action is chosen in terms of the anticipated meaning and how that action appears to us in that time and place, based on how other actions are seen in the sphere of possibilities that are open to us. From Dewey's perspective, it is in the looking forward that meaning appears to emerge and in the imagination of what the range of possibilities hold.

[1] Being is capitalized to indicate "being" in the philosophical sense, as the central aspect of who a person is.

Dewey also suggested that often meaning is not conscious, rather it becomes conscious when action undergoes reconstruction through the art of imagination. As Alexander (1990) stated, "imagination must contend with the alternative possible meanings of the situation: possibilities will present themselves not in neutral light but as candidates for being the meaning of our actions" (p. 338). The situation can of course include others and it is in the relationship with others, of imagining the possibilities with others, that meaning emerges, where a thing or an event involves making something common between two centers of action and imaging what the consequences will be. This transaction is further explained by Garrison (2002), who identified that "any private meaning people may have, they make from meaning that originated in social transaction" (p. 14).

Both Heidegger and Dewey indicate that meaning occurs in context. From Heidegger's perspective it is in the horizon of being in the world that we primarily understand things; we come to an understanding of things in the context of past and present. From Dewey's perspective meaning lies in the transaction, of imagining the possibilities and what lies in the future. The work of Heidegger and Dewey is also significant in that they both espouse the view that there is a connection between the person and the world, that a person cannot be separated from the context in which he or she lives and that the person and context are part of one another. It is because of this connection that meaning needs to be considered as arising from the interaction of person and context, which includes objects, the world and others in the world.

Heidegger described this unique relationship as "Being-in-the-World"; from his point of view it is the characteristic way in which a person exists. It is the world that places us in context with other people, tools, equipment and everything else we are aware of or unaware of. We become familiar with the world through our engagement in our everyday existence. Familiarity with the world allows us to make sense of it based on experience. We come to understand something based on how we have used it or seen it used in the past, and it is from our engagement with that tool or piece of equipment that the meaning emerges. It is in the transaction between person, object and the world that meaning is made explicit and as we become aware of the ways in which the world around us is available to us, we come to understand how the world and the things in the world become meaningful.

Similarly Dewey's notion of "organism-in-the-environment-as-a-whole" (Dewey and Bentley 1949, p. 109) suggests a continuity of person and world, which is more than being part of one another. It suggests that a person and environment should be considered as co-defining. This is explained further in that human beings are transactional in their participation with the world. The participation requires a transaction of human and non-human things, which in turn modifies the person and the environment. Furthermore, no transaction stands alone; it is enmeshed in a body of activities. Dewey extended this further by suggesting that:

> …human life itself, both severally and collectively, consists of transactions in which human beings partake together with non-human things of the milieu along with other human beings, so that without this togetherness of human and non-human partakers we could not even stay alive, to say nothing of accomplishing anything. From birth to death every human being is a *Party*, so that neither he nor anything done or suffered can possibly be understood when it is separated from the fact of participation in an extensive body of transactions. (1948 p. 198)

4.3 Perspectives on Meaning Uncovered by Research

A phenomenological study (Reed et al. 2010) explored the meaning of occupation for 12 New Zealand adults who had experienced a disruption to their occupations. For the purposes of the study, the disruption was seen as a "way in" to begin the conversations and gather the stories of the ordinary occupations of the participants' everyday lives. The study, informed by the work of Heidegger, called for conversational interviews where participants were asked to describe things they had done over the previous week to 10 days. Following transcription, the interview data were analyzed by identifying key themes and engaging in a hermeneutic process of thinking and writing, which included going back to the work of Heidegger. The findings suggested that when life is disrupted and occupation can no longer be performed in a non-thinking manner, the occupation's meaning comes to light. Three themes emerged from the study; Being-with, the Call, and Possibilities, each intertwined and inter-connected with the others. These themes draw out the richness of the meaning of occupation from an experiential perspective and in the framework of being in relationship with others and in the dynamic and ever changing world.

We will focus on the theme of Being-with, as this theme best illustrates how the meaning of occupation is connected to others in the world, rather than being individually derived. Heidegger described Being-in-the-World as a world shared with others and suggested that "Being-with" others is the fundamental nature of human existence. He used the term "Dasein" to describe the unique characteristic that people have of reflecting on and wondering about their existence. In being able to reflect and wonder about our life we come to understand the meaning of being in context. We exist in a world that we cannot be separated from and thus because we are in the world we are in context with other people, tools and equipment. According to Heidegger, "Being-with is an existential characteristic of Dasein even when factically no Other is present-at-hand or perceived" (1962, p.156). Heidegger was not necessarily concerned with the dynamics of the relationship, rather he was more concerned with the influences of others on our being and how a person understands him or herself by being-with others. It is through being with others that we get a sense of who we are, by reflecting on similarities and differences between them and us, how others respond to our actions or non action, and how we navigate what is the right or wrong thing to do based on what has been determined by others as being correct or legitimate.

While the connections people have with others are influential, they are often hidden or lost in the everydayness of doing. The meaning and importance of being in relation to other people was, however, revealed in the participants' stories of occupation that had been changed by the disruption they were experiencing. Specifically their occupations revealed meanings of being wanted, being there, intimacy, working together, sharing an interest, and/or having a special bond. To illustrate this claim one of the participants from the study, a 66-year-old business owner called Frank, described how his ability to walk was restricted following an accident and that he was now not able to engage in his regular weekly walk with one of his granddaughters. Instead he had been spending time with another of his grandchildren who he did not usually see. Together they played games of dominoes, snakes and ladders, and cards. He described playing games:

> We had not been that close because she is usually pretty active, but she loved it and I realized that by actually sitting down and playing these games we formed a very special bond. She would ring up and say 'I bet you [won] granddad, when are we playing again?'

It is through the occupation of playing board games that Frank was able to connect with his granddaughter in a manner that had not been present before. The connection struck Frank as being important, how in the moment of engaging in the occupation there was a coming together as grandfather-and-granddaughter. The meaning becomes apparent in the transaction of the two of them. It is the Being-with and the nature of the relationship that gave the occupation meaning. There is a sense that while Frank felt this connection, so too had his granddaughter. It was through the occupation and the transaction that occurred during the occupation that a mutual connection was created. It was thus in the social transaction that the meaning of the occupation originated, sitting within a context of past experiences and future possibilities. One imagines that playing board and card games are not Frank's favorite occupations per se, but playing them with the granddaughter he loves made the experience meaningful and precious. It is from a place of looking back and imagining future possibilities that the meaning sits, perhaps never to be experienced in the same way or with the same person ever again.

Another example of meaning in relation to being-with comes from Pearl, a 27-year-old woman who had left full time work to become a student. She described two experiences of cooking a meal at home with the woman she rooms with:

> Usually when I cook it is with a particular flat mate. Often we plan what we will be having during the day with a few phone calls until a decision is made about what we will have and who will buy what. My flat mate has her own way of doing things. I usually do a lot more of the preparation and cleaning up and she does more of the actual cooking. We work together like a well-oiled machine. When we are cooking we will be chatting and having a glass of wine. When I cooked alone it wasn't nearly as much fun, in the end it felt like something that needed to be done. All I did was cook and watch a bit of television.

For Pearl, the cooking of the meal with her flat mate appears to be much more than just cooking the food. There is an air of occasion, excitement and anticipation which builds up over the day as they make their plans to purchase and cook the food. There is a sense of them imagining what the meal will be like, how good it will be, and how they will enjoy each other's company both during the cooking and eating of the meal. They come together and are both involved in the negotiation and decision making, they work as a team. There is a bond and synergy that shows itself in the way they are together, in the sense of enjoyment they get from each other's company and in working together. In contrast, Pearl's experience of cooking alone gives the sense that the meaning of occupation has changed in response to not having the other physically present. The memory remains but the transactional nature of the occupation is significantly different. Cooking alone became something that needed to be done; it was lonely, dreary and routine. The story from Pearl highlights how the meaning of occupation changes depending on the presence of the other. To cook with a friend is lively and fun; to cook alone merely a task, the kitchen dull and uninviting.

Frank and Pearl's stories and others in the study challenge the idea that the meaning of occupation is individually derived. The meaning of occupation is situated in the context in which the occupation occurs, and is not just an individualistic understanding; rather there are multiple layers that are related to the context and the people in the person's world. Even when the occupation is done in isolation from another person, there is connection to previous experiences of that occupation either involving others or having a link to others in some way. The idea that the meaning of occupation is contextual and transactional relates to Heidegger's notion of Being-in-the-world and Dewey's notion of organism-in-the-environment-as-a-whole. The experience of the participants shows that a person is always connected to the world and others in the world. Participating in an occupation modifies the person, other people, and/or the non-human environment. They are interconnected and inseparable. It is through this inseparable connection that meaning evolves. It is the transactions that occur with others and the world that brings meaning to the fore and it is this connection, the transaction, that allows meaning to exist.

4.4 Implications for Occupational Therapy and Science

The meaning of occupation exists in context and in the transactional nature of occupation that occurs with other people and non-human things. The complex layers of meaning are not necessarily obvious and tend to remain hidden, both to the individual and to those in the world of that person, even when the occupation is done in isolation. In the delivery of occupational therapy services, therapists need to appreciate the context in which the occupation occurs, of the others who are engaged in the occupation or who influence the occupation past or present and how the occupation modifies or is modified by the environment. Enabling a person to tell their story from an occupational perspective will allow the meaning of occupation to be revealed. Narrative that focuses on a person telling his or her story from an occupational perspective requires a change in focus and requires time, which could be constrained by service delivery expectations such as managing a caseload, accounting for time spent with a person or meeting other service expectations. Adapting practice so that assessment processes and intervention plans focus on meaning will allow for more authentic occupational therapy practice by creating more significant relationships to develop with clients and focusing the outcomes of practice beyond function and performance. Eliciting narratives in order to understand the contextualized meaning of clients' occupations, however, will call for a change in the way that occupational therapists work in some settings, and requires evidence that will demonstrate the value of this approach to health service administrators.

While early definitions of occupation proposed by occupational scientists almost always referred to the meaning of occupation, studies that have addressed the meanings occupations hold are sparse. Among those published, few have considered the meaning of occupation in context, focusing instead on the meanings experienced at an individual level. Yet Reed's (2008) study showed that even mundane occupations hold complex layers of meaning. Those meanings are circumstantial, shaped by the transactional interplay of people, competing demands, imagined futures, and the environment. As life in Western society becomes busier and busier there is less time to reflect on what is meaningful, or explore the complex relationship of person and environment or how doing impacts on one's personal development. If, as Frankl (1984) and King et al. (2006) have suggested, finding meaning in life is key to positive functioning, then occupational scientists have the potential to make a significant contribution to understanding meaning in life through occupation, in particular how the meaning of occupation contributes to the health and well-being of individuals and communities. This idea is supported by Bailey and Jackson (2005) who identified that "occupational scientists tend to devote time to the mundane, everyday aspects of life. They do so because complexity often lurks below the surface of ordinary occupations. Occupational scientists recognize that it is in the doing of taken-for-granted occupations that life unfolds" (p. 57).

To understand how the meaning of occupation could be further explored, we suggest that the impact the social context has on meaning-making through occupation could be a suitable starting point. This could include exploring how family, cultural and social connections influence the occupations people pursue and the meaning people give to those occupations. This could be expanded to consider how technological advances affect meaning-making. For example, the advent of internet-based social networking tools has changed the way we build, sustain and maintain relationships. In this chapter, we have highlighted that the meaning of occupation is connected to being-with others. What is not so well understood is the impact on the meaning of occupation when the mode of Being-with changes. Exploring how life course development, occupational disruptions, obstacles and uncertainty in the human and non-human environment affect the meaning of occupation also are areas worthy of investigation. Developing understandings from the perspectives of children, those in their middle years, older adults and those from different cultural groups will bring new insights. Existing work provides a platform from which to build such understandings as well as evidence regarding meaning and occupation that brings culture, aging, leadership, responsibility, continuity and disruption and lack of responsibility for social outcomes into the mix (Asaba 2008; Heatwole Shank and Cutchin 2010; Hocking et al. 2002; Reed 2008; Russell 2008). Understanding the meaning of occupation as a transactional process suggests a need to continue to explore the meaning of occupation from the perspective of lived experience, not as something that is individually derived but as something that is connected to the broader context of the world.

4.5 Conclusion

Occupation is incredibly complex (Dickie 2010) and made up of interwoven layers of meaning. This meaning includes who the occupation is done with, the situation in which the occupation occurs, and how the occupation is contextualized and integrated in terms of past, present and future. This chapter has argued that the meanings of occupations are situated in the context of people's everyday experiences and need to be resituated and explored in that context. A transactional perspective brings to light the complexity of the meaning of occupation, and the philosophical work of Dewey and Heidegger provide a useful lens from which to view the interconnected and complex layers of meaning. This requires moving beyond an individual perspective to one where the situated context of person, others in the world, and the world itself are considered in their entirety. After all, occupation matters, for each one of us is always within a mode of being-occupied. It is the very essence of being human.

References

Alexander, T. M. (1990). Pragmatic imagination. *Transactions of the Charles S Pierce Society, 29*, 325–347.

Asaba, E. (2008). Hashi-ire: Where occupation, chopsticks and mental health intersect. *Journal of Occupational Science, 15*, 74–79.

Bailey, D., & Jackson, J. (2005). The occupation of household financial management among lesbian couples. *Journal of Occupational Science, 12*, 57–58.

Berman, M. (1993). Why modernism still matters. In S. Lash & J. Friedman (Eds.), *Modernity and identity* (pp. 33–58). Oxford: Blackwell.

Blumer, H. (1969). *Symbolic interactionism: Perspective and method*. Englewood Cliffs: Prentice-Hall.

Bruner, J. (1990). *Acts of meaning*. Cambridge: Harvard University Press.

Dewey, J. (1922). *Human nature and conduct: An introduction to social psychology*. New York: H. Holt and Company.

Dewey, J. (1948). Common sense and science: Their respective frames of reference. *The Journal of Philosophy, 45*(8), 197–208.

Dewey, J. (2008). In J. A. Boydston (Ed.), *John Dewey: The later works, 1925–1953: vol. 3: 1927–1928, Essays, reviews, miscellany, and "Impressions of Soviet Russia"*. Carbondale: Southern Illinois University Press.

Dewey, J., & Bentley, A. F. (1949). *Knowing and the known*. Boston: Beacon.

Dickie, V. (2010). Are occupations 'processes too complicated to explain'? What we can learn by trying. *Journal of Occupational Science, 17*, 195–203.

Frankl, V. E. (1984). *Man's search for meaning* (3rd ed.). New York: First Washington Square Press (Original work published in 1963).

Garrison, J. W. (2002). Habits as social tools in context. *Occupational Therapy Journal of Research, 22*(Supplement), 11–17.

Hasselkus, B. R. (2002). *The meaning of everyday occupation*. Thorofare: Slack.

Heatwole Shank, K., & Cutchin, M. (2010). Transactional occupations of older women ageing in place: Negotiating change and meaning. *Journal of Occupational Science, 17*, 4–13.

Heidegger, M. (1962). *Being and time* (J. Macquarrie & E. Robinson, Trans.). Oxford: Blackwell. (Original work published in 1927).

Hocking, C., Wright-St. Clair, V., & Bunrayong, W. (2002). The meaning of cooking and recipe work for older Thai and New Zealand women. *Journal of Occupational Science, 9*, 117–127.

Jackson, J., Carlson, M., Mandel, D., Zemke, R., & Clark, F. (1998). Occupation in lifestyle redesign: The well elderly study occupational therapy program. *American Journal of Occupational Therapy, 52*, 326–336.

Kielhofner, G. (1995). *A model of human occupation: Theory and application* (2nd ed.). Philadelphia: Williams and Wilkins.
King, M. (2001). *A guide to Heidegger's being and time*. Albany: State University of New York Press.
King, L. A., Hicks, J. A., Krull, J. L., & Del Gaiso, A. K. (2006). Positive affect and the experience of meaning in life. *Journal of Personality and Social Psychology, 90*(1), 179–196.
Laliberte Rudman, D., Valiant Cook, J., & Polatajko, H. (1996). Understanding the potential of occupation: A qualitative exploration of seniors' perspectives on activity. *American Journal of Occupational Therapy, 51*, 640–650.
Liew, S. L., & Aziz-Zadeh, L. (2011). The neuroscience of language and actions in occupation: A review of findings from brain and behavioral sciences. *Journal of Occupational Science, 18*, 97–114.
Magnus, E. (2001). Everyday occupations and the process of redefinition: A study of how meaning in occupation influences redefinition of identity in women with a disability. *Scandinavian Journal of Occupational Therapy, 8*, 115–124.
Nelson, D. L. (1987). Occupation: Form and performance. *American Journal of Occupational Therapy, 42*, 633–641.
Persson, D., Erlandsson, L. K., Eklund, M., & Iwarsson, S. (2001). Value dimensions, meaning and complexity in human occupation: A tentative structure for analysis. *Scandinavian Journal of Occupational Therapy, 8*, 7–18.
Putman, H. (1975). *Mind, language and reality. Philosophical papers* (Vol. 2). Cambridge: Cambridge University Press.
Reed, K. (2008). *Resituating the meaning of occupation in the context of living*. Doctoral thesis, Auckland University of Technology, Auckland, New Zealand. Retrieved from http://aut.researchgateway.ac.nz/handle/10292/398
Reed, K., Hocking, C., & Smythe, E. (2010). The interconnected meanings of occupation: The call, being-with, possibilities. *Journal of Occupational Science, 17*, 140–149.
Reker, G. T., & Wong, P. T. P. (1988). Aging as an individual process: Toward a theory of personal meaning. In J. E. Birren & V. L. Bengtson (Eds.), *Emergent theories of aging* (pp. 214–246). New York: Springer.
Russell, E. (2008). Writing on the wall: The form, functioning and meaning of tagging. *Journal of Occupational Science, 15*, 87–97.

Chapter 5
Conceptual Insights for Expanding Thinking Regarding the Situated Nature of Occupation

Debbie Laliberte Rudman and Suzanne Huot

5.1 Introduction

Research within occupational science has tended to neglect or de-emphasize ways in which the occupations of individuals and collectives are situated within macro-level political, economic and socio-cultural factors (Hocking 2000; Kantartzis and Molineux 2010; Laliberte Rudman 2010; Whiteford 2010). Within this chapter, we use the term "situated" to refer to the complex embeddedness of occupations within contexts. This situated nature of occupation, as articulated by Whiteford et al. (2005), means that "no human action is independent of the social, cultural, political and economic contexts in which it occurs. These contextual forces, to a greater or lesser extent, shape the form and performance of occupation as well the meaning ascribed to it by an individual or group" (p. 10). A similar concern regarding neglect of the ways in which contexts are always part of what humans do, particularly articulated in relation to the pervasive influence of individualism and dualistic thinking in occupational science, was part of the impetus for the introduction of transactionalism into the occupational science literature (Cutchin 2004; Dickie et al. 2006). Thus, the primary point of connection between this chapter and the meta-theoretical perspective of transactionalism is a shared interest in more fully developing a contextualized, or situated, view of occupation.

The Deweyan concept of transaction proposes a relational, holistic perspective on the interpenetration of individuals and contexts, working against a dualistic

D.L. Rudman (✉)
School of Occupational Therapy, and Occupational Science Field,
Health and Rehabilitation Sciences Graduate Program, Western University,
London, ON, Canada
e-mail: drudman@uwo.ca

S. Huot
School of Occupational Therapy, Western University, London, ON, Canada

M.P. Cutchin and V.A. Dickie (eds.), *Transactional Perspectives on Occupation*,
DOI 10.1007/978-94-007-4429-5_5, © Springer Science+Business Media B.V. 2013

perspective that articulates persons and contexts as separable entities (Aldrich 2008). In turn, it has been argued that Dewey's concept of transaction, which addresses ways in which people and environments continually co-define and co-constitute each other (Cutchin and Dickie 2012), provides a fruitful way forward to study occupation as a "transaction joining person and situation" and "a way to functionally coordinate the intimate person-situation relationship" (Dickie et al. 2006, p. 90). However, Dewey has also been critiqued for primarily focusing on how humans functionally coordinate their actions to achieve harmony within situations, and not adequately attending to ways that relations of power impact on various actors' possibilities for action, as they possess differential resources and attributes within a situation (Cutchin et al. 2008; Stuhr 2003). As articulated by Stuhr (2003), "Thus Dewey talked confidently about *the* indeterminate situation that *we* experience, but he never asked directly the relevant political questions: Who are "we"? Whose situation is indeterminate? How was this indeterminate situation produced? By whom? Whose interests are served…?" (p. 162).

The assumption of homogeneity of interests and experiences and the neglect of inequities and power are important to re-address as Dewey also articulated that actions in situations are influenced by perceptions of possibilities (Joas 1996). If possibilities, and perceptions of them, are themselves differentially shaped, then it becomes necessary to consider how social relations of power shape transactions and, in turn, how occupations are always politically, socially and culturally situated. In particular, drawing on concepts from two bodies of critically located social theory, specifically, governmentality studies and Bourdieu's theory of practice, this chapter aims to outline ways occupational scientists can further consider power when examining the dynamic transactional relations of contexts and people. The section on governmentality studies is primarily written by Laliberte Rudman, drawing on her experiences utilizing governmentality studies to examine the contemporary re-structuring of retirement. The section on Bourdieu is primarily written by Huot, drawing on her experiences applying the concepts of field, habitus and capital in her doctoral critical ethnography exploring the integration experiences of French-speaking newcomers from visible minority groups in London, Ontario, Canada.

5.2 Governmentality Studies: Shaping Occupational Possibilities

Within Dewey's work, the situation, or the context of action, is viewed as generative of action in that it sets the stage for the possibilities of action (Cutchin and Dickie 2012). Concepts developed within Foucauldian-informed governmentality studies can be drawn upon to consider how power, also seen as productive or generative of action, operates to shape possibilities for occupation in ways tied to, and reproductive of, broader political values and aims (Laliberte Rudman 2010). Connecting this with Dewey, if actions in situations are influenced by perceptions of possibilities, governmentality studies provide a way to consider how such perceptions are shaped through technologies of government which enact power in accord with broader systems of thought regarding how best to govern populations and individuals.

Governmentality Studies is a diverse interdisciplinary field (Nadesan 2008; Rose et al. 2006). In this section, I draw on authors within governmentality studies whose work seeks to explicate how the governance of everyday life in contemporary societies occurs. Key concepts essential to understanding governmentality studies are first outlined, including government, power, rationalities, technologies, and subjectivity. Finally, the concept of "occupational possibilities" is described and briefly illustrated.

Governmentality scholars adopt Foucault's broad conceptualization of government as the "conduct of conduct" (Foucault 1991); that is, as "any attempt to shape with some degree of deliberation aspects of our behavior according to particular sets of norms and for a variety of ends" (Dean 2010, p. 18). The term broadens the notion of government beyond the actions of the state to include the plurality of agencies and authorities, such as health care professionals, organizational managers, educators, or self-help "experts," who seek to shape how individuals and groups come to understand themselves and how they act in the world. The term government also encompasses government of the self, that is, the processes through which individuals reflect upon and manage their own behavior. These processes of government of the self are themselves viewed as intimately linked to the broader circulation of knowledge regarding how this should best be done and towards what ends. Of particular relevance to occupational science, government is seen as intimately linked to occupation, that is, to how people think about what they should and can do in everyday life and the subsequent forms of doing they engage in. For example, Foucault (1982) indicated, "To govern, in this sense, is to structure the possible field of actions of others" (p. 790).

In considering how government is enacted, governmentality scholars draw on Foucault's conceptualization of power as intimately linked to knowledge and the production of "truths" (Foucault 1980). Rather than see power operating through repressing possibilities for action, power is seen as operating through the production and circulation of knowledge, or "truths," that seek to shape how people come to understand and act upon themselves in order to work towards particular idealized outcomes (Rose 1999). Although the thoughts and actions of individuals are not necessarily determined by truths, such knowledge comes to be taken-for-granted within beliefs and practices of individuals and collectives. Understanding how these truths are shaped, circulated, and become embedded, taken-for-granted aspects of everyday life requires attending to technologies of government. Technologies of government include non-discursive and discursive means, such as policies, media, consumer products, and types of programs, used to shape "the conduct, aspirations, needs, desires capacities of specific categories of individuals" (Dean 1994, p. 156) towards particular aims in line with broader political goals. Within a particular socio-historical context, a broader system of thought regarding how best to govern and towards what ends, termed "political rationality," guides the ways power is enacted through technologies. These rationalities address questions such as who and what needs to be governed, why they should be governed, how best to govern, and what the outcomes of governing should be. Thus, possibilities for action shaped through government are themselves shaped within broader rationalities such as neoliberalism, a particular rationality of contemporary prominence in Western societies, which emphasizes the need to govern in ways that shape individuals who are enterprising, prudential, and take up responsibility for themselves in a wide array of life areas (Rose et al. 2006).

To illustrate the ways in which governmentality scholars tie these various concepts together, I draw on Mitchell Dean's example of dieting as a practice of self-government. Dean (2010) discussed dieting as a practice of self-government shaped and idealized through the production and circulation of knowledge, via media, health care professionals, and other social authorities, regarding healthy eating and ideal body shapes. Such knowledge is presented in ways that enlist people to engage in dieting practices to work towards the achievement of a particular version of a "good," "responsible," or "controlled" body. This idealized body comes to be taken-for-granted as a healthy body, and also aligns with the interests of various social authorities to deflect attention away from larger social forces contributing to rising obesity rates or to the differential access of individuals to the resources required to engage in idealized healthy eating practices. While individuals are free to act outside of this particular version of a "good" or "controlled" body, engagement in the occupations associated with eating outside those deemed as ideal within such "truth regimes" may be viewed as abnormal, unnatural, and perhaps, morally transgressive (Rose 1999).

5.2.1 Discourses

Discourses, which consist of groups "of statements that provide a language for talking about a topic and a way of producing a particular kind of knowledge about a topic" (du Gay 1996, p. 43), are a particular type of technology of government through which "truths" are shaped and circulated (Bennett 2003). Several contemporary governmentality theorists emphasize that subjectivity is an essential object and target of contemporary discourses within neoliberal and advanced liberal contexts. Discourses addressing subjectivity are produced and circulated in ways that "make up" particular kinds of ideal subjects and seek to act upon peoples' sense of who they are and who they strive to be (Hacking 1986; Dean 1999; Rose 1999). As articulated by Ainsworth and Hardy (2004), discourses addressing subjectivity shape possibilities for identity. In turn, people take up such discourses in various ways as they negotiate and manage who they are and what they want to do in the world. Such discourses also outline "practices of the self," that is, how individuals need to act upon the self to work towards the achievement of ideal subjectivities (Rose 1999; Rose et al. 2006).

For example, in my critical discourse analysis work of Canadian media articles addressing retirement (Laliberte Rudman 2006), I outlined how four ideal subjectivities were shaped. Within this work, media articles are conceptualized as a technology of government that both reflects and contributes to the construction of dominant discourses. Within contemporary Western society, media plays a pivotal role as a site of discourse production that interplays with scientific, academic and other forms of texts and circulates discourses within peoples' everyday lives (Fairclough 1998; Smith 2007). The ideal subjectivities shaped in the Canadian media articles revolved around production-based and consumer-based subjectivities seeking to either defy age or reduce the risks of aging. Each of these idealized subjectivities was discursively constructed as an ideal subjectivity to work towards with aging, and sets of practices of the self were promoted as means to achieve idealized goals such as age-defiance, autonomy, and social inclusion. Placing these within the larger political rationality of neoliberalism, this analysis raised concerns regarding how such ideal subjectivities call upon aging individuals to engage in relentless practices of self-reflection and improvement, self-marketing, risk management, lifestyle maximization and body optimization, while simultaneously shifting problems of aging to the individual level and obscuring the need for state or societal forms of support such as pensions or health care programs. Moreover, positive subjectivities for aging individuals who experience disability, poverty, or other so-called "risks" of aging were absent, and indeed such individuals were sometimes framed as irresponsible, failed citizens.

It was in the midst of the analysis of the Canadian media texts addressing retirement that I began to see how the same discourses that shaped particular types of subjectivities as ideal, also marked out particular types of occupations as ideal, possible and appropriate for aging individuals. Based on subsequent discourse analysis studies of media texts, all focused on aspects of aging and retirement, I proposed the concept of occupational possibilities, as the "ways and types of doing that come to be viewed as ideal and possible with a specific historical context, and that come to be promoted and made available within that context" (Laliberte Rudman 2010, p. 55). Underpinned by key concepts drawn from governmentality studies, occupational possibilities are proposed to be integral to contemporary forms of government, such that a multiplicity of social actors seek to govern the occupations of individuals and collectivities via the use of technologies of government which shape particular occupations as ideal, possible, and ethical for particular individuals or collectives, while simultaneously marking out others as not possible, non-ideal, or unethical. This proposition overlaps with that of governmentality scholars who have noted a rise of activation technologies of government in neoliberal and advanced liberal societies. Such technologies seek to remake individuals and collectivities defined as at-risk of dependency and inactivity, such as the unemployed and those with disabilities, into active citizens who engage in an array of activities to ensure self-reliance and productivity, while simultaneously minimizing or neglecting societal barriers to their active engagement (Rose 1999; Mann 2007; Ilcan 2009). Although the ideal subjectivities and occupations outlined within discourses do not determine who individuals strive to be and how they will act, other research examining the individual negotiation of "positive aging" discourses points to various ways aging individuals incorporate such discourses in understanding themselves as aging individuals, choosing activities, and planning for the future (Kemp and Denton 2003; Cardona 2008).

5.2.2 *Differential Shaping of Occupational Possibilities*

Returning back to the argument that drawing on governmentality studies will enable consideration of how possibilities for action, and perceptions of possibilities are shaped, the concept of occupational possibilities provides one lens to critically consider how particular occupations come to be possibilities for particular types of people in particular situations, while simultaneously considering what other possibilities for occupation are neglected, downplayed, or shaped as non-ideal. Rather than take such possibilities for action as natural or as equally harmonious to all those involved in a situation, governmentality studies points to the need to consider questions related to how power is taken up, by whom, and towards what ends in the differential shaping of occupational possibilities. Thus, merging a governmentality perspective with a transactionalist perspective can enable examination of how relations of power differentially influence the possibilities for action available for various types of actors within situations.

For example, in a critical discourse analysis study addressing occupational possibilities shaped within discourses regarding ideal housing options for later life, the ways in which such discourses marked out particular occupations, connected to specific idealized places, as ideal and possible for the aging housing consumer were examined (Laliberte Rudman et al. 2009). Although these idealized occupations, which revolved around consumer activity, physically active leisure, and "cultured" occupations may open up occupational possibilities for those aging individuals financially and physically able to become part of idealized retirement homes and communities, they simultaneously set boundaries on what were seen as the "right" occupations for aging persons in such places. Moreover, these discourses excluded aging persons who face bodily, physical, financial and social challenges from taking up the subjectivity of the ideal aging housing consumer or the idealized occupations associated with this subjectivity.

5.3 Bourdieu's Theory of Practice: Voicing the Unspoken

Concepts drawn from Bourdieu's theory of practice fit well with a Deweyan-informed understanding of transactionalism, because both seek to bridge the socially constructed dichotomy of structure and agency, or environment and person. A theoretical framework guided by Bourdieu's concepts of field, habitus and capital was applied in my doctoral research exploring the integration experiences of French-speaking newcomers from visible minority groups in London, Ontario, Canada. The theory was used to stress the "dialogical" relationship between agency and structure and to highlight the reciprocal influence of human activity and the social context where it occurs (Layder 1994). Bourdieu's work addresses elements of social structure, which are often implied or ignored within research focusing on individuals, and further attends to how these are related to power and are unintentionally reproduced through everyday practice. Thus, Bourdieu highlights the importance of elements of the social structure for setting the conditions in which individuals routinely, and habitually, enact and shape identity through everyday social interactions and when engaging in occupation within particular places. This reflects Cutchin and Dickie's (2012) transactional argument that there is a need to move beyond a dualistic understanding of people as separate from the environment. This section of the chapter briefly describes two of Bourdieu's key concepts, field and habitus, and then provides an example taken from my research that illustrates how such a theory attends to power when exploring the situated nature of occupational engagement.

Bourdieu's theory suggests that all individuals within a given society do not have the same knowledge of, and access to, social rules and resources that shape the conditions of their existence and his conceptualization of power emphasizes how one's situation is inherently tied to one's social position. Specifically, he proposes that people's sense of social reality is related to the field of "doxa" and influences their degree of agency. Doxa is described as "that which is taken for granted" (Bourdieu 1993, p. 161) and refers to seemingly natural perceptions and opinions that are connected to fields and habitus. Thus, doxa can be understood as the pre-reflexive intuitive knowledge mediated by fields, which becomes internalized through one's habitus (Deer 2008). Different social settings, or "fields of practice," exist within the larger field of doxa and contextualize individuals' engagement in occupation. "Fields" are characterized by norms that over time become naturalized and self-evident. The more stable an "objective" structure, the more likely it is that individuals reproduce it on a day-to-day basis, and the more likely it is to be taken for granted. Social norms are thereby developed within a particular context where the natural and social worlds come to be viewed as self evident. Individuals' senses of limits are developed according to these norms, and the resulting conditionings associated with their circumstances of existence within particular fields produce their habitus (Bourdieu 1991; Thomson 2008).

"Habitus" refers to one's dispositions that have been acquired over time within a particular context (Bourdieu 1990) and can be understood as "a system of durable, transposable dispositions which functions as the generative basis of structured objectively unified practices" (Bourdieu 1979, p. vii). Habitus contributes to the routine nature of daily life and the reproduction of social structures by tacitly organizing people's practices. Indeed, Bourdieu (1990) argues that people are located within "real activity" (p. 436), they are actively present within the world and have practical relation to it on an ongoing basis, which serves to manage their words and actions "without ever unfolding a spectacle" (p. 436); that is, in an innate manner. One's habitus thus influences one's actions "more reliably than all formal rules and explicit norms" (Bourdieu 1990, p. 438). According to Thibodaux (2005), habitus exists as part of the social structure in relation to which an individual defines oneself, and as a result, it cannot be changed at will. Her interpretation of Bourdieu further suggests that habitus is a form of "envelope" for one's identity, in which one's past, present, and future ways of being are embodied or held together. Such embodied knowledge remains uncontested because "it is generated by the actions and interactions of the person himself or herself within the space he or she occupies in the social world" (Thibodaux 2005, p. 509). Similarly, Judith Lynam et al. (2007) described habitus as a 'comfort zone': "the physical places and social spaces in which we do not need to 'look for clues' to know how to participate" (p. 29).

Habitus inherently serves to organize people's occupations by shaping their tendencies, ways of being, and habitual states (Bourdieu 1977) and can thereby be linked to an occupational perspective based on processes of doing, being, becoming, and belonging. Indeed, Maton (2008) argued that habitus "focuses on our ways of acting, feeling, thinking and being. It captures how we carry within us our history, how we bring this history into our present circumstances [...]" (p. 52). Cutchin et al. (2008) also link Bourdieu's notion of practice to occupation by arguing that regular actions occur "in social contexts; contexts which are themselves produced by a combination of habitus, capital and field" (p. 162). The contextual nature of habitus thus serves to influence the way people of the same group (e.g., social group or class) commonly perceive, conceive, and objectify things, and the way they act; which may be distinct from the habitus of a different social group or class (Bourdieu 1977; Girard and Bauder 2007). By integrating a particular group of people through the production and reproduction of their ordering principles, rules and norms, habitus can serve as a mechanism of exclusion. Field and habitus are described by Bourdieu as interconnected, meaning that they must always be considered together as they are mutually reinforcing. Transactionalism, informed by Dewey's pragmatism, has also been described as a relational theory (Cutchin and Dickie 2012) because it can be applied to explore and better understand the relation *among* things, such as a person and his or her environment, rather than *within* them. Thus, explorations of occupation must go beyond the occupations themselves (i.e. what occurred) and consider the social space in relation to which particular occupations take place (Thomson 2008).

Within my doctoral research, participants discussed how negotiating the myriad transitions they experienced following international migration entailed having to learn "how things worked" within their host communities in order to move toward integration. This was in part due to their habitus becoming situated within fields outside which it had been developed. The resulting disjuncture between their habitus and the fields within which they found themselves following migration led to their uncertainty regarding their doing and being, affected their sense of belonging, and ultimately threatening who they felt they could become within their new and different context. Considering how people functionally coordinate their environments, as Garrison's (2001) discussion of Dewey suggests, promotes a more holistic understanding of the person-environment relationship. Yet also drawing on Bourdieu further enables a critical exploration of one's capacity, or lack thereof, to engage in such functional coordination. I briefly draw on data from one of the respondents, Makane (pseudonym), to illustrate why a transactional view of occupational engagement that specifically attends to power is essential for understanding the situated nature of occupation. The interviews were conducted in French and the quotations provided are translations.

5.3.1 Makane: A Case in Point

Makane had been in Canada approximately 10 years and had experienced a number of transitions to a variety of occupations related to the process of international migration. He emphasized the lack of fit he continued to experience between his habitus and the various fields he engaged in and described how this sense of not being sure how to "be" and "do" within particular contexts affected his engagement in occupation. For example, Makane discussed challenges in negotiating the Canadian labor market in general, and his workplace in particular. He explained that at work he initially had to learn how to "walk on eggs without breaking them," and that while he was now more used to the situation, he continued to find his job frustrating and stressful, in part because he worried about unintentionally breaking an "unwritten rule" of the workplace. He said that the most simple and mundane things were the most difficult in Canada, and that taking things lightly and making assumptions about what seemed perfectly natural to him could end up causing him problems. He argued that learning the subtleties of Canadian life, including everyday occupation, was essential to integration:

> You can't succeed here if you don't want to, it's a universal language, a common language that everyone speaks, you have to speak it, there are ways of doing,…. Canada is, the people are so, they are open, they accept everyone but,… you have to reflect on everything that you do. In your unconscious you have to say oh, maybe there are other ways of doing,… if you don't start, they will never tell you. They will leave you in your little world.

He emphasized the need to learn to perform appropriately within particular contexts and to a certain extent did so by "acting how they act and not how you perceive things." By trying to function in this way, he explained that he was always looking back to evaluate his actions and questioning his way of doing. As a result, he argued that he did not see a situation in which he could not adapt himself. Placing the onus on himself to change his ways of doing and being reflected his argument that people can act on themselves but not on others. Notwithstanding such efforts on his part, Makane still did not fully feel he belonged in the host society; this despite having become a Canadian citizen, owning a home and car, and having a full time job—all traditional markers of successful integration. While he discussed learning to perform accordingly within particular fields (e.g., the workplace), this was ultimately not a simplistic process of learning to "act Canadian." Because occupation is related to habitus, shifting one's occupational performance to suit a given context also entails a more fundamental alteration of one's habitus. A negotiation occurs as newcomers may no longer tacitly know how to perform and have to reflect upon their naturalized dispositions prior to engaging in occupation. Ultimately, using stronger language, Makane described integration as a form of "jihad" upon oneself, whereby rather than make excuses for why he would not be able to succeed, he sacrificed himself to do what was necessary in order to find a job that provided stability for his family.

While Makane's wording above implies that he views the learning of social norms largely as an individual process that takes place over time, other comments he made suggest that he nonetheless recognizes the challenges to doing so are not entirely in one's control, emphasizing social power relations that can restrict agency. For instance, he addressed the issue of institutional racism he felt existed within the Canadian labor market. He explained that the discrimination newcomers from visible minority groups faced was often not overt. He said that "when you send the CV a thousand times and no one calls you, the people just look by family name. You don't have any chances." He used this example to explain that discrimination is often implicitly connected to one's social identity. For instance, he saw those from the "non-visible majority" getting jobs while he continued to face difficulty in integrating into the workforce:

> [I]t is not the same market for visible minorities.... but you come from somewhere that, I don't know, from the Congo, you come, you want to do management, administration, you could have ten doctorates but you won't find work, you have to be rational. If you want to return home, so much the better, but here it's not, those jobs, it doesn't reflect your portrait. The market is well structured, there are jobs where it's not for everyone....

Yet, the discrimination newcomers face may not be solely tied to their visible markers of social identity (e.g., race). In considering the discussion of habitus above, if migrants are uncertain of how to act within a particular field, they may not be marginalized simply because they look different, but also because they may "do" things differently. While alternative ways of doing and being are not as easily recognizable, a newcomer's habitus may thus become "racialized."

Using the theoretical concepts of field and habitus taken from Bourdieu's theory of practice serves to emphasize the necessity of considering social power relations in discussions of transactionalism. As people seek to coordinate with their environments, their agential capacity to do so is always related to their particular situation within the larger social structure. The habitus of dominant social groups within particular fields of practice ultimately serves as a source of power which enables some to engage in occupation in a taken-for-granted manner, while others may struggle with learning the unwritten rules of society and performing according to them. Thus, individuals who experience a disjuncture between habitus and field may face challenges to occupational engagement, in part due to their resulting uncertainty of how to do and be within particular situations, but also due to the assumption on the part of powerful groups that "others" with a different habitus will not know how to act accordingly within the situation or that their ways of doing occupation are problematic.

5.4 Conclusion

Transactionalism challenges occupational scientists to think differently about occupation, particularly in ways that consider occupation as embedded in relations between people and contexts, and attend to how people and their environments co-define and co-constitute each other (Cutchin and Dickie 2012). Both governmentality studies and concepts from Bourdieu's theory of practice have previously been identified as potentially commensurate with a transactional approach. Cutchin and Dickie have argued that work drawing upon governmentality scholarship to examine discursive effects upon occupation is generally supportive of a transactional approach as it offers a way "to understand relational dynamics between contextual elements and people in situations." Cutchin et al. (2008) also argued for the commensurability of several aspects of the work of Dewey and Bourdieu, similarly arguing that Bourdieu's greater emphasis on elements of power can lead to new insights into the transactional view of occupation. Within this chapter, we have further explored potential points of connection between these various theoretical perspectives, despite possible ontological or epistemological differences.

We propose that addressing ways in which power operates within and through social relations will further enable occupational science to take up transactionalism. Governmentality studies and Bourdieu's theory of practice provide two lenses through which inter-connections between power and occupation can be considered. Both these lenses point to the importance of considering the productive nature of power and its effects on what people, and collectives, come to take-for-granted regarding what they and others should and can do. As well, these lenses enable consideration of how people and collectives marked out socially by age, gender, language, class, and other identifiers have differential access to knowledge and resources that enable engagement in occupations in taken-for-granted, idealized, and "functional" ways.

Within the introduction to this chapter, we articulated that the primary point of connection between this chapter and the meta-theoretical perspective of transactionalism is a shared interest in more fully developing a contextualized, or situated, view of occupation. In addition, in line with Dewey's commitment to using theory and research to create a better world and enriching opportunities for people to grow through acting in the world, the ideas outlined in this chapter provide theoretical tools that occupational scientists can draw upon to imagine and promote more equitable possibilities for doing and being.

References

Ainsworth, S., & Hardy, C. (2004). Critical discourse analysis and identity: Why bother? *Critical Discourse Studies, 1*, 225–259.

Aldrich, R. M. (2008). From complexity theory to transactionalism: Moving occupational science forward in theorizing the complexities of behavior. *Journal of Occupational Science, 15*, 147–156.

Bennett, T. (2003). Culture and governmentality. In J. Z. Bratich, J. Packer, & C. McCarthy (Eds.), *Foucault, cultural studies and governmentality* (pp. 47–66). Albany: State University of New York Press.

Bourdieu, P. (1977). *Outline of a theory of practice*. London: Cambridge University Press.

Bourdieu, P. (1979). *Algeria 1960: The disenchantment of the world: The sense of honour: The Kabyle house or the world reversed*. New York: Cambridge University Press.

Bourdieu, P. (1990). Structures, habitus, practices. In C. Lemert (Ed.). *Social theory: The multicultural and classic readings* (2004, pp. 435–440). Boulder: Westview Press.

Bourdieu, P. (1991). *Language and symbolic power*. Cambridge: Harvard University Press.
Bourdieu, P. (1993). Structures, habitus, power: Basis for a theory of symbolic power. In N. B. Dirks, G. Eley, & S. B. Ortner (Eds.), *Culture, power, history: A reader in contemporary social theory* (pp. 155–199). Princeton: Princeton University Press.
Cardona, B. (2008). 'Healthy ageing' policies and anti-ageing ideologies and practices: On the exercise of responsibility. *Medical Health Care and Philosophy, 11*, 475–483.
Cutchin, M. P. (2004). Using Deweyan philosophy to rename and reframe adaptation-to-environment. *American Journal of Occupational Therapy, 58*, 303–312.
Cutchin, M. P., & Dickie, V. (2012). Transactionalism: Occupational science and the pragmatic attitude. In G. Whiteford & C. Hocking (Eds.), *Critical perspectives in occupational science: Society, inclusion and participation* (pp. 23–37). London: Wiley.
Cutchin, M. P., Aldrich, R. M., Bailliard, A. L., & Coppola, S. (2008). Action theories for occupational science: The contributions of Dewey and Bourdieu. *Journal of Occupational Science, 15*, 157–165.
Dean, M. (1994). A social structure of many souls: Moral regulation, government and self-formation. *The Canadian Journal of Sociology, 19*(2), 145–168.
Dean, M. (1999). *Governmentality: Power and rule in modern society*. London: Sage.
Dean, M. (2010). *Governmentality: Power and rule in modern society* (2nd ed.). London: Sage.
Deer, C. (2008). Doxa. In M. Grenfell (Ed.), *Pierre Bourdieu: Key concepts* (pp. 119–130). Stocksfield: Acumen.
Dickie, V., Cutchin, M. P., & Humphry, R. (2006). Occupation as transactional experience: A critique of individualism in occupational science. *Journal of Occupational Science, 13*, 83–93.
du Gay, P. (1996). *Consumption and identity at work*. London: Sage.
Fairclough, N. (1998). Political discourse in the media: An analytical framework. In A. Bell & P. Garrett (Eds.), *Approaches to media discourses* (pp. 142–162). Oxford: Blackwell.
Foucault, M. (1980). Two lectures. In C. Gordon (Ed.), *Power/knowledge: Selected interviews and other writings 1972–1977* (pp. 78–108). New York: Pantheon Books.
Foucault, M. (1982). The subject and power. *Critical Inquiry, 8*(4), 777–795.
Foucault, M. (1991). Governmentality (P. Pasquino, Trans.). In G. Burchell, C. Gordon, & P. Miller (Eds.), *The Foucault effect: Studies in governmentality* (pp.87–104). Chicago: University of Chicago Press.
Garrison, J. (2001). An introduction to Dewey's theory of functional "trans-action": An alternative paradigm for activity theory. *Mind, Culture, and Activity, 8*, 275–296.
Girard, E. R., & Bauder, H. (2007). Assimilation and exclusion of foreign trained engineers in Canada: Inside a professional regulatory organization. *Antipode, 39*(1), 35–53.
Hacking, I. (1986). Making up people. In T. C. Heller et al. (Eds.), *Reconstructing individualism* (pp. 222–236). Stanford: Stanford University Press.
Hocking, C. (2000). Occupational science: A stock take of accumulated insights. *Journal of Occupational Science, 7*, 58–67.
Ilcan, S. (2009). Privatizing responsibility: Public sector reform under neoliberal government. *Canadian Review of Sociology, 46*, 207–234.
Joas, H. (1996). *The creativity of action*. Chicago: University of Chicago Press.
Kantartzis, S., & Molineux, M. (2010). The influence of Western society's construction of a healthy daily life on the conceptualization of occupation. *Journal of Occupational Science, 18*, 62–80.
Kemp, C. L., & Denton, M. (2003). The allocation of responsibility for later life: Canadian reflections on the roles of individuals, governments, employers and families. *Ageing & Society, 23*, 737–760.
Laliberte Rudman, D. (2006). Shaping the active, autonomous and responsible modern retiree: An analysis of discursive technologies and their links with neo-liberal political rationality. *Ageing and Society, 26*, 181–201.
Laliberte Rudman, D. (2010). Occupational possibilities. *Journal of Occupational Science, 17*, 55–59.

Laliberte Rudman, D., Huot, S., & Dennhardt, S. (2009). Shaping ideal places for retirement: Occupational possibilities within contemporary media. *Journal of Occupational Science, 16*, 18–24.

Layder, D. (1994). *Understanding social theory*. Thousand Oaks: Sage.

Lynam, M. J., Browne, A. J., Reimer Kirkham, S., & Anderson, J. M. (2007). Re-thinking the complexities of 'culture': What might we learn from Bourdieu? *Nursing Inquiry, 14*(1), 23–34.

Mann, K. (2007). Activation, retirement planning and restraining the 'third age'. *Social Policy & Society, 6*, 279–292.

Maton, K. (2008). Habitus. In M. Grenfell (Ed.), *Pierre Bourdieu: Key concepts* (pp. 49–65). Stocksfield: Acumen.

Nadesan, M. H. (2008). *Governmentality, biopower and everyday life*. New York: Routledge.

Rose, N. (1999). *Powers of freedom: Reframing political thought*. Cambridge: University of Cambridge Press.

Rose, N., O'Malley, P., & Valverde, M. (2006). Governmentality. *Annual Review of Law and Social Science, 2*, 83–104.

Smith, J. L. (2007). Critical discourse analysis for nursing research. *Nursing Inquiry, 14*, 60–70.

Stuhr, J. J. (2003). *Pragmatism, postmodernism and the future of philosophy*. New York: Routledge.

Thibodaux, L. R. (2005). Habitus and the embodiment of disability through lifestyle. *American Journal of Occupational Therapy, 59*, 507–515.

Thomson, P. (2008). Field. In M. Grenfell (Ed.), *Pierre Bourdieu: Key concepts* (pp. 67–81). Stocksfield: Acumen.

Whiteford, G. (2010). Occupation in context. In M. Curtin, M. Molineux, & J. Supyk-Mellson (Eds.), *Occupational therapy and physical dysfunction: Enabling occupation* (6th ed., pp. 135–149). London: Elsevier.

Whiteford, G., Klomp, N., & Wright-St. Clair, V. (2005). Complexity theory: Understanding occupation, practice and context. In G. Whiteford & V. Wright St. Clair (Eds.), *Occupation and practice in context* (pp. 3–15). Sydney: Churchill Livingston.

Chapter 6
Exploring the Transactional Quality of Everyday Occupations Through Narrative-in-Action: Meaning-Making Among Women Living with Chronic Conditions

Sissel Alsaker, Staffan Josephsson, and Virginia A. Dickie

6.1 Introduction

Most of us would agree that humans' everyday occupations are complex and multifaceted and that to understand them properly we must look beyond the individual. The fluidity and emergence of engagement in everyday occupations multiplies the complexity. Because occupations take place within local cultures, it is necessary to think about the role of culture in occupation, but to do so without relying on artificial dualisms that set up barriers to our understanding of fluidity, emergence, and holism of occupation. Yet even with the best intentions, we often fall back on the use of factors, components, and characteristics to describe occupational life rather than understanding the more holistic, ongoing processes that emerge in everyday experience.

A transactional perspective on occupation has been presented as a way to access knowledge about processes of occupation (Dickie et al. 2006). Still, the focus of research in occupational science (OS) and occupational therapy (OT) largely remains aimed at developing knowledge of components and characteristics of human occupational experience, without attending to the challenge of the relationship of individual actions and experiences within their contexts. In this chapter, we take this challenge as a point of departure. The chapter begins with a discussion of everyday occupations as embedded in local cultural perspectives to demonstrate how this embeddedness is to be understood in the light of women living with chronic conditions.

S. Alsaker (✉)
Department of Health and Social Care, Sør-Trøndelag University College, Trondheim, Norway
e-mail: sissel.alsaker@hist.no

S. Josephsson
Department of Neurobiology, Care Sciences and Society, Division of Occupational Therapy, Karolinska Institutet, Stockholm, Sweden

V.A. Dickie
Department of Allied Health Sciences, Division of Occupational Science and Occupational Therapy, University of North Carolina at Chapel Hill, Chapel Hill, NC, USA

M.P. Cutchin and V.A. Dickie (eds.), *Transactional Perspectives on Occupation*,
DOI 10.1007/978-94-007-4429-5_6, © Springer Science+Business Media B.V. 2013

We then present the position of narrative-in-action (Alsaker et al. 2009), originating from the French philosopher Paul Ricoeur (1991), with the goal of addressing the challenge and extending the transactional view. In doing so, we suggest that the phenomenological and hermeneutic perspective of Ricoeur may give access to transactional qualities of everyday occupation and offer a complimentary perspective to the Dewey-informed approach (Cutchin 2004; Dickie et al. 2006; Cutchin and Dickie 2012). Stories elicited from the everyday life of women living with chronic conditions are then used to illustrate our argument (Alsaker and Josephsson 2010, 2011). Finally, we elaborate on the possibilities and hazards associated with using the concept of narrative-in-action to access transactional dimensions of human occupation.

6.2 Everyday Occupations as Transactions Within Local Cultures

Without conscious consideration, most people highly value their everyday tasks and activities, or what in OT and OS are called occupations. If, when affected by illness or disability, individuals cannot engage in their everyday occupations in the same way as they are used to, the value and meaning of everyday occupations surface and become important issues. An exemplary position in the OS literature suggested that everyday occupations are productive, pleasurable and restorative, and that these aspects are intermingled and difficult to separate (Pierce, 2001). Others have argued that everyday occupations are best portrayed as ongoing processes where specific activities are folded together or linked in a variety of ways instead of appearing as separate (Kielhofner 1997, 2008; Zemke and Clark 1996).

A theoretical way to better understand the integration of entities and how they are related in the contexts of evolving experience has only recently been proposed. Dewey's transactional perspective illustrated by the metaphor "organism-in-environment-as-a-whole" was proposed by Dickie et al. (2006) as a way to begin to perceive the holistic and dynamic nature of occupations and their contexts. In our reading of the transactional perspective on everyday occupations, we understand occupations as connecting person and environment in ongoing action (DeFalco 2010). Here the person and the environment are integrated and functionally coordinated through occupation (Dickie et al. 2006). The personal meaning and experiences of the individual transact with general cultural meanings, socially and metaphorically, through the performance of everyday tasks and activities (Alsaker and Josephsson 2010). In the following we elaborate on the enactment of everyday activities as conceptualized by narrative-in-action, an ongoing process of meaning making.

6.3 "Narrative-in-Action": Meaning Making Endeavors

The ongoing everyday life of people consists of activities with different quality and substance based on place, condition and sociality. However, the pace, the meanings, the shifting and the overall variety that characterize such everyday activities are difficult to grasp both in research and therapy. Knowledge from OT theory and practice provides us with a rather extensive understanding of everyday activity. Nonetheless, the emphasis in this literature is mainly on a set of characteristics as opposed to the ongoing quality of occupation. We will exemplify how narrative-in-action might serve as a resource to access the ongoing quality of occupation by presenting and discussing how narrative meaning occurs in and through occupation. This understanding was developed through an ethnographic study of how women with chronic conditions related to and created meaning in their everyday occupations (Alsaker 2009). By establishing a conceptual framework of narrative-in-action (Alsaker et al. 2009), a narrative understanding of how meaning is managed in the women's everyday occupations was developed. That understanding showed how the on-going processes were fluid and embedded with challenges and contradictions for the women. By suggesting that occupation produces communication between individual practices and cultural practices, this work contributed to the on-going exploration of the transactional perspective of occupation and narrative-in-action. Data from the study will be presented in more detail below.

The term "narrative" is used in different ways in the literature (Josephsson et al. 2006). In health research, narrative is mainly understood as verbal storied text concerning someone's experiences, from fiction or real life. The storied form with a plot structure is dominant and a constituent of the narratives (see Hydèn 1997 for a review). Stories are created by linking together events and happenings emplotted by the individual in the moment and circumstances where the telling takes place (Mattingly 1998a; Ricoeur 1984a). Meaning is thus embedded in the plots, and in line with narrative theory, the plots of such stories differ. When telling someone of an event, the teller will adjust the story according to her perception of who the teller is and in what context the telling takes place. Consequently narrative meaning is created by the teller and may vary according to the listener and the situation where the telling takes place (Charmaz 1999; Werner et al. 2003; Ville and Khlat 2007).

In another view of narrative, meaning is connected to and embedded in occupation (Ricoeur 1984b, 1991). When people are doing everyday occupations, they produce images that they may connect to prior experiences or to future events. The actual doing produces images that relate to the past or to the future, and that are brought together into a possible story. This forms a narrative structure of action and experience that emerges because actors are searching for meaning, as noted by Mattingly (1998a, b). She wrote that particular actions "... take their meaning by belonging to and contributing to, the story as a whole" (p. 46). Following Aristotle (1920) Ricoeur referred to this human possibility of enacting meaning as *mimesis*. Ricoeur's advancement of Aristotle's mimesis has been used in health care research, but mostly in analyses of verbal material (Lindseth and Norberg 2004; Nygren et al. 2007; Stamm et al. 2008; Taïeb et al. 2008).

Ricoeur (1984b) developed this idea as a threefold mimesis: (1) unconscious praxis or action, not yet uttered or verbalized, (2) configuration, where praxis or action are processed into possible conscious plots, and (3) communication, where praxis or action are verbalized as emplotted stories. In a mimesis process, action or occupation is crucial, by that the actual doing producing images of possible stories from the person's real-time context. When linking images to possible plots, the person creates a situational interpretation taking the structural form of a story with a beginning, middle and end and linked together by a plot. Listeners to share the story and to confirm, negotiate, or affirm its meaning is necessary for a story to be communicative. Stories are always social and contextualized.

This communicating ability of stories can be outlined in more detail as follows. *Mimesis first fold* contains the acting human's general view of existence, action and time and is put into use in a particular acting situation. By doing everyday occupations, new images are produced and brought into the already ongoing mimesis. In *Mimesis second fold* interpretations take place by linking the images from action to the overall situation of the person's everyday life and culture, initiating or making up the story of that moment. In some respects this is similar to Dewey's concept of *dramatic* rehearsal, part of the transactional perspective on occupation (Fesmire 2003; Cutchin et al. 2008; also see Chap. 2). In *Mimesis third fold*, possible meaning and potential plots are formed into a story with clear meaning (plot) that is told to someone. When stories are told, listeners interpret and respond, creating situational communications. Ricoeur (1991) underscored that meaning needs to be both enacted and communicated to be configured into narratives.

Unlike verbal narratives, enacted narratives are clearly linked to occupation by situating the actors in a social and material world and putting an emphasis on real time action. The above conceptualization of mimesis first fold implies doing/occupation and thus underscores the importance of occupation in local culture/context when understanding ongoing everyday occupational life. This is not enough, however, to understand how occupations unfold and are changed. Consequently using the concepts of enacted narratives and narrative-in-action might be a fruitful way to gain access to the ongoing occupational processes and their transactional qualities. In DeFalco's (2010) analyses of Dewey's perspective on occupation, he argued that occupation is transactional and that meaning and morals as well as action comes together in such processes, qualities that we invoke in our argument of narrative-in-action as a way to unpack the transactions in occupation. By providing the readers with the above conceptualization we have situated ourselves before proceeding to examples of transaction from the narrative-in-action perspective.

6.4 Everyday Transactions, Meaning Making in Everyday Occupations

The concepts of "everyday life" and "everyday" are often used interchangeably in the literature, but rarely defined. When used in occupational therapy, the term "everyday occupations" generally means what individuals do as time is passing (Hasselkus 2006). Also included in the profession's use of the term are concerns for how individuals perform, where they perform, and the assumption that such occupations are embedded with meanings.

Based on these notions, we understand "everyday occupations" to be the everyday doings of people in their local cultures, which includes both situational performance and the natural occurring conversation that take place in the context. This implies that communication is on-going within a general culture, both socially and materially (Gullestad 1996). Additionally, due to the mundane and repetitive quality of everyday life and occupations, we need to consider that day-to-day occupation provide the individual with experiences, habits and routines that establish structure and predictability for the individual and allow for novel experiences and experiments such as creative endeavors (Clark 2000; MacKinnon and Miller 2003; Dubouloz et al. 2004). This implies that we consider everyday life to be where cultural acts (Gullestad) happen, and where everyday occupations mean acting in a temporal and cultural world, an understanding that is consistent with transactionalism, where transactions are actions that integrate the individual with and within its local culture.

Women living and everyday life with chronic conditions are part of these transactional endeavors, as the examples below from our research show (Alsaker 2009). The following case of Lily is described from field notes.

> Lily is a middle aged married woman who has been living off a disability pension for many years due to a severe rheumatic condition. She is strongly engaged in a user organization and the following situation is part of her work for this organization. This particular morning, the researcher accompanied her on a trip to city centre to deliver some materials to someone. Lily did the driving to town, and along the way she told me about the importance of finding a parking space wide enough so that she could open the door of her side of the car completely, as she needed a lot of space to get out due to her limited range of body movement. Her shoulders, hips and trunk were stiff. I commented on the spaces for the disabled, but she disclaimed my comments. "I want a space in the regular parking areas," she said, "because the lots designated for disabled people are either occupied or too narrow for me," and she added that those spaces are meant for people with wheelchairs or walkers.
>
> Eventually we found a parking space with an open space on the driver's side, and we got out and strolled along the pavement. Just before leaving the car she reached out and removed her disability parking sign away from the car window and put it into the glove compartment. When we approached the car again, Lily stopped for a moment and said, "You can understand my problems because you are with me for longer periods and do things together with me, but others see me as normal when I am walking down the street. You see, this is about the distance I can walk without slowing down or starting to limp".

This story is an example of transaction in everyday occupation, showing Lily's way of becoming part of her local culture. In Deweyan terms this would be referred to as functional coordination of a problematic situation (Cutchin and Dickie 2012). For others walking along the street at that moment, Lily and the researcher did not draw attention—they melted into the moving street crowd. But Lily has designed this everyday process to fit her interpretation of how "walking along the streets" takes place in her local community. Her way of orchestrating navigating her space and carrying out her task could be seen as an example of how such attention to the manner of engaging in occupation can situate Lily within the ordinary life of her city. Her careful and somewhat automatic planning was not objectively observable and would have been difficult to access through interviews. Thus to understand the manner in which she functionally coordinated problematic situations (Cutchin 2004) required a research approach of being with her in the moment.

Thus, the need to gain access to transactional experiences (i.e., to be with people in those experiences) has consequences for methodological choices when planning research (Alsaker et al. 2009), but it also affects planning and implementing interventions, something that we will attend to in the following. We argue that on-going occupational processes are only accessible within their context. What this means is that, for example, participation in occupation puts us in contact with issues that arise in the moment of action. Additionally such situated actions extend into past experiences and possible futures and are possible sources of meaning (the narrative function) and motivation.

In the above example a plot surfaced in Lily's everyday occupation tapping into her strong wish be and act just as anyone else, like an ordinary woman (Alsaker and Josephsson 2010). This exemplifies a transaction, where meaning and moral choices were embedded in her everyday occupation. Lily was enacting her urge to be ordinary and this transaction shows how she enacted "organism-in-environment-as-a-whole" (Dewey and Bentley 1949, p. 109) through an everyday occupation. Transactions within a context infuse the occupation with individual meaning. A narrative analysis allows access to that meaning.

6.5 Everyday Transactions in Local Cultures

Gullestad (1996) understood everyday life as social acts happening in a culture. She proposed that culture in itself is not a set phenomenon but is created, adjusted, and negotiated by acting people in what she called "local circumstances." We use the term *local culture* here to characterize the experience of everyday life in specific, identifiable localities, in contrast to global cultures in which the phenomenon of everyday life is identifiable globally in many geographic localities (Gubrium and Holstein 1997; Frerer and Vu 2007). Local culture comprises ordinary people's interpretation of what and how to act in the circumstances of their everyday living. Additionally their interpretations embed their moral values and interests, as well as their feelings of appropriateness and comfort.

Culture and its content of "everyday social acts" is thus viewed as on-going and continuously changing, which contrasts with a view of culture as something set or clearly framed (Gullestad 1996). Inherent to it are the activities and the practical and moral aspects temporally ascribed to the idea of ordinariness (Kralik 2002). Gullestad argued that everyday life was the way people established integration in their immediate life world by setting up and maintaining a meaningful connection between social roles, activities and circumstances, an argument which we draw upon here. Local culture is infused with metaphors and meaning (Ricoeur 1974) that the individual cannot avoid when acting but is also a source that offers opportunities for action and meaning – an enactment that make everyday life easier to manage and negotiate (Alsaker and Josephsson 2004). Thus individuals are in transaction with their local culture through their actions.

Others have argued that Western society is based on a kind of generalized normality in all aspects of everyday life, marked by fluidity (Rosenfeld and Faircloth 2004). This means that people living in a local culture have tacit knowledge of what "normal" means and how this works in their everyday life. Owing, however, to the fluid quality of normality, such knowledge may change at any moment. This generalized normality contains what is morally good in a local culture. Similarly, Mattingly (1998a) identified the "good" as what constitutes moral and practically appropriate action given the exigencies of a particular situation. This requires relating to and being in on-going communication with a local culture and the geographical, social and material circumstances that individuals meet in their everyday life (Gubrium and Holstein 1997). Further, the "good" is constantly adjusted by people acting in local cultures over time (Polkinghorne 2004; Stern 2004).

Our use of the notion of the "good" is grounded in Aristotle's understanding of practical action and practical reasoning, as outlined by Mattingly (1998a, b). A moral "good" is always in question, as it is embedded in action, not divided from it. Aristotle further pointed out that to understand the general moral truths in a society, the "universals", it is not enough to relate to the "good", as one also needs to consider the particulars. Mattingly (1998b) further asserted that particulars are always concerned with action. This implies that the individual meets with and negotiates her relations with the universals of a society by her practical action. When acting, individuals practice their interpretation of the universals. In this way universals are interpreted and become embedded in particulars through actions (Polkinghorne 2004). This is another way of understanding how individuals through occupations are communicating with their local culture and thus making "in the moment" interpretation that connects the particulars and universals. Additionally, in the small moments of doing (Stern 2004), the individual person establishes images and relations based on her knowledge of and experiences from previous actions in similar circumstances. Thus, when acting, she establishes links between herself and her prior experiences and her ideas and wishes for a future, a process identified as narrative (Mattingly 1998a; Ricoeur 1984b).

Mattingly based her understanding of narratives on Ricoeur's conceptualization, using the concept of narrative in a rather ordinary but restricted sense (Mattingly 1998a; Ricoeur 1984b). She identified narrative as a discourse featuring human adventure and suffering, a discourse, which connects motives, acts and consequences into causal chains. Further, Mattingly expressed this discourse as a process fundamental to story construction (Mattingly 1998a, 2006). This story-making discourse allows the narrator to understand personal meanings and experiences in the light of broader social and political contexts, and even to use such experiences to understand and critique such contexts. In other words, when activities are done in a social setting, a communication is established between universals and particulars, between the individual "good" and society's "good". Narratives like this also include processes of exploring and negotiating visions of the future "good" (Mattingly 1998b) by linking to the past through the present and into a possible future. In an everyday setting, stories are not complete with a beginning, middle and end and a clear plot.

They are narratives in the making, and are presented as events and happenings partly linked or not linked at all, but embedded in individuals' practical action in specific circumstances, here called local cultures.

Also of interest here is Mattingly's (1998a, b) argument that biomedicine offers a language, a mode of perception and an organization of therapeutic practice that denies narrative its moral status. In a biomedical frame, client's narratives are not heard; their moral dilemmas are not considered important. In everyday occupations, following the mimesis three folds (Ricoeur 1991) the individual establishes causal links in the form of possible stories, stories that convey meanings in that moment of time, meanings that may be communicated, in that they are expressed to persons participating in the acting situations (Alsaker and Josephsson 2010). In this way, individuals relate to society's "good" through their practical actions and receive feedback from society which in return they interpret and add to their existing narratives. This discourse or communication is central in individual lives, showing how everyday action connects to moral questions, challenges and dilemmas, establishing narrative meaning-making processes which have transactional qualities. An example of such a process follows for a woman living with a chronic condition, showing her everyday transactions and inherent moral issues from a narrative perspective (Alsaker and Josephsson 2011):

> Esther, now 79, had lived with fibromyalgia for close to 30 years. "When I was diagnosed my physician told me I turned out positive on all thirteen points from his diagnostic scheme," she said. "He wanted me to stop working, I worked as a clerk in a bank, but I endured it for a long time, even when the bank entered the computing area and the screen work made my working days extra exhausting", she said when we were having a coffee break together in her sitting room. Esther and I met regularly in her home and talked on the telephone for about half a year. At every encounter she told me, "there are no changes to my life or my condition". She told of how she kept her situation stable and controlled her condition with six Paracet per day and 20 minutes on her exercise bicycle, exercises in a sling attached to the roof, together with regular outside walks. Her everyday life was routine with crossword puzzles, reading, cooking and keeping her apartment in impeccable order. "You know, I have the best of equipment, both a Kirby and a Mièle[1] vacuum cleaner, and my children assist me when there is a need to air the carpets", she said. When I complimented her on all her wall decorations she told me that she had had a passion for embroidery and enjoyed displaying them in her sitting room, a room which she had kept unchanged since her husband died.
>
> "And additionally I am remembering," she added, "I read in my diaries and remember". She said she had been writing her diaries for 25 years, still did a couple of sentences every day. "I remember most of it, but need to catch up with time and dates", she said. "Every day after dinner I sit down in my armchair and reflect and rest, I need a lot of rest", she said, adding with a smile "but I know the "art of living with" after all these years…"
>
> On my first visit to her home I realized that every now and then a train passed just outside and when I asked Esther if she was disturbed by it she answered, "I do not hear the train, I have always lived by the railway, my father worked there, the railway has

[1] Kirby and Mièle are expensive vacuum cleaners of high quality, but with slightly different functions.

always been close". Esther also said that she greatly enjoyed reading travel books and atlases, and that she travelled to "Syden" once a year with a consumers' travel agency, staying at a rehab centre, "but just for two weeks" she said, "that's enough". On this year's trip she had had some bad experiences: "You know the physiotherapy (PT) treatment is usually good for my condition, but this time the treatment hurt and I told the PT that it was not good for me, but he put a considerable pressure on me to endure the pain even when I told him that my physician has said that I am not to do exercises that pass my pain limit. And additionally the whole group with which I was travelling had to handle the luggage on our own, owing to new security regulations in airports, so I think this was my last trip", she said.

Esther lived on the second floor of a two-storey house which the couple had bought when they moved to this town some 60 years ago. She had grown-up children, two of whom lived in separate flats on the first floor and Esther made them dinner every day. The third child had a family and lived in another part of the country. They all spent time together at Christmas and other occasions, and Esther described their last family gathering as follows: "We had sooo much fun all Christmas..." and when I asked what they were doing, she said "just being together".

In our analysis, the plot of this story is composed by the contradictions between Esther's chosen authorities and her on-going everyday experiences. She worked hard to do what the doctors told her to do, keeping up a stable everyday life, balancing between exercise and rest, taking the prescribed medication and keeping up her everyday routines according to their recommendations. She seemed to regulate her everyday activities so that she prioritized following the doctors' advice, and then attended to her own wishes and interests. In our interpretation she has given biomedicine authoritative power in her everyday life at home, not just regarding her condition. She seems to conform to the universals of biomedicine, and in our interpretation she was accepting that her condition in a way "was herself". She could have put her individual everyday interests first and adapted to the doctors' advice, but we found that she preferred to do it the other way.

Yoshida and Stephens (2004) reported that individuals often make their priority doing valued activities in their everyday life at the expense of managing their arthritis. For Esther, however, we argue that her actions can be seen as similar to conforming to society's "good" (Mattingly 1998b), that her actions were the right things to do. She acted for her personal moral "good", in which her values and interests were prioritized at the same level as those of the biomedical expertise.

When Esther's actions made her meet with events that challenged her "story", she became frustrated and avoided such activities, like travelling to Syden (Norwegian expression for southern latitudes) to a treatment centre for a couple of weeks, where, on her latest tour, she was treated by a physiotherapist who told her to change her exercises and routines. Esther expressed frustration and in our interpretation she avoided considering these new ideas of treatment and exercises by saying that she would not travel any more. Instead Esther kept up her habitual everyday activities in which her actions did not put her in connection with challenges that forced her to alter her story. She resisted changing the causal links that she had established that made up her narrative (Alsaker and Josephsson 2011).

The story shows a woman who belongs to a generation and social class where the moral "good" was to work hard and to do the right things. Her interpretation of the moral "good" in society and biomedicine was similar to her individual moral "good", and not to be challenged, though it may seem to limit her engagement in everyday living. In a way, she was stuck (Mattingly 1998b) within the plot of her story.

The way we interpret her narrative, Esther literally lived the contradictions inherent in a cultural narrative between the universals and the particulars, or the moral good for a group or population with chronic conditions, in contrast with the moral good of particular individuals with a chronic condition. Esther enacted the everyday transactional processes in a way that was coherent with her values and morals, keeping a meaningful everyday life for herself.

Another story shows transactions from different angle (Alsaker and Josephsson 2010):

> May is 36, married with three children, and works for organizations that try to benefit people with particular disabilities or illnesses. She said, "After they gave me my diagnosis I thought the pain would disappear, but it did not happen. Then I decided that the diagnosis was wrong and acted like that. But when I eventually met with people from the user organization I discovered you still could have fun even with such a diagnosis". May's main aim is to change the way the organizations work; she wants to offer the members something else apart from coffee breaks, small talk and raffles. She created a group for young adult members and their families and today she had arranged a meeting for them. Before the meeting started she said, "I'm on mega doses of cortisone to keep me going, have decided to follow this arrangement through, we are about to hear lectures from health persons on avoiding back pain in everyday life and some theory about relations, you know many attending here are married to a chronic condition person, and of course it affects the relationships, and then we are serving lots of good food and talking". Then she continued, smiling, "tomorrow I'm going to have a collapse". We had met regularly for nearly two years, and she had told me similar stories before, how she used all her energy in similar projects and managed to forget her symptoms while engaged, and then spent the following days in bed. "You know it's the way I can get things done, but I'm so sorry it's not possible to adjust to a working environment, I was so sorry I had to stop working, but the employers were not even interested in negotiating with my working capacity", and she continued, "I then realized the advantages this could give regarding spending time with my family and work for my user organisation".
>
> When ending the lectures on relations, the lecturer cited a poem written by May long ago; "My partner lupus –you want to make all the decisions – but you know we're supposed to be two in a partnership…"

In this example, May's reflections show how she has chosen a way of life that provides her with meaning, by spending time and energy towards causes that she has chosen, attending to family occupations, and engaging in matters of importance for the user group she belongs to. She creates transactional experiences for herself by playing her part in meaning making processes with her family and user group. One can imagine the struggle she experiences by opposing biomedical recommendations regarding not overexerting herself. However, her way of acting is clearly embedding her everyday life with meaning and grounding her in her environment.

6.6 Everyday Occupational Transactions Enacted and Embedded in Local Culture

Based on the perspectives of three women living their everyday life with chronic conditions, we have shown examples of how transaction with the culture through everyday occupations can be understood by using theoretical resources from narrative-in-action. The fluidity and complexity of everyday occupations are revealed in the above narratives, showing enactment of meaning in action in local cultures as transactional processes. In contexts like the above, there are also several other narratives or plots that are enacted by others such as family members, but they were deliberately put aside for this analysis.

Ricoeur (1984b) discussed the importance of entering into the world of "as if", when meaning is to be understood. In the mimesis second fold the options and possible interpretations are tested. Similar to Dewey's concept of dramatic rehearsal, the idea of "as if" is central in our discussion of transaction; i.e., processes are ongoing in everyday occupations and are constantly adjusted and negotiated in the occupational context (the local culture where the occupations take place). In "real life" (historical) narratives the access to this "as if" world is connected to the options that are made available by doing occupations. Occupations are literally temporal and culturally localized; they take place in a context. What this means is that in an acting context you relate to available social and material surroundings, which evokes images and interpretations of previous experiences and cultural forms. Persons who act have access to cultural metaphors, to try out different interpretations, and change or rearrange them. However, they have to be figured out during the acting, as Lily did when parking her car in a regular space and removing the special parking sign from the car window.

For the women in this study, our analyses show that this possibility of enacting a variety of "as ifs" or alternative interpretations in their everyday life also made them able to work with significant issues by communicating with the general cultural issues and metaphors, and by that the transactional opportunities are made available for them.

Even if not all possible plots were constituted into full stories, motion was established and flexibility and possibilities were kept open. The women acted within contexts that provided them with many options for narrative interpretations, challenging the notion of meanings as stable traits. This "trying out" function in occupations is important and has implications for the personal transformation and change that is central in therapy.[2] Yet the bottom-line message of this chapter is that narrative-in-action is a useful approach to access the transactional nature of occupation and to thereby provide the conceptual means of intervening positively in people's lives.

[2] Moreover, 'trying out' is another instance of the connection to the transactional perspective where experimental inquiry is seen as an essential part of everyday activity (see Chap. 2).

References

Alsaker, S. (2009). *Narrative in action: Meaning-making in everyday activities of women living with chronic rheumatic conditions*. PhD-thesis, Norwegian University of Science and Technology, NTNU, Trondheim, Norway.

Alsaker, S., & Josephsson, S. (2004). Negotiating occupational identities while living with chronic rheumatic disease. *Scandinavian Journal of Occupational Therapy, 10*, 167–176.

Alsaker, S., & Josephsson, S. (2010). Occupation and meaning: Narrative in everyday activities of women with chronic rheumatic conditions. *OTJR: Occupation, Participation and Health, 30*(2), 58–67.

Alsaker, S., & Josephsson, S. (2011). Stories stirring the quest of the good: Narratives of women living with chronic rheumatic conditions. *Scandinavian Journal of Disability Research, 13*(1), 53–70.

Alsaker, S., Bongaardt, R., & Josephsson, S. (2009). Studying narrative-in-action in women with chronic rheumatic conditions. *Qualitative Health Research, 19*(8), 1154–1161.

Aristotle. (1920). *Aristotle on the art of poetry*. New York: Oxford University Press.

Charmaz, K. (1999). Stories of suffering: Subjective tales and research narratives. *Qualitative Health Research, 9*(3), 362–382.

Clark, F. (2000). The concepts of habits and routine: A preliminary theoretical synthesis. *OTJR: Occupational Therapy Journal of Research, 20*, 123–135.

Cutchin, M. P. (2004). Using Deweyan philosophy to rename and reframe adaptation-to-environment. *American Journal of Occupational Therapy, 58*, 303–12.

Cutchin, M. P., Aldrich, R. M., Bailliard, A., & Coppola, S. (2008). Action theories for occupational science: The contributions of Dewey and Bourdieu. *Journal of Occupational Science, 15*, 157–65.

Cutchin, M. P., & Dickie, V. (2012). Transactionalism: Occupational science and the pragmatic attitude. In G. Whiteford , C. Hocking (Eds.), Occupational science: Society, inclusion, participation (pp. 23–37). Oxford: Wiley-Blackwell.

DeFalco, A. (2010). An analysis of John Dewey's notion of occupations: Still pedagogically valuable? *Education and Culture, 26*(1), 82–99.

Dewey J., & Bentley, A. (1949). Knowing and known. Boston: Beacon Press.

Dickie, V., Cutchin, M. P., & Humphry, R. (2006). Occupation as transactional experience: A critique of individualism in occupational science. *Journal of Occupational Science, 13*(1), 83–93.

Dubouloz, C.-J., Laporte, D., Hall, M., Ashe, B., & Smith, C. D. (2004). Transformation of meaning perspectives in clients with rheumatoid arthritis. *The American Journal of Occupational Therapy, 58*(4), 398–407.

Fesmire, S. (2003). John Dewey and the moral imagination: Pragmatism in ethics. Bloomington, IN: Indiana University Press.

Frerer, K., & Vu, C. M. (2007). An anthropological view of poverty. *Journal of Human Behavior in the Social Environment, 16*(1/2), 73–86.

Gubrium, J., & Holstein, J. (1997). *The new language of qualitative method*. New York: Oxford University Press.

Gullestad, M. (1996). *Everyday life philosophers*. Oslo: Scandinavian University Press.

Hasselkus, B. R. (2006). The world of everyday occupation: Real people, real lives. *The American Journal of Occupational Therapy, 60*(6), 627–640.

Hydèn, L.-C. (1997). Illness and narrative. *Sociology of Health & Illness, 19*(1), 48–69.

Josephsson, S., Asaba, E., Jonsson, H., & Alsaker, S. (2006). Creativity and order in communication: Implications from philosophy to narrative research concerning human occupation. *Scandinavian Journal of Occupational Therapy, 13*(2), 125–132.

Kielhofner, G. (1997). *Conceptual foundations of occupational therapy* (2nd ed.). Philadelphia: F A Davis Company.

Kielhofner, G. (2008). *Model of human occupation: Theory and application* (4th ed.). Baltimore: Wolters Kluwer/Lippincott Williams & Wilkins.

Kralik, D. (2002). The quest for ordinariness: Transition experienced by midlife women living with chronic illness. *Journal of Advanced Nursing, 39*(2), 146–154.

Lindseth, A., & Norberg, A. (2004). A phenomenological hermeneutical method for researching lived experience. *Scandinavian Journal of Caring Sciences, 18*(2), 145–153.

MacKinnon, J. R., & Miller, W. C. (2003). Rheumatoid arthritis and self esteem: The impact of quality occupation. *Journal of Occupational Science, 10*(2), 90–98.

Mattingly, C. (1998a). *Healing dramas and clinical plots: The narrative structure of experience*. Los Angeles: University of California Press.

Mattingly, C. (1998b). In search of the good: Narrative reasoning in clinical practice. *Medical Anthropology, 12*(3), 273–297.

Mattingly, C. (2006). Reading medicine: Mind, body, and meditation in one interpretive community. *New Literary History, 37*(3), 563–581.

Nygren, B., Norberg, A., & Lundman, B. (2007). Inner strength as disclosed in narratives of the oldest old. *Qualitative Health Research, 17*(8), 1060–1073.

Pierce, D. (2001). Untangling occupation and activity. *American Journal of Occupational Therapy, 55*, 38–146.

Polkinghorne, D. (2004). *Practice and the human sciences: The case for a judgement-based practice of care*. New York: State University of New York Press.

Ricoeur, P. (1974). Metaphor and the main problem of hermeneutics. *New literary History, 6*(1), 95–110.

Ricoeur, P. (1984a). *Time and narrative* (Vol. I–III). Chicago: The University of Chicago Press.

Ricoeur, P. (1984b). *Time and narrative* (Vol. I). Chicago: The University of Chicago Press.

Ricoeur, P. (1991). *From text to action: Essays in hermeneutics*. Evanston: Northwestern University Press.

Rosenfeld, D., & Faircloth, C. (2004). Embodied fluidity and the commitment to movement: Constructing the moral self through arthritis narratives. *Symbolic interaction, 27*, 507–529.

Stamm, T., Lovelock, L., Stew, G., Nell, V., Smolen, J., Jonsson, H., et al. (2008). I have mastered the challenge of living with a chronic disease: Life stories of people with rheumatoid arthritis. *Qualitative Health Research, 18*(5), 658–669.

Stern, N. D. (2004). *The present moment in psychotherapy and everyday life*. New York: W.W. Norton.

Taïeb, O., Révah-Lévy, A., Moro, M. R., & Baubet, T. (2008). Is Ricoeur's notion of narrative identity useful in understanding recovery in drug addicts? *Qualitative Health Research, 18*(7), 990–1000.

Ville, I., & Khlat, M. (2007). Meaning and coherence of self and health: An approach based on narratives of life events. *Social Science & Medicine, 64*(4), 1001–1014.

Werner, A., Isaksen, L. W., & Malterud, K. (2003). "I am not the kind of woman who complains of everything": Illness stories on self and shame in women with chronic pain. *Social Science and Medicine, 59*, 1035–1045.

Yoshida, K., & Stephens, M. (2004). Living with rheumatoid arthritis: Strategies that support independence and autonomy in everyday life. *Physiotherapy Theory and Practice, 20*(4), 221–231.

Zemke, R., & Clark, F. (1996). *Occupational Science: The evolving discipline*. Philadelphia: F A Davis Company.

Part II
Case Studies

Chapter 7
Navigating Cultural Spaces: A Transactional Perspective on Immigration

Shoba Nayar and Clare Hocking

7.1 Introduction

Immigration is an international phenomenon, with the result that the majority of developed countries are now considered diverse, multiethnic societies (Kağitçibaşi 2007). The growth in immigrant populations has prompted the drive for research to better understand immigrants' needs and the impact of immigration on society at large. Hence, research focussing on aspects of immigration such as why people immigrate, what happens in the act of immigration and how the settlement process unfolds for new immigrants continues to proliferate internationally (Ward and Rana-Deuba 1999).

As a field of interest, immigration has been closely studied by anthropologists, sociologists, psychologists, and researchers in other disciplines such as geography; however, it is only within the last decade that occupational scientists have turned their attention to immigrants as an increasingly important group (Nayar and Hocking 2006; Martins and Reid 2007; Boerema et al. 2010; Huot and Laliberte Rudman 2010; Nayar et al. 2012). Immigration has particular value as a field of study for occupational scientists because immigration implicitly means a change of physical, political, cultural, societal, and economic context and the settlement process requires many immigrants to adapt and adjust valued occupations. That is, the occupations of immigrants have the potential to reveal new insights into the relationship between occupation and environment, and the human response to a pervasive demand to change what they do.

The stance taken in this chapter is that immigrants' occupations offer a unique opportunity to examine the transactional nature of occupation because, unlike the

S. Nayar (✉) • C. Hocking
Department of Occupational Science and Therapy,
Auckland University of Technology, Auckland, New Zealand
e-mail: shoba.nayar@aut.ac.nz

M.P. Cutchin and V.A. Dickie (eds.), *Transactional Perspectives on Occupation*,
DOI 10.1007/978-94-007-4429-5_7, © Springer Science+Business Media B.V. 2013

phenomenological methods more typically employed in the study of occupation, a transactional perspective brings the environment into focus. In the case of immigrants endeavoring to settle in a new country, the transactions that occur with person and environment are made more visible because they take place in an historical, cultural and environmental context that is unfamiliar. An occupational perspective on immigration has much to offer current understandings of migration and acculturation which, to a large extent, fail to understand settlement in a new country as a transactional process. A process that is defined by how immigrants, to varying degrees, embrace their situations and reconstruct their occupational routines, traditions and practices; and how the resources, practices and attitudes in the host country change in response to the immigrants' presence.

This chapter begins with a brief review of current understandings of immigration and settlement, with a particular focus on the concept of acculturation. The following section reveals how profound the impact of immigration actually is, for both the immigrant and the receiving society at large, when considered in combination with Dewey's notions of "habit" and "situation." The complex and transactional nature of the settlement process is illustrated with a case study that stems from a larger study used to generate the Theory of Navigating Cultural Spaces, a substantive theory of how Indian immigrant women settle and create a place for themselves and their families in New Zealand (Nayar 2009). Presenting an occupational perspective, this theory suggests that immigration and the settlement process is dynamic and in flux, influenced by immigrants' interpretation of the personal and situational demands and others' attitudes and actions. This discussion highlights some of the limitations of current understandings of immigration and settlement. Finally, this chapter will consider how an appreciation of the transactional nature of the immigration process reveals new avenues for both science and society in supporting immigrants, from assisting them to locate familiar resources and navigate employment relations, to interpretation of local practices and cultural values. At a policy level, it also suggests the need to promote community readiness to host its new members.

7.2 Current Perspectives on Immigration and Settlement

In the context of immigration, settlement is largely considered as a two way process which requires the active participation of both parties; that is, the willingness of immigrants to learn about the new society and the willingness of the host society to become better informed of immigrants' cultural practices. The relationship between cultural groups, where one group forms the majority and the other group constitutes a minority, and the resulting changes in cultural attitudes, values and behaviors, is commonly referred to as acculturation; a concept that originated within anthropology and has been used to describe the process by which immigrants acquire, and adapt to, a new culture (Berry 1992, 2001; LaFromboise et al. 1993; Nesdale et al. 1997; Lopez et al. 2002). In principle, acculturation is a neutral term that implies that change may take place in either or both groups (Bailey 1937).

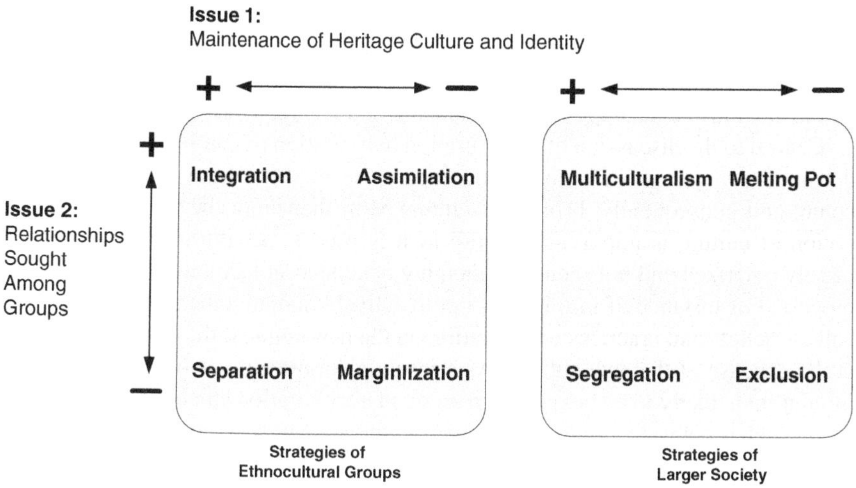

Four acculturation strategies based on two issues – view of ethnocultural groups (left) and of larger society (right)

Fig. 7.1 Berry's model of acculturation (Berry 2003, p. 23). Copyright © 2002 by the American Psychological Association. Adapted with permission. The use of APA information does not imply endorsement by APA)

However, in the late 1980s and 1990s, research tended to focus on what happens for the minority group when living in the dominant culture. This aligns with Berry's (1990) observation that "in practice acculturation tends to induce more change in one of the groups than in the other" (p. 294). More recently, trends in acculturation research indicate a shift in focus back to the intended process of mutual change (Berry 1997; Bourhis et al. 1997).

Acculturation permeates all facets of immigrants' daily living including language, foods, cultural connections, beliefs and attitudes. Whether immigrants retain or lose their traditional culture, and to what degree, are questions central to acculturation research. Berry has attempted to redress the issue of acculturation being presented as a bi-polar model, wherein immigrants either retain or lose their culture. He developed a typology in which ethnic identity and mainstream identity can run parallel to one another (Berry et al. 1986, 2006; Berry 1992). Accordingly, individuals can take on a mainstream identity, without necessarily losing their ethnic identity. The use of this typology has increased over the last decade (Ward et al. 2001) and it is widely cited in migration research discussing the concept of acculturation (Kağitçibaşi 2007). Berry's model of acculturation is depicted in Fig. 7.1.

Berry's model is based on the answers to two questions that pertain to the immigrant: (a) Is my cultural identity of value and to be retained? and (b) Are positive relations with the larger society sought? Individuals' answers to these questions result in four possible outcomes: assimilation, separation, marginalization and integration. For example, in assimilation, migrants are seen as foregoing their cultural values and beliefs and taking on those of the new country. Separation is the reverse process whereby migrants keep within their cultural ways of knowing and doing. Marginalization is when the immigrant group fits neither with the dominant or their traditional culture, and integration enables newcomers to continue to practice their cultures but also encourages them to adapt to and engage with the host society.

Central to the discussion of acculturation in migration research is the recognition that minority groups will have some experience of the culture from which they come, and consequently, bring that culture with them into the new society. The notion of culture is important because as it is used in acculturation models, it is largely polarized and not seen as something beneficial in facilitating the settlement process. For instance, if immigrants opt to actively maintain their original cultural values, beliefs and practices while settling in the new country, they are seen to do so at the expense of the new culture. As a result, as in the case of Berry's model, the immigrant is likely to be boxed into a mode of acculturation labeled "separation"; a term which is not welcoming and lacks recognition of a wider context—the historical, societal and encompassing nature of culture. Indeed, Dewey contended that culture surrounds us; we cannot be taken out of our culture (Sullivan 2000). For example, research with Indian immigrant women settling in New Zealand revealed that some women actively chose to engage in occupations reflective of their ethnic culture, and thus a mode of separation, as this provided them with a sense of safety and accomplishment (Nayar et al. 2012), important elements in facilitating successful settlement. The benefits the women experienced from participating in occupations arising from a different context illustrate that individual habits are created and shaped by cultural customs at a society level (Dewey 1957) to the extent that "cultural constructs that structure us *are* us" (Sullivan 2000, p. 26). We cannot be separated from our culture; yet immigrants who choose to engage in occupations that spring from their cultural roots are viewed as resisting or being unwilling to "integrate" into their new community.

Studies of acculturation primarily focus on changes in attitudes or values, and few have specifically considered the changes in everyday occupations—such as grocery shopping, parenting or using public transport—and the impact that these changes have on successful settlement. The following discussion considers immigration and settlement from a transactional perspective, which highlights occupation as the core dynamic of both the transaction and immigration process.

7.3 A Transactional Perspective on Immigration and Settlement

Immigration is an event of both enormous magnitude and scope, in that it does not exist within a single location of time or place. From Dewey's (1981, pp. 126–127) perspective, immigration is an event, wherein, "Events, being events and not rigid and lumpy substances, are on-going and hence as such unfinished, incomplete, indeterminate". Thus, immigration is a process, a possible response to individual aspirations or social problems that are experienced at the time, and the possible instigator of individual benefits or social problems still to come. Therefore acculturation theories are incommensurate with the migration processes that serve as the basis for them. A transactional perspective on immigration offers the possibility of more than one mode of acculturation to be active at any particular time.

Immigration can also be conceptualized as what Dewey would call a meaningful action, which for many individuals drives them to seek a new, perhaps better, life. According to Dewey (1957), the origins of such action can be conceptualized as "conflicts" and conflicts "represent ruptures in the human-environment continuity" (Cutchin 2001, p. 34). Another way of considering the human-environment continuity may be to consider the notions of biography (human) and history (environment) as discussed by sociologist C. Wright Mills.

> We have come to know that every individual lives, from one generation to the next, in some society; that he lives out a biography, and that he lives it out within some historical sequence. By the fact of his living he contributes, however minutely, to the shaping of society and to the course of its history, even as he is made by society and by its historical push and shove (Wright-Mills 1967, p. 6).

Immigration is a process in which the intersection between history and biography comes to the fore. Transitioning between old and new environments is a chapter in the developing biographical stories of immigrants. However, this transition means that immigrants enter a different historical sequence mid-stream, one of which they might have little understanding. The template for interaction between self and society needs to be re-designed as immigrants establish their place as part of a new historical sequence.

Personal history, a place, and a possible future are three components in which people who move, such as immigrants, are embedded (Cutchin 2001). Current models of acculturation and settlement acknowledge the past, in as much as it is something that immigrants hold on to and which may prevent them from integrating or becoming part of the new society. However, those models fail to explicitly look at how immigrants actively use their past to assist with settlement in the present and future. An occupational model of immigration and settlement, grounded in a transactional perspective, allows for that complex consideration.

7.3.1 Navigating Cultural Spaces: A Case Study

Navigating Cultural Spaces is a theory of how Indian immigrant women settle in New Zealand. Extensive interviews and participant observations with 25 Indian women who had immigrated to New Zealand were analyzed through the theoretical lens of symbolic interactionism and the methodological process of dimensional analysis, to develop this grounded theory (Nayar 2009). Navigating Cultural Spaces is a continuous process that unfolds with each occupational situation the women encounter and is, therefore, fundamental to how Indian immigrant women perform activities on a daily basis for the purpose of settling in a new environment.

Table 7.1 Dimensions of Spaces

Indian Space	New Zealand Space	Private Space	Public Space
Religious diversity	Legislation – The Treaty of Waitangi[a]	The home	Community perceptions and opportunities
Geographical diversity	History as an immigrant nation	Construction of the personal cultural context	Social and political context
Migration history of the Indian communities in New Zealand	Formation of Pākehā[b] values	Personal values and beliefs	External representation of what it is to "be Indian"

[a]The Treaty of Waitangi is a living document that was signed between the Crown representative and Māori chieftains in 1840, at Waitangi, New Zealand. The Treaty established a partnership between the Crown and Māori and formed the basis of biculturalism as it informs New Zealand's socio-political climate

[b]There are no definitive oral or written records about the exact origins of the term 'Pākehā' and even today, many have difficulty defining its exact meaning. Initially a Pākehā was that person who came from England, and settled or worked in New Zealand, but the word Pākehā is used more commonly now to refer to a New Zealander of Caucasian descent

Engaging in occupations is a transactional process the women participate in, either by themselves or with others, interacting with their environment and moving between cultural boundaries. Occupations occur in conjunction with different environments, involve a variety of skills, engage individuals and collective groups, and are performed consciously and unconsciously. In Navigating Cultural Spaces, the environments within which occupations are performed have been conceptualized as spaces: Indian, New Zealand, Private and Public. The women constantly journey through and move between each of the four cultural spaces, needing to keep themselves safe, knowing their capabilities and making the most of opportunities for exploring new ways of doing everyday activities. The women encounter each of the spaces through their occupations, which they engage in from one of three perspectives: Working with Indian Ways, Working with New Zealand Ways, or Working with the Best of Both Worlds. Each of the spaces, Indian, New Zealand, Private and Public, is interwoven and reveals different dimensions, to varying degrees. These dimensions are depicted in Table 7.1.

The following case study showcases the complexity of Navigating Cultural Spaces from a transactional perspective, through the occupation of parenting that Nina, an Indian immigrant woman settling in New Zealand, engages in on a daily basis.

> It's balancing that Indianness now, where you want to push your child and you feel that okay I don't want my child, like no matter how balanced I try to be in front of you right now, I'm still a mum who'll absolutely whip my daughter's ass if she's going to be with a partner, who is not married to him and living with him under one roof. I mean I don't care if any Kiwi or any Indian Kiwi or any Fijian Kiwi tells me that I'm being a conservative bitch, but I just do not believe my daughter's body is a commodity for any guy who she perceives as fit at that point in time, to be played with. So that's how I feel at this stage. I don't know how I'm going to feel at, when she's 20 or 30, but when I ask my husband, he said, 'no I'm not going to whip my daughter's ass, I'm just going to kill her'. No, you know we're not literally going to do

> that, but this is the way we're going to feel it's, because what, that's the one thing that has stayed intact with me. I've changed everything about myself, to some extent, I've changed the way I've dressed, I've changed the way I speak, my accent has changed in a way without really realizing it, the words and the content of what I speak has changed, my outlook has changed, my skills have changed, everything has changed. But the core of what I am when I came here, the values that are what's brought in the Catholic environment are still there… it's again having a balance between that closed and open mind where I want to say 'okay daughter, here are your values' which I want her to be in a Catholic school and say 'okay baby you want to make your choices, but these are the values that I'm going to give you and then make your choices keeping in mind my values and what your values are'.

A transactional perspective "assumes no pre-knowledge of either organism or environment alone as adequate" (Dewey and Bentley 1989, p. 114). In this case study, the spaces, their dimensions, and the individuals cannot be understood independently of each other. Nina's statement reveals her role as an Indian immigrant mother and her attempt to make sense of differing values; those she brought with her from her old environment, those she experiences in the new environment and how they play out in her interactions with her daughter. The analysis of this case study will draw on the dimensions of spaces as outlined in Table 7.1 and Dewey's notions of "habit" and "situation" to reveal how a transactional perspective extends our understanding of the settlement and acculturation process for immigrants.

The construct of place has received much attention in the occupational science literature and must be considered here, for what is immigration if not a change in place? In this instance, Nina carries out the occupational role of parenting her child in the immediate place of "the home" a dimension of the Private space. In the home she can freely express her thoughts and beliefs in a strong statement such as, "I'm still a mum who'll absolutely whip my daughter…." The Private space allows the expression of "individual values and beliefs," without judgment from others or having to fit in with "community perceptions," a dimension of the Public space.

However, a Deweyan understanding of situation is something that extends beyond the immediate environment in which an occupation occurs. Situation incorporates connections with other areas, which for immigrants might include family and economic ties, or cultural media. Thus situations contextualize human experience and are "transitions to and possibilities of later experiences" (Dewey 1980, p. 236). For Nina, the occupation of parenting extends to consideration of the New Zealand and Indian spaces and the respective dimensions of "history as an immigrant nation" and "migration history of the Indian communities in New Zealand." As Nina talks, she acknowledges the cultural diversity that exists in New Zealand: "I don't care if any Kiwi or any Indian Kiwi or any Fijian Kiwi tells me that I'm being a conservative bitch." In doing so, she situates the occupation of parenting not just within her private home, but within a wider community—the national space—and thus indicates the transactional character of her occupation (parenting). Nina recognizes that others in her environment will have beliefs about parenting and what is or is not good practice. In this instance she chooses not to be influenced by others in society, but nevertheless, she recognizes that other cultural groups and their beliefs do exist and that this could affect her parenting.

Another way in which the transactional character of parenting reveals itself is through the interaction of the three dimensions: "social and political context" (Public space), "formation of Pākehā values" (New Zealand spaces), and "individual values and beliefs" (Private space). In her account, Nina reveals her desire to retain beliefs about not living with a man before marriage, beliefs which are grounded in her Indian culture and upbringing in the Catholic faith. These beliefs conflict, however, with New Zealand Pākehā values, reflective of the "New Zealand" space, in which many members of society consider it acceptable for a man and woman to live together and not be married.

For Nina, the root of her struggle with parenting her daughter in New Zealand lies in the conflicting values held by each culture. Originating within respective cultures are social customs which have become entrenched in ways of knowing and doing and out of which, Dewey contended, individual habits arise (Cutchin 2007). Actions are formed in part by habits and, in turn, habits are formed by those embedded social customs and value systems (Dewey 1957). For instance, Nina brings Catholic Christian values to her parenting (dimension: "religious diversity," space: Indian). These are values that have been embedded in Nina as part of her upbringing in the Catholic environment back in India, and they are values which she hopes to impart to her daughter by enrolling her in a Catholic school. Nina acknowledges that elements of herself have been altered, "I've changed everything about myself, to some extent, I've changed the way I've dressed, I've changed the way I speak…." Yet her core values remain even as she is living in a different cultural environment. This ongoing dynamic, of changing some ways of being and retaining others, highlights the transactional nature of occupation and the settlement experience which is not captured in current models of acculturation.

Berry (1997) posited that over the course of acculturation, individuals are likely to explore different acculturative strategies before settling on one that is more useful and satisfying than the others. However, what models of acculturation fail to address with regard to time, is everyday experience. Experience is a temporal aspect of human life in which the past, present and future are integrated (Dewey 1989). While she might display the acculturative strategy of assimilation by changing the way she dresses and speaks (in the present), Nina also enacts a strategy of separation by holding on to her Christian values (drawing on the past). Furthermore, she demonstrates openness to integration (looking to the future) when she says to her daughter, "then make your choices keeping in mind my values and what your values are." Thus, through the occupation of parenting, we can make sense of how values from the past and present are transactionally mediated through "situation" and "habit" as Nina, an Indian immigrant woman, constructs a life for herself and her family in New Zealand.

7.4 Implications for Science and Society

In this section, the implications of a transactional perspective for understanding the settlement process immigrants undertake are considered. In particular, the insights arising for occupational science research and societal practice, including practical support and construction of policy, are addressed.

7.4.1 Occupational Science Research

When occupational science first emerged as an academic discipline, Yerxa and colleagues (1990) contended that there was a need to be interdisciplinary and synthesize ideas from other disciplines that had something to say about occupation. In this assertion lies a challenge for occupational science researchers to move beyond what is currently known and actively employ theoretical or philosophical perspectives from other disciplines, such as environmental psychology or geography, to consider how we frame our understandings of occupation. This chapter has demonstrated how a transactional perspective is critical for understanding the ways in which cultural context, self, occupation and connections interact in the process of immigration. It has long been acknowledged within occupational science that occupation is contextual, yet understandings of how occupation mediates person-place interactions have been limited. Navigating Cultural Spaces is fundamentally a transactional theory that arises from the interactions immigrants have with their environment and the subsequent meanings created from these interactions. Occupational science researchers need to be interdisciplinary in their study of occupation and go beyond static descriptions of an environment-occupation-person interface to capture the dynamic, lived experience of participating in occupation with contexts. Concurrently, occupational scientists must employ their knowledge and understandings of occupation to inform other fields of research, such as studies of acculturation which, to date, have overlooked the centrality of everyday occupation in immigration and settlement processes. This chapter has shown that the discipline of occupational science can bring a unique and rich perspective to migration and acculturation studies.

Another challenge for occupational science researchers is the need to move beyond a focus on individuals and individual engagement with occupation. Dewey (1986) contended that, "In actual experience, there is never any such isolated singular object or event; an object or event is always a special part, phase or aspect of an environing experienced world—a situation" (p. 72). In embracing a transactional perspective on occupation, researchers need to expand their view to people acting in situations that involve others' values and customs. The case study includes not only Nina, but also her husband and daughter, family and friends in India who await news of the family's New Zealand experience, the Indian and Pākehā communities in New Zealand, and the men Nina's daughter might meet. All of these people create the situation in which Nina expresses her own beliefs and values, and envisions future occupations. Further, Dewey argued that a transaction always implies consequences (Garrison 2001). Thus, research needs to move beyond immigrants' immediate experiences of engagement in occupation to the impact of that engagement, both where they come from and where they are currently residing. In Nina's case, how does changing the way she dresses and speaks influence her relationship with her family back in India? How does her refusal to give up her Catholic values impact her relationship with other New Zealanders and her daughter? Such questions broaden and deepen the meaning of occupation and the understanding of the immigrant experience.

7.4.2 *Societal Practice*

Employing a transactional perspective on immigration has implications, from the way the settlement process is conceptualized through to the delivery of social services and formulation of policy that address the everyday needs of immigrants as they settle in an unfamiliar environment. Current policy tends to conceptualize settlement in terms of acculturation models, whereby immigrants adopt one of four modes of acculturation: separation, marginalization, assimilation or integration. Many of the settlement goals, and thus immigration support services, are targeted at longer term roles and occupations representative of integration, such as paid employment or becoming a homeowner. However, an appreciation of the transactional nature of the immigration process suggests a variety of avenues for supporting immigrants, from assisting them to locate familiar resources and navigating employment relations to interpretation of local practices and cultural values.

Taking a transactional perspective also highlights two other issues. Firstly, support services do not enter into immigrant transactions to enhance them until immigrants know about the services they offer and how to gain access to the support when it is needed. The challenge is how to make such services more responsive to immigrants. Two mechanisms for action are suggested. First, many places need better availability of volunteers who can provide "hands on" assistance to immigrants who want to perform everyday activities out in the community. Establishing support groups within the local community that new immigrants can attend and share their experiences of trying to do things in a new environment would assist with creating an extended network of support. Second, immigrant support services could enter into immigrant transactions through working with members of the local community to develop host preparedness. Educating the local community of the benefits immigrants bring to their adopted society, with the aim of diminishing personal and institutional attitudes and practices that could be perceived as unwelcoming or racist, would be a valuable role for immigrant support services in facilitating the settlement of new immigrants.

Understanding immigration as a transactional process, at the core of which are the everyday occupations people perform, suggests a need for society to promote community readiness to host its new members. Community readiness extends from the increasing awareness of differences in cultural practices with respect to "language," to addressing the "actions" of the host society. Promoting community readiness so that members of the host society are aware of the impact their words and actions might have for new immigrants is a critical step towards welcoming immigrants and helping them feel settled in an unfamiliar environment. Yet the concept of promoting community readiness is not new; as noted by Butcher et al. (2006) who identified the need to "promote the development of knowledge and understanding in the host population with regard to the backgrounds and situations of new settlers" (p. vii).

Thus, public policy needs to actively promote settlement as a two-way process. Members of the host society gain from receiving specific knowledge on the potential benefits of welcoming immigrants into society as well as from more general information regarding the cultures and philosophies that shape immigrants' interactions and everyday activities. Importantly, there must be opportunities for practical experience of interacting with diverse immigrants, as research has shown that "the more direct contact people have with immigrants, the more positive and tolerant they are on virtually all immigration issues" (Spoonley et al. 2007 p. vii). Immigrants gain from interacting with members of the host community who, if not attuned to their specific needs, at least appreciate that immigrants have occupational needs.

7.5 Conclusion

This chapter has revealed that a transactional perspective on immigration and settlement challenges current understandings of acculturation, such that immigration is seen not as something that happens in stages, with the ultimate goal of integration, but as a process that is dynamic and experienced through everyday occupations. Accordingly, it is a mistake to think of immigration only in terms of what happens when immigrants enter the country and start to adapt and adopt the occupations that will make up their everyday lives. As Dewey pointed out, experience is situational and temporally continuous; any experience is integrated with the past, present, and future. Therefore if occupational scientists are to consider the settlement experience of new immigrants, we cannot just consider what is happening to them now and in the future in their new country. We need to think back to where they have come from, what they bring with them, and how that will influence the present and future situations they experience. Moreover, this transactional perspective must be shared with services that exist to support immigrants, policy makers, and members of the public, as all of them make up the situations immigrants encounter.

References

Bailey, A. G. (1937). *The conflict of European and Eastern Algonkian cultures 1504–1700: A study in Canadian civilization* (Monograph Series, Vol. 2). St. John: New Brunswick Museum.

Berry, J. W. (1990). Psychology of acculturation. In J. Berman (Ed.), *Cross-cultural perspectives: Nebraska symposium on motivation* (pp. 201–234). Lincoln: University of Nebraska Press.

Berry, J. W. (1992). Acculturation and adaptation in a new society. *International Migration, 30*, 69–85.

Berry, J. W. (1997). Immigration, acculturation and adaptation. *Applied Psychology, 46*, 5–68.

Berry, J. W. (2001). A psychology of immigration. *Journal of Social Issues, 57*(3), 615–631.

Berry, J. W. (2003). Conceptual approaches to acculturation. In K. M. Chun, P. Balls Organista, & G. Marin (Eds.), *Acculturation: Advances in theory, measurement and applied research* (pp. 17–37). Washington, DC: American Psychological Association.

Berry, J. W., Trimble, J. E., & Olmedo, E. L. (1986). Assessment of acculturation. In W. J. Lonner & J. W. Berry (Eds.), *Field methods in cross-cultural research* (pp. 291–324). Thousand Oaks: Sage.

Berry, J. W., Phinney, J. S., Sam, D. L., & Vedder, P. (2006). Immigrant youth: Acculturation, identity and adaptation. *Applied Psychology: An International Review, 55*(3), 303–332.

Boerema, C., Russell, M., & Aguilar, A. (2010). Sewing in the lives of immigrant women. *Journal of Occupational Science, 17*(2), 78–84.

Bourhis, R., Moise, C., Perreault, S., & Senecal, S. (1997). Towards an interactive acculturation model: A social psychological approach. *International Journal of Psychology, 32*, 369–386.

Butcher, A. P., Spoonley, P., & Trlin, A. D. (2006). *Being accepted: The experience of discrimination and social exclusion by immigrants and refugees in New Zealand.* Palmerston North: New Settlers Programme.

Cutchin, M. P. (2001). Deweyan integration: Moving beyond place attachment in elderly migration theory. *International Journal of Aging & Human Development, 52*(1), 29–44.

Cutchin, M. P. (2007). From society to self (and back) through place: Habit in transactional context. *OTJR: Occupation, Participation and Health, 27*, 50S–59S.

Dewey, J. (1957). *Human nature and conduct: An introduction to social psychology*. New York: The Modern Library (Original work published in 1922).

Dewey, J. (1980). *The quest for certainty: A study of the relation of knowledge and action.* New York: Perigee (Original work published in 1929).

Dewey, J. (1981). Experience and nature. In J. A. Boydston (Ed.), *John Dewey: The later works* (Vol. 1, pp. 1–409). Carbondale: Southern Illinois University Press (Original work published in 1925).

Dewey, J. (1986). Logic: The theory of inquiry. In J. A. Boydston (Ed.), *John Dewey, The later works, 1925–1953* (Vol. 12, pp. 1–529). Carbondale: Southern Illinois University Press (Original work published in 1938).

Dewey, J. (1989). *Experience and nature* (2nd ed.). LaSalle: Open court (Original work published in 1929).

Dewey, J., & Bentley, A. (1989). Knowing and the known. In J. A. Boydston (Ed.), *John Dewey: The later works* (Vol. 16, pp. 1–279). Carbondale: Southern Illinois University Press (Original work published in 1949).

Garrison, J. (2001). An introduction to Dewey's theory of functional "trans-action": An alternative paradigm for activity theory. *Mind, Culture and Activity, 8*(4), 275–296.

Huot, S., & Laliberte Rudman, D. (2010). The performances and places of identity: Conceptualising intersections of occupation, identity and place in the process of migration. *Journal of Occupational Science, 17*(2), 68–77.

Kağitçibaşi, Ç. (2007). *Family, self and human development across cultures: Theory and applications* (2nd ed.). Mahwah: Erlbaum Associates.

LaFromboise, T., Coleman, H., & Gerton, J. (1993). Psychological impact of biculturalism: Evidence and theory. *Psychological Bulletin, 114*, 395–412.

Lopez, E. J., Ehly, S., & Garcia-Vazquez, E. (2002). Acculturation, social support and academic achievement of Mexican and Mexican American high school students: An exploratory study. *Psychology in the School, 39*, 245–257.

Martins, V., & Reid, D. (2007). New immigrant women in urban Canada: Insights into occupation and sociocultural context. *Occupational Therapy International, 14*(4), 203–220.

Mills, C. W. (1967). *The sociological imagination.* Oxford: Oxford University Press.

Nayar, S. (2009). *The theory of navigating cultural spaces.* Unpublished doctoral thesis, AUT University, Auckland, New Zealand.

Nayar, S., & Hocking, C. (2006). Undertaking everyday activities: Immigrant Indian women settling in New Zealand. *Diversity in Health and Social Care Journal, 3*(4), 253–260.

Nayar, S., Hocking, C., & Giddings, L. (2012). Using occupation to navigate cultural spaces: Indian immigrant women settling in New Zealand. *Journal of Occupational Science, 19*(1), 62–75.

Nesdale, D., Rooney, R., & Smith, L. (1997). Migrant ethnic identity and psychological distress. *Journal of Cross Cultural Psychiatry, 28*(5), 569–588.

Spoonley, P., Gendall, P., & Trlin, A. (2007). *Welcome to our world: The attitudes of New Zealanders to immigrants and immigration*. Palmerston North: New Settlers Programme.

Sullivan, S. (2000). Reconfiguring gender with John Dewey: Habit, bodies, and cultural change. *Hypatia, 15*(1), 23–42.

Ward, C., & Rana-Deuba, A. (1999). Acculturation and adaptation revisited. *Journal of Cross-Cultural Psychology, 30*(4), 422–442.

Ward, C., Bochner, S., & Furnham, A. (2001). Social identification theories. In C. Ward, S. Bochner, & A. Furnham (Eds.), *The psychology of culture shock* (pp. 98–121). East Sussex: Routledge.

Yerxa, E. J., Clark, F., Frank, G., Jackson, J., Parham, D., Pierce, D., et al. (1990). *An introduction to occupational science: A foundation for occupational therapy in the 21st century*. Binghamton/New York: Haworth.

Chapter 8
The Situated Nature of Disability

Sharon Dale Stone

8.1 Introduction

For the able-bodied population, common sense seems to suggest that disability is something that happens to an individual's body, so that people *have* disabilities. Indeed, rather than referring to disabled people, it is common in everyday language to refer to people *with* disabilities, so that disability is conceptualized as a property of the individual body rather than as an individual's most salient characteristic. This conceptualization does not allow for understanding disability in terms of a transactional relationship involving person and situation. My purpose in this chapter is to argue that it is useful to understand disability as a relational, situationally specific concept, rather than a trans-situational characteristic that an individual can have. The argument is grounded in and illustrated with excerpts from my research on experiences of disability. As well, I draw on symbolic interactionist theory, as well as insights from critical disability studies and the social model of disability.

I begin the chapter with a brief overview of contemporary attempts to conceptualize disability, which allows for an understanding of the significance of definitions and measures of disability. I then move to a discussion of findings from distinct research projects examining experiences of disability, to illustrate the point that disability is necessarily situational. I discuss this with reference to three over-riding themes: situational identification; strategic identification; and avoiding stigma. Finally, I move to a more theoretical consideration of the significance of findings about people's willingness to identify as disabled, to highlight the extent to which this is dependent on whether they were or were not constrained in their ability to pursue desired occupations. Rather than bodily limitations, an inability to engage in desired occupations was experienced as disabling.

S.D. Stone (✉)
Department of Sociology, Lakehead University, Thunder Bay, ON, Canada
e-mail: sdstone@lakeheadu.ca

M.P. Cutchin and V.A. Dickie (eds.), *Transactional Perspectives on Occupation*,
DOI 10.1007/978-94-007-4429-5_8, © Springer Science+Business Media B.V. 2013

8.2 Conceptualizing Disability: An Overview of Recent Controversies

An understanding of disability as something an individual can have is built into the World Health Organization's (WHO) conceptualization of disablement in its International Classification of Impairments, Disabilities and Handicaps (ICIDH) (World Health Organization 1980). In this influential document, translated into 13 languages by the time it was reprinted in 1993, disablement is conceptualized as a linear process that begins with bodily disease, which may lead to bodily *impairment* (defined as bodily dysfunction). When impairment adversely affects an individual's ability to engage in a range of activities, the individual is then said to experience *disability*, defined as "any restriction or lack (resulting from an impairment) of ability to perform an activity in the manner or within the range considered normal for a human being." This may then lead to the individual having a *handicap*, defined as a social disadvantage. Thus, according to the ICIDH, individuals *have* disabilities and handicaps on account of an underlying pathology. As pointed out by Bickenbach et al. (1999), the ICIDH problematically assumes that:

> the social and physical world is immutable and benign. The underlying model does not clearly acknowledge that the presence of social barriers and the absence of social facilitators play any sort of role in the creations of the disadvantages that a person with a disability experiences (pp. 1175–1176).

This conventional understanding of disablement is in stark contrast to the politicized conceptualization offered by many disability rights advocates, who subscribe to what is known as the social model of disability—a model developed in the UK by a group called the Union of the Physically Impaired Against Segregation (UPIAS). According to this model, disability is defined as "the disadvantage or restriction of activity caused by a contemporary social organization which takes no or little account of people who have physical impairments and thus excludes them from participation in the mainstream of social activities" (UPIAS 1976, p. 14). Disability, in other words, does not reside in an individual's body as something that someone may *have*, but is defined as the loss of opportunity resulting from discrimination. To some extent the social model concept of disability is analogous to the ICIDH concept of handicap, but the key difference is that the ICIDH conceptualizes handicap as something someone can have as a consequence of a disease process, whereas the social model conceptualizes disability in terms of oppression that is unjustly imposed on those with impairments (Abberley 1987). The social model solution is not to change the individual, but to remove disabling barriers.

From the perspective of disability studies, disability is socially created through practices that deny the ubiquity of impairment (cf. Zola 1993). As I have argued elsewhere (Stone 2008), we need to recognize that impairment is not always experienced as troublesome, and impairment is not inherently disabling. Thus, someone with an impairment such as paraplegia is not disabled because of an inability to walk, but is disabled in *situations* where the expectation is that someone ought to be able to walk. Disability is, therefore, always contextual. Treating disability and impairment as tragic or as necessarily involving suffering is what typically contributes to the experience of disablement which, ultimately, is what causes suffering.

8.2.1 The International Classification of Functioning, Disability and Health (ICF)

Almost as soon as it was created, disability activists and scholars began critiquing the medicalized approach to disability embedded in the ICIDH (Barnes and Mercer 2010; Bickenbach et al. 1999). The critique largely centered on the assumption that disability and handicap were necessarily caused by impairment. Controversy over the utility of the ICIDH led the WHO to replace it in 2001 with the ICF, which conceptualizes disablement in terms of the discrete domains of *impairment, activity limitations* and *participation restrictions* (World Health Organization 2002). A major advance over the linear ICIDH model, in the ICF disability is conceptualized as arising from the interaction between these three domains in a specific social or physical environment such as work, home or school. The ICF posits disability as a universal human experience, and recognizes that the environment plays a role in the disablement process. In creating the ICF, the WHO wrote:

> ICF puts the notions of 'health' and 'disability' in a new light. It acknowledges that every human being can experience *a decrement in health* and thereby experience some disability. This is not something that happens to only a minority of humanity. ICF thus 'mainstreams' the experience of disability and recognizes it as a universal human experience ... Disability is a complex phenomena that is both a problem at the level of a person's body, and a complex and primarily social phenomena (World Health Organization 2002, p. 3, 9 italics added).

Even though there is now recognition that social factors also play a role, the ICF, like the ICIDH before it, continues to posit disability as a problem with an individual's body. Moreover, the ICF does not move away from conceptualizing disability as a health matter, as proponents of the social model argue is necessary (e.g., see Oliver 1990; Barnes and Mercer 2004). Indeed, the ICF explicitly identifies disability as "a decrement in health." As Bickenbach et al. (1999) commented:

> [It] remains a health classification, so the scope of participation issues is restricted to disablement, that is, to those experiences that are linked to a health condition of some sort. The ICIDH-2 [ICF], like its predecessor, is a classification of consequences of health conditions, (p. 1184).

In other words, the ICF does not allow for the possibility that disability may be situationally created, regardless of the presence or absence of a health condition.

As numerous critics have pointed out, the ICF pays insufficient attention to the significance of contextual factors in creating disability (Badley 2008; Conti-Becker 2009; Imrie 2004). For example, the ICF treats *participation* as though it can be defined without regard for social factors such as gender, age, culture or socio-economic status, as though it can be understood in terms of individual performance abstracted from contextual factors, and as though subjective perspectives about the situation are irrelevant (Hammel et al. 2008). *Participation,* according to Hammel et al. needs to be recognized "as a multifaceted, *transactive* process involving interaction with and within physical, social, cultural and political environments and communities" (p.1458, emphasis added). These critiques of the ICF make it clear that the usefulness of the ICF for understanding disability is limited by a failure to sufficiently highlight the central role played by the environment in creating disability. As Badley (2008) stated the issue:

> In particular, this analysis reaffirms the role of the environment as being a scene-setter for disability and not just as a facilitator or barrier, particularly for problems with tasks and societal involvement. This ... sees disability as the product of an interaction between the individual and his/her environment (p. 2343).

The call for recognizing disability as the product of person/environment interaction, as outlined above, clearly underscores the need for the application of a transactional perspective for understanding disability. It is an error to reify the concept of disability, treating it as something unchanging that can be objectively observed by onlookers; rather, disability is always situationally created, its presence (or absence) is necessarily contingent upon contextual factors including the willingness of situational actors to variously recognize or disavow disability. Using a transactional perspective allows us to emphasize the co-constitutive relationship of person and situation, and their ongoing coordination that redefines the relationship, in understanding disability (Cutchin and Dickie 2012). Moreover, establishing the presence (or absence) of disability is an ongoing accomplishment—as the transactional relationship of person and situation proceeds, understandings of disability and its presence or absence may change.

8.3 Research Projects: Support for the Transactional Perspective on Disability

That disability is both relational and an ongoing accomplishment can be illustrated with reference to the experiences of three distinct groups of people with impairments that are sometimes disabling, sometimes not. These individuals were interviewed as part of four different research projects.

Group One: Stroke Survivors. This group was made up of 28 women who survived a hemorrhagic stroke before age 50, most of whom were left with residual impairments such as varying degrees of one-sided weakness, lack of stamina, or cognitive difficulties such as aphasia. For the most part, their impairments were not obvious to casual onlookers. I interviewed these stroke survivors for a qualitative research project about their post-stroke experiences.[1]

---

[1] "Women Survivors of Hemorrhagic Stroke." Funded by a grant from the Social Sciences and Humanities Research Council of Canada, 2002. Details about research methods can be found in Stone (2007).

Group Two: Injured Workers. This group was made up of 77 men and women who had a variety of permanent impairments due to workplace injury, most commonly musculoskeletal injuries. Like members of the first group, members of this group were also likely to have impairments not obvious to casual onlookers. I and my research assistants interviewed these injured workers for two distinct research projects about the experiences of injured workers.[2]

Group Three: Academics with MS. This group was made up of 35 men and women with multiple sclerosis (MS) who work or have worked as university professors. Most of these academics had obvious impairments (as indicated, e.g., by use of a cane or wheelchair). Some experienced no impairment at all at the time of interview, and some of them, like members of the other two groups, had impairments not obvious to casual onlookers. For example, they commonly reported becoming easily fatigued. My co-researchers interviewed members of this group for a study about the experience of chronic illness in the academic workplace.[3]

Below, I highlight themes that cut across all three groups regarding the willingness of research participants to identify as disabled. Altogether, what participants had to say serves to illustrate the point that disability is necessarily transactional.

8.3.1 Situational Identification

In each of the three groups, there were people who did not identify as disabled, even though they had impairments that limited their ability to engage in desired occupations. Indeed, in the group of 35 academics with MS, 12 (slightly more than one third) rejected a disabled identity even though 6 of these 12 used a mobility aid. For example, a wheelchair user with MS, when asked whether she identified as disabled, said: "… earlier in having MS I probably was more inclined to say I was disabled than I am now. Um, I don't think of myself as disabled. … I prefer the term 'differently abled'."

The wheelchair user was not asked to elaborate on her understanding of disability or why she changed her mind about how to identify herself, but it would be reasonable to surmise that she did not view the term "disabled" positively. Likely, she chose to identify as "differently abled" as a way of drawing attention away from

[2] One group was interviewed for a research project titled "Injured Workers in Northwestern Ontario and the Effectiveness of Peer Support" funded by a grant from the Workplace Safety and Insurance Board (Ontario), 2001. Details about research methods can be found in Stone (2003). A second group was interviewed for a research project titled "Workers Compensation and the Consequences of Workplace Injury" funded by a Community-University Research Alliance grant from the Social Sciences and Humanities Research Council of Canada, 2006 (Principal Investigator Emile Tompa). Details about research methods are as yet unpublished.

[3] "Chronic illness and the knowledge worker." Funded by a grant from the Social Sciences and Humanities Research Council of Canada, 2008 (Principal Investigator Valorie A. Crooks). Details about research methods can be found in Crooks et al. (2011).

what she was unable to do (e.g., walk unassisted) and focusing attention on what she could do. Although disability studies scholars such as Linton (1998) are adamant that euphemistic terms for disability such as "differently abled" ought to be eschewed in favor of unequivocally claiming disability, in the minds of many disabled people use of the term "differently abled" can be a way of denying the presence of disability while simultaneously celebrating ability (cf. Watson 2002).

Another handful of academics with MS explained that whether they adopted a disabled identity depended on the situation. For example, one woman with invisible impairments, when asked whether she identified as a person with a disability, said "Um, it depends, at times I do." Another woman, who used a walker, used virtually the same words in responding to the question: "Um, it depends, professionally I don't." She went on to say that she would, however, identify as such when with friends and family.

Several injured workers, as well as several stroke survivors, made similar comments about identification depending on the situation. One stroke survivor, for example, said that for the most part she did not consider herself disabled, but:

> … sometimes I have considered myself, you know, disabled I guess, in some ways with certain things, [like] when it comes to people asking me to play softball or this or that… So I would say that I definitely have a disability 'cause I mean, for me to throw the ball, like for some reason, this finger likes to just do its own thing, so I go to throw, I mean, it stays out here. And then there goes the ball, and it's *embarrassing*, I mean, you know, I can't, so you know [in that situation] I'd say I am. [emphasis added]

Others concurred that being recognized as disabled was embarrassing. For example, a woman who had been an art therapist working with disabled children before her stroke at age 28 tried to articulate why she recoiled against calling herself disabled, even though she had become aphasic and had great difficulty walking:

> Because I think disability is someone in a, a wheelchair and, uh—you, you know, it's funny because when I'm on the other side, where I'm a therapist then I talk about all this and try to convince the clients why it's not the end of the world. But when it's actually happening to *you*, it has changed. And [extended pause] it's like it's just overwhelming. … I, I don't use the—I don't say I'm disabled. Um, because I feel *embarrassed* [emphasis added].

Some injured workers also said they were embarrassed by being recognized as disabled. One woman who had chronic pain due to a neck injury felt embarrassed that she could not join her husband in socializing either at or away from home. In her words, "Well, it's *embarrassing*. I feel like shit because you do want to be down there socializing." Also a man who had chronic pain due to a back injury said that when others discovered that he was unable to lift heavy objects:

> It makes me feel uh, challenged uh, you know. Um, for example if, you go buy let's say a couple of cases of pop or something … you know, you don't want to ask, oh can I get somebody to carry this out for me. You know. It's uh, a little bit *embarrassing*. Right? [emphasis added]

In addition to the noteworthy use of the term embarrassing by injured workers, it is also noteworthy that the man with the back injury said that he felt challenged when his limitations became obvious. Based on other comments he made about his experiences when interviewed, it was clear that he did not usually think of himself as either disabled or having limitations. To be reminded of this, therefore, was what was challenging and embarrassing. Like the woman with a neck injury, and like others quoted above, he only felt disabled when in situations where he needed to call attention to his limitations. The presence of disability was contingent on the demands of the situation and the attitudes of situational participants. Accordingly, academics with MS, stroke survivors and injured workers alike continually adjusted their ideas about what was possible and what they wanted to do. Clearly, research participants actively negotiated each situation anew, which underscores the point that the relationship between person and situation is co-constitutive and coordinated in an ongoing manner.

8.3.2 Strategic Identification

Others offered comments to show that adoption of a disabled identity was often not only situational, but strategic. For example, some of those who rejected a disabled identity for themselves were nevertheless willing to identify as disabled when seeking accommodations such as accessible parking. One academic with MS who used a cane said that she identified herself as disabled when applying for a disabled parking permit, but that otherwise she did not consider herself disabled. She was clear that she would only adopt the identity if she were unable to accomplish what she desired. As she said: "But I can sort of do what I normally do, … there's nothing I … can't do that I want to do."

Gaining access to a disabled parking sticker was an accommodation sought by many people in all three research groups: stroke survivors, injured workers, and academics with MS. While many would publicly disavow a disabled identity, regardless of the visibility of their impairments or use of mobility aids, many nevertheless had difficulty with walking and so needed access to a parking spot close to where they were going. Thus strategically claiming a disabled identity in order to get access to a needed accommodation such as disabled parking was a pragmatic move. This is further evidence of the situational contingency of disability. From the outside, it might appear that people were getting undeserved benefits by strategically claiming disability, but in reality, they were getting what they needed in order to pursue desired activities on the same basis as everyone else. If calling themselves disabled or going to a doctor to be certified as disabled was going to get them what they needed, then they generally did not hesitate to bow to the dictates of the situation, but they were quick to drop the identity once they left the situation (cf. Crooks et al. 2008). It was as though at one moment they were disabled, at the next moment they were not.

Just as adoption of a disabled identity could be strategic, non-adoption of a disabled identity could be strategic. The injured workers who were interviewed were likely to reject a disabled identity for themselves because they had a vested interest in being recognized and gaining rights *as injured workers*, as opposed to being lumped in with and treated the same as other disabled people. For them, the politics of naming was of great concern. They typically did not recognize organizations for disabled people as relevant to their lives, but sought to be recognized as a distinct group that had suffered on account of workplace injury, and deserved compensation on account of injuries sustained while working for an employer.

Research participants who were stroke survivors were also likely to reject a disabled identity for themselves, even though all but one of the 28 participants had residual impairments that hampered their ability to do as they pleased. One woman, for example, was prone to extreme fatigue which meant that she could not work for more than a few hours at a time. Consequently, she was unable to find paid employment and she was at the time of interview in the process of applying to the government for disability benefits. She strategically identified as disabled for the purpose of applying for a pension, yet privately, she rejected a disabled identity for herself. In her words: "I wouldn't say I classify it as a disability. I'm … it's more of a challenge."

8.3.3 Avoiding Stigma

Some stroke survivors commented on adopting a disabled identity, not so much because they truly felt disabled, but because of the attitudes of others. As one woman said, she was "definitely disabled" due to hemiplegia, yet:

> I don't, hmm, in my mind I'm not disabled in that respect but I'm sure people meeting me think I'm disabled when they watch me having to do everything with the one hand, and they try to help me and I say, 'it's OK, I don't need the help, thank you.' And I guess that offends a lot of people 'cause it's, their nature to want, they *want* to help.

This woman then felt obliged to restrain herself from letting others see her perform one-handed actions. Otherwise, the situation simply became uncomfortable all around. Disability intruded in her life, not because of her hemiplegia, but because of the attitudes of others.

Similar comments were made by several other stroke survivors, as well as a few academics with MS. One academic, for example, said that she did not want to identify as disabled because:

> I don't want people to see me as somebody with a disability, and it probably goes back to … the time when I was diagnosed when the people close to me would sort of call up and say, 'How are you feeling today, how are you feeling?' instead of you know the casual, 'Hi, how are'—it was like, 'Are you okay, are you okay?' And it was this, this whole like tiptoeing around me that I didn't, I didn't want to take on the illness role, like the sick role.

In the same vein, a woman who sustained a brain injury while working commented on how her relationships with family members had changed. As a consequence of her brain injury, she was easily fatigued. She said:

> You go from this person who's walking your dog and going to the gym and having fun, to a person who's laying on the couch all the time … I mean, even my mum went through a period where … she'd say like, 'What is *wrong* with you? You're always tired. You're this, you're that!' Everybody loses patience, I guess, eventually.

Elsewhere in the interview, she talked about how she did not usually think of herself as disabled and she disliked having others comment negatively on her limitations. She worked to actively resist a disabled identity, because if she were to take that on, she would feel obliged to stop doing all that she did (e.g., she continued in full-time employment while also being responsible for maintaining order in her household).

People in the injured workers group were especially likely to comment on being wary of being pigeon-holed as disabled, because they were well aware of the negative attitudes towards disability that routinely circulate in mainstream society. Most of them were unemployed yet interested in finding paid employment, even if only on a part time basis. Most of them also felt that to the extent that they could not find satisfactory work, it was due to the unreasonable prejudices of potential employers. Accordingly, they did not want to be stereotyped as disabled and therefore incapable of productive labor. A construction worker, for example, attributed his success in finding a series of jobs to his ability to hide his missing fingertip from public notice. He said:

> I've lost the last quarter tip of my finger, so when my hand is closed nobody can tell. Nobody can see anything at all. All they can see is a normal hand. The way I position my hand, most people can't … notice it … Most bosses don't know about it because I don't tell them …For example, a job interview. If you're trying to get a job, you don't want them to know that you are injured. So you don't want them to say, 'Oh, you would be great for the job, but I don't know if you could handle it.' I just don't want that to be an option. So I hide it. Then other times when you're in a fine setting or other times when maybe you're not in a fine setting but you make a joke out of it and you bring it out. Most of the time you don't show it unless needed. [It depends on] the crowd, the situation. If it's appropriate or not.

Clearly, disability is something that can be produced as relevant to a situation or not. It is never unambiguously present or absent. This same construction worker, for example, also talked about going out of his way while working to hide his inability to perform certain tasks on account of his missing fingertip. He put a great deal of energy into finding ways to do things in non-standard ways or, when that was not possible, he tended to make a joke out of not feeling well enough to do a job. In other words, even though he was himself well aware of his impairment and how that limited him, he worked to make it irrelevant. With no one else aware of his impairment, he was able to avoid having the specter of disability enter into the transactional situation. To be able to say that disability is present, it must always be acknowledged as relevant to the situation.

8.4 Conclusion

Comments from all three groups of research participants illustrate the point that, regardless of how they saw themselves, others were often inclined to treat them as disabled. Depending on the situation, they were not always able to successfully present themselves as able-bodied, even when they protested that they were not disabled. The work of Goffman on presentation of self (1959) and on the relational nature of stigma (1963) is relevant here. Goffman's work was grounded in the sociological perspective of symbolic interactionism, a tradition with roots in the pragmatist thought of John Dewey and George Herbert Mead. Accordingly, there are close parallels between symbolic interactionism and a transactional perspective: in particular the view that people act on the basis of the meaning ascribed to a situation, and meaning is always situationally dependent or transactional. In any case, Goffman drew attention to the ways in which actors attempted to manipulate situations such that they would be recognized as "normal," competent individuals and avoid both embarrassment and stigmatization. He identified disability as an especially embarrassing and stigmatizing characteristic that individuals would try to hide from others as they engaged in social interaction. In the same vein, Davis (1961) studied the interactions of people who had been disabled by polio and coined the term "deviance disavowal" to refer to the practice of disabled people to pretend that they were able-bodied so as to avoid stigmatization.[4]

More recently, after anthropologist Murphy (1987) became paralyzed due to a spinal cord tumor, he systematically observed the reactions of others to his changed abilities. He noted that when he began using a wheelchair, formerly friendly colleagues and acquaintances appeared to go out of their way to avoid interaction with him. Interestingly, however, he also noted that his students as well as many women with whom he had not formerly been acquainted did not appear to be threatened by him, but were willing to engage in social interaction. Murphy's observations illustrate the symbolic interactionist point that disability is not inherently meaningful. Rather, meaning must be continually established and re-established by interacting participants as they negotiate the definition of the situation. Situational participants will then act based on how they interpret the social context. In the case of Murphy's experiences, what changed was not the visibility or extent of his impairments, but the different ways that others assigned meaning to his impairments. Formerly friendly colleagues were likely to act as though Murphy was no longer a competent or interesting actor, while those who belonged to groups of people that would otherwise be considered as subordinate to him began treating him as their social equal.

Similar observations are peppered throughout the disability studies literature reviewing personal experience. Wheelchair-user Keith (1996), for example, analyzed her own experiences with prejudicial attitudes, to note that "doing disability all day long can be an exhausting process" (p. 71). From Keith's perspective, the

[4] Both Goffman and Davis published these works before the rise of the disability rights movement or the development of a social model of disability to counter the hegemony of biomedicine. Accordingly, they wrote as though all reasonable people unquestionably accept the legitimacy of mainstream horror in the face of disability, and they used terms such as "physically handicapped" rather than modern terminology about disability. This limits the usefulness of their works for understanding disability in the contemporary context, yet as interview extracts suggest, there are still many disabled people with self-understandings similar to those studied by Goffman and Davis.

problem is not that she needs a wheelchair for mobility; the problem is having to deal with other peoples' preconceptions and misconceptions about her abilities. Given a choice, Keith might opt to have disability considered irrelevant to social interaction, but she is rarely given this choice. Instead, she becomes disabled by the attitudes and actions of others in transactional situations. The significance of this for occupational science is that she is thereby prevented from exercising her ability to engage in desired occupations. This, the crux of disabling oppression from a social model perspective (Abberley 1987), is what is experienced as disabling.

The interview extracts presented in this chapter can collectively be understood as examples of people being actively prevented from pursuing desired occupations either on account of how others define the situation, or on account of their own fear of being seen in a negative light due to impairment. Indeed, this chapter can offer only a small sampling of the examples illustrating this that abound throughout interview transcripts for each research project. Particularly for people with impairments, occupation is clearly not something to be pursued in the abstract. Self-initiated occupation, which is what is valued in our individualistic society, can only be pursued to the extent that an individual is able to adopt an understanding of her/himself as competent to perform the task at hand. People with impairments, however, are continually vulnerable to being defined as incompetent.[5] At the same time, they know based on experience that their vulnerability is always situationally specific. Just as they might be defined as disabled and hence incompetent in one situation, or at one moment, there is always the chance that in the next situation, or the next moment, they might be redefined as competent to meet the demands of the situation/moment. They need, therefore, to continually find ways to maintain control over the definition of the situation, or at least maintain control over how they are perceived by others in the situation. Their identity is not necessarily a matter of individual preference. It is negotiated within the context of a situation, and the outcome of that negotiation has repercussions for what it is possible to do. Perhaps, if disability were not so widely understood as an individual problem, they might feel more comfortable pursuing occupations that they cherish. As it is, they are often too occupied with working to maintain a sense of dignity.

References

Abberley, P. (1987). The concept of oppression and the development of a social theory of disability. *Disability & Society, 2*(1), 5–19.

Badley, E. M. (2008). Enhancing the conceptual clarity of the activity and participation components of the International Classification of Functioning, Disability, and Health. *Social Science & Medicine, 66*, 2335–2345.

Barnes, L., & Mercer, G. (Eds.). (2004). *Implementing the social model of disability: Theory and research*. Leeds: The Disability Press.

Barnes, L., & Mercer, G. (2010). *Exploring disability* (2nd ed.). Cambridge: Polity Press.

[5] As are all people continually vulnerable to being defined as incompetent.

Bickenbach, J. E., Chatterji, S., Badley, E. M., & Üstün, T. B. (1999). Models of disablement, universalism and the international classification of impairments, disabilities and handicaps. *Social Science & Medicine, 48*, 1173–1187.

Conti-Becker, A. (2009). Between the ideal and the real: Reconsidering the International Classification of Functioning, Disability and Health. *Disability and Rehabilitation, 31*(25), 2125–2129.

Crooks, V. A., Chouinard, V., & Wilton, R. D. (2008). Understanding, embracing, rejecting: Women's negotiations of disability constructions and categorizations after becoming chronically ill. *Social Science & Medicine, 67*, 1837–1846.

Crooks, V. A., Stone, S. D., & Owen, M. (2011). Problem-focused coping strategies used by Canadian academics with multiple sclerosis to enable university teaching. *Canadian Journal of Occupational Therapy, 78*(1), 45–49.

Cutchin, M. P., & Dickie, V. A. (2012). Transactionalism: Occupational science and the pragmatic attitude. In G. Whiteford & C. Hocking (Eds.), *Critical perspectives on occupational science: Society, inclusion, participation* (pp. 23–37). London: Wiley.

Davis, F. (1961). Deviance disavowal: The management of strained interaction by the visibly handicapped. *Social Problems, 9*, 120–132.

Goffman, E. (1959). *Presentation of self in everyday life*. New York: Anchor.

Goffman, E. (1963). *Stigma: Notes on the management of spoiled identity*. Englewood Cliffs: Prentice-Hall.

Hammel, J., Magasi, S., Heinemann, A., Whiteneck, G., Bogner, J., & Rodriguez, E. (2008). What does participation mean? An insider perspective from people with disabilities. *Disability and Rehabilitation, 30*(19), 1445–1460.

Imrie, R. (2004). Demystifying disability: A review of the International Classification of Functioning, Disability and Health. *Sociology of Health & Illness, 26*, 287–305.

Keith, L. (1996). Encounters with strangers. In J. Morris (Ed.), *Encounters with strangers: Feminism and disability* (pp. 69–88). London: The Women's Press.

Linton, S. (1998). *Claiming disability: Knowledge and identity*. New York: New York University Press.

Murphy, R. (1987). *The body silent*. New York: Henry Holt.

Oliver, M. (1990). *The politics of disablement*. London: Macmillan.

Stone, S. D. (2003). Workers without work: Injured workers and well-being. *Journal of Occupational Science, 10*, 7–13.

Stone, S. D. (2007). *A change of plans: Women's stories of hemorrhagic stroke*. Toronto: Sumach.

Stone, S. D. (2008). Resisting an illness label: Disability, impairment, and illness. In P. Moss & K. Teghtsoonian (Eds.), *Contesting illness: Processes and practices* (pp. 201–217). Toronto: University of Toronto Press.

UPIAS. (1976). *Fundamental principles of disability*. London: Union of the Physically Impaired Against Segregation.

Watson, N. (2002). Well, I know this is going to sound very strange to you, but I don't see myself as a disabled person. *Disability & Society, 17*(5), 509–527.

World Health Organization. (1980). *The International Classification of Impairments, Disabilities and Handicaps (ICIDH)*. Geneva: WHO.

World Health Organization [WHO]. (2002). *Toward a common language for functioning, disability and health: ICF, the International Classification of Functioning, Disability and Health*. Geneva: World Health Organization.

Zola, I. (1993). Disability statistics: What we count and what it tells us. *Journal of Disability Policy Studies, 4*(2), 9–39.

Chapter 9
Place Integration: A Conceptual Tool to Understand the Home Modification Process

Karin Johansson, Malcolm P. Cutchin, and Margareta Lilja

9.1 Introduction

Aspects of a transactional perspective have been utilized to understand aging in context as well as the provision and effects of services for older people (Law et al. 1996; Cutchin 2001, 2003; Cutchin et al. 2003; Johansson et al. 2009a, b). A fundamental basis of the transactional perspective is that research that does not recognize the transactional, or relational and dynamic, character of human life will overlook important dimensions of its subject matter (Cutchin 2003, 2004; Dickie et al. 2006). Moreover, because of a traditional focus on individuals as the cause of changes in quality of life, non-transactional perspectives struggle to explain the role of service organizations in such changes and how they are addressed (Griffiths 2001; Fischer 2003; Grape et al. 2006). Constituting a promising perspective to develop adequate knowledge about aging in context and the provision and effects of services, the transactional perspective also is associated with methodological challenges, as noted by the above researchers. In this chapter we utilize a particular conceptual tool developed on the basis of a transactional perspective to improve our understanding of human occupation. More specifically, we discuss how the concept of place integration can be applied to enhance understandings of older persons' everyday situation at home. In addition, we discuss how place integration can inform intervention design and implementation to support older adults' everyday activities to their satisfaction.

K. Johansson (✉) • M. Lilja
Department of Neurobiology, Care Sciences and Society, Division of Occupational Therapy, Karolinska Institutet, Stockholm, Sweden
e-mail: karin.e.johansson@ki.se

M.P. Cutchin
Department of Allied Health Sciences, Division of Occupational Science and Occupational Therapy, University of North Carolina at Chapel Hill, Chapel Hill, NC, USA

M.P. Cutchin and V.A. Dickie (eds.), *Transactional Perspectives on Occupation*,
DOI 10.1007/978-94-007-4429-5_9, © Springer Science+Business Media B.V. 2013

Interventions to improve older people's everyday lives do not always succeed. This most likely reflects a failure of both methods for assessment of needs and the design of services to recognize the ever-changing nature of an older person's situation (Vik 2008; Alsaker et al. 2009; Johansson et al. 2009b). Thus, in order to provide more successful interventions to support older persons in their everyday life, there is a need for a shift of the focus in research and practice from predefined phenomena to the emergent situation as a whole (see Chap. 12). In line with the larger purpose of this book, this chapter argues that there is an urgent need for the development of theoretical tools to grasp the dynamic relationships involved in older people's everyday activities in home environments. To do so would aid greatly in the development of more appropriate interventions. In this chapter we present insights from a research project to illustrate how the concept of place integration can be useful in the efforts to generate advances in research and interventions along these lines.

9.2 Aging in the Home Environment

Performing everyday activities in home environments when aging with functional limitations constitutes specific situations that pose particular challenges to older people and those that care for them. Increasing age is associated with increasing risk for health problems that might lead to functional decline and reduced possibilities to perform everyday activities (Jagger et al. 2001; Iwarsson 2005; Ahacic et al. 2007). As one grows older, characteristics of the home situation often change. For example, social (who is living in the home and in the neighborhood), physical (the indoor and outdoor physical environment), or financial aspects (ability to manage home-related tasks) can change. Such changes often constitute a challenge since they demand changes in the person's habits and activity performance so that they can functionally coordinate with the home environment in meaningful ways (Cutchin et al. 2008). Interventions for older adults living at home with functional limitations typically address this situation without theorizing it as such (Gitlin 2003; Iwarsson 2005; Wahl et al. 2009). Yet the need of older adults to engage in everyday occupations is well known, and a transactional perspective would further inform interventions such as home modification programs.

9.3 Place Integration

The concept of place integration was developed by Cutchin (1999, 2003) as a philosophically-based conceptual tool useful for framing the dynamics of people and their concrete situations. The concept is based on the geographical understanding of place and the philosophy of pragmatism, more specifically, the work of John Dewey who developed the transactional perspective. In contemporary social and cultural geography, place is understood as a process, a continuously changing and integrated socio-culturally and physically experienced setting (Cutchin 2003; Wiles 2005). Dewey's pragmatism focused on the ever-changing and integrated character of human action and experience (Cutchin 2008). The objects of inquiry are the time-specific situations in which experiences and actions occur, and the transactional relationships that form the interdependencies in those situations. The primary connection between the geographic perspective and pragmatism is the situation/place through which action occurs. In line with those concepts, the place integration process is understood as a process of continuous transactions into new situations. Changes in the person-place whole may lead to what Dewey (1998) called "problematic" or "undetermined" situations. The threat of disintegration of the person-place whole through the problematic or undetermined situation prompts reflection and the emergence of possibilities for change through creative thoughts and actions (Cutchin 1999, 2003). The place integration process can be described as a spiral of transactions into new situations rather than as a linear process in which causes and consequences follow a unidirectional chronology or a circular process of repeated and predictable situations (Johansson et al. 2009a, b). As such, older people's lives, especially the components related to the home environment, can be understood as a process of continual place integration (Cutchin 2003; Johansson et al. 2009a, b). We argue that the concept of place integration is relevant in particular to generate understanding of how problems of older people in home environments occur and are handled. Understanding interventions such as home modifications for older people as an important part of the place integration process is therefore a promising approach to generate knowledge about how needs and expectations for interventions are developed and how interventions are integrated into older persons' everyday lives.

9.4 Older Persons in Their Homes: The Swedish Case

The example presented here is taken from a research project focusing on home modifications for older persons in Sweden. The project was developed because traditional theories did not manage to capture the complexity involved in older persons' relationships with their homes. Furthermore, little was known about how needs for home modifications were caused, understood, and defined by older persons. In addition, the effects of home modifications in relationship to those dimensions of need were unknown. In a more practical sense, there was a lack of knowledge about what problems older persons hope to be solved by a home modification, and how interventions can manage to meet such hopes and expectations. Therefore, the project aimed to collect in-depth data about the processes involved in home modification for older adults living at home and to generate new theoretical insights about how home modifications are integrated into older persons' everyday lives.

The project focused on home modification processes within the Swedish home modification system. In Sweden every municipality is obliged by law to provide Home Modification Grants (HMG) for home adaptations that are assessed to be necessary for the performance of daily living activities for individuals with permanent functional limitations (Ministry of Health and Social Affairs 1992). Grants can be provided for modifications in rented as well as owned homes, irrespective of the applicants' financial situation. The grant covers modifications of permanent physical features in the indoor and immediate outdoor home environment, for example, the creation of ramps, rebuilding of bathrooms, and introduction of automatic stair lifts. Decisions about HMG are made by municipal administration officers who base the decision on an application, a referral, and sometimes a home visit. Health care professionals write referrals, and when the applicant is an older person, referrals are often written by an occupational therapist who specializes in primary care. Applications for HMGs can be made in collaboration between the applicant and the health care professional, but they must be signed by the applicant. The municipal administrative officers make the final assessment of needs and match those with solutions available on the open market to determine the size of the grant.

9.4.1 Methodological Development of the Project

The project included 102 persons, aged 40 or older who had applied for home modification grants. 90% were 65 years or older. Two thirds were women, and the participants reported a variety of health problems, such as neuromusculoskeletal and heart and respiratory problems (Johansson et al. 2007). The methods for data collection included (a) a structured instrument for collection of data on self-perceived activity performance from all 102 older persons; (b) retrospective interviews with four older persons who had received home modifications, focusing on how the participants navigated through the service system to get access to appropriate home modification services; and (c) repeated interviews in connection with focused participant observations with four other older home modification grant applicants, focusing on relationships between actions taken by the older persons to handle experienced problems in everyday life, and the service process related to home modification services. (For further details on data collection methods see Johansson et al. 2007, 2009a, b).

Preliminary analysis of data collected through interviews and participant observation with older persons who had applied for home modification grants shaped the direction the project eventually took. Early findings identified that the older persons' hopes and expectations regarding home modifications were closely interconnected with their efforts at handling problems related to everyday activities in the home. In search for a theoretical perspective and associated methods to grasp the process of problem-handling, the concept of place integration was identified as an appropriate tool to meet the aim of the project.

After initial analysis, the data were re-visited and data related to place integration were identified, coded, and further interpreted. A hermeneutic approach (Gustavsson 2000) was used in the final analysis to integrate the data collected with different methods. In this analytical approach, the dialectic relationship between data and the theoretical perspective related to the concept of place integration were interpreted. The goal was to achieve an understanding of the relationships between older persons efforts at handling problems and the home modification services. Through this methodological approach, questions based on the concept of place integration were developed.

One question addressed the situation in which a need for home modifications occurs and how it is defined. This question was formulated as: "What constitutes a problematic situation in the presence of physical barriers for activity performance in the home environment?" As will be described in the following section, the answers to this question were represented with the theme "threatened possibilities for action." This finding guided the development of the question: "How do creative thoughts and actions emerge from a problematic situation constituted by threatened possibilities for action?" Through the analysis, the overarching answer to this second question was represented by the theme "through struggles to regain possibilities for action." In order to understand the relationships between creative thoughts and actions and the subsequent situation (that might or might not include a home modification in the end), the third question was formulated as: "How is the situation emerging as a result of struggles for possibilities for action?" Data identified as providing answers to these questions were further interpreted with the goal of gaining a deeper understanding of connections between the participants' experiences and problem-solving in everyday life and the home modification service process.

9.5 Aspirations for Possibilities for Action: A Central Driving Force

Following from the theory-driven analysis, we found that the place integration process was largely influenced by the participants' primary concern for being in situations where they had possibilities to perform activities as they wanted. Through the analysis, the situations desired were conceptualized as ones that offered possibilities for action. The intention of this concept was to highlight the fact that the older persons' aspirations were not directed towards performance of specific activities; rather, they were oriented towards developing situations where they would have possibilities to perform various activities in accordance with their overriding values and preferences (see Johansson et al. 2009b). A central aspect of this was a desire to have the possibility to make spontaneous choices about when and how to perform everyday activities. For instance, possibilities for action could include having the opportunity to take a shower when the older person perceived it was needed for hygienic reasons, or when he or she had the energy for doing it, as opposed to when it fitted to schedule of formal or informal helpers. Possibilities for action also represented situations through which spontaneous choices could be made about what to eat or what groceries to buy.

9.5.1 A Problematic Situation

Participants concern for doing what they wanted to do meant that a situation became problematic when their possibilities for action were restricted. This was illustrated by data from interviews and participant observation, as well as by the data from structured instruments. Home modification applicants often performed activities independent of assistance from another person but with considerable difficulties. Those difficulties and the unsafe and complicated activity performance that accompanied them were experienced as threats to present and future possibilities for action that they foresaw as desirable; i.e., the difficulty and risk were viewed as a risk to present and future freedom of action. Following from their functional limitations, and from physical barriers in the home, the participants were concerned about becoming dependent on help from others to perform everyday activities. The modifications most commonly applied for were related to showering. Problems associated with being dependent on help from others to shower can be exemplified by Anders, who expressed it this way:

> They come, well, they come today around 10:30. Somebody comes with the newspapers, but drat it, who wants to wait half the day to shower? Showering, that's something you do in the morning.

There were problems associated with activities beyond self-care. One of the participants described a situation where she wanted to bring some flowers to a funeral. To make this possible she had to pay for getting the flowers delivered to her home. She also had to coordinate the time of this delivery with her order of transport services instead of being able to "just roll down the road [to the flower shop] with the walker" and take transport service from there. As illustrated in the above examples, being dependent on help from others was not perceived as a problem in itself, but because such dependence included adjusting activity performance to the more rigid schedules and preferences of a service organization, relatives, or friends, it was perceived as problematic. Moreover, the character of the problematic situation also was shaped by the information an older participant had and what his or her expectations were about changing the situation. Perceptions, aspirations, and expectations of what a situation could become—sometimes based on what other older people had told our participants about their own experiences—were part of how our older participants understood their current situation to be problematic. This dynamic relationship between the present and future of the situation was an important part of how the situation evolved.

9.5.2 Struggling to Create Possibilities for Action

We found the participants' actions emerging from a problematic situation were focused in two directions. On one hand, participants directed creative thoughts and actions towards changes in how and when to perform everyday activities. On the other hand, they also tried to find ways of gaining access to home modification services. Those strategies included complex ways of negotiating the relationship among their own physical capabilities, aspects of the physical environment, and different social agents in the service process. Because this complexity included a lot of resistance in the form of physical barriers, physical capacity, as well as social relationships and organization, the term "struggling to regain possibilities for action" was used to denote the difficulty.

Strategies focused on activity performance could include challenging one's own physical capacity and existing physical barriers by managing to perform activities (in accordance with values and preferences) through extra physical efforts and complicated re-organization of activity. The data illustrated how the older persons used a large amount of creativity, physical effort and complicated planning to remain or generate possibilities for action. For example, Anna described how she developed an approach to showering so that she could be free of structure and bureaucracy of home help:

> I sit on the stool, and then I move one leg over the bath tub, and grab the bar on the wall, and then lift the other leg - standing there. I sometimes think you need to be an octopus with roller skates, having many arms to hold with. It has gone well. I do it in the morning, because I don't dare to shower in the evening, I have to be rested. [......] But I am stubborn, and want to get along by myself (laughing) maybe it's silly at times but I want to be able to do it, I don't want to wait. I'm allowed to shower once a week. I want to take a shower two, three times a week.

Part of the participants' strategies to perform activities as they desired was the use of assistive devices. This was illustrated in interviews and observations, but also by the documentation from quantitative data, showing that 101 out of 102 participants used some kind of assistive device. The participants most frequently reported that they performed everyday activities with support from assistive devices and without support from others but with high levels of difficulty. This indicated that the use of assistive devices did support possibilities to perform activities when preferred, but such use did not reduce difficulties in activity performance.

Some participants noted that having the chance to undertake spontaneous activities outside the home was important to them. For example, two participants who could not get in and out of their homes on their own had each developed strategies in response to that situation. Their common solution was to coordinate their personally desired activities with scheduled health care activities outside the home, for which transport services were already organized. One participant arranged the return trip from heath care appointments so that there was extra time to "roll around for a while" in a wheelchair within a suburban center.

Strategies focusing on getting access to home modification services included more activities and challenges than filling in the application form. After we identified that participants' expectations, experiences, and actions with services were directed by their mental maps of the organizations, "the geographical map" was used as a metaphor to explain participants' mode of coordinating with services. A geographical map is constructed by the symbolization of what is chosen as meaningful for understanding and navigating through the geographical landscape (Cutchin 2007). In this study, maps used by the participants were constructed by participants' symbolizations of what was meaningful for understanding and navigating through the organizational landscape, including descriptions of what institution was responsible for providing what services and what was required to be eligible for such services.

The participants' navigation by their maps guided them in their choice of what professionals and institutions to communicate with and how to present their personal situation. In other words, the character of the navigation process varied across participants. We discovered that when the older person and professionals differed in their understanding of responsibilities and eligibility in the service system, the participants continued their navigation process, trying to convey their situation in another way or to another professional. By this, the home modification process was not only a matter of applying for a home modification and having it installed, but could be a prolonged process of reshaped actions and negotiations.

9.5.3 *Negotiating Threatened Possibilities for Action into Technical Solutions*

Threatened possibilities of action were translated into technical solutions such as home modifications through a negotiation process between the older persons and those involved in providing home modifications. In this negotiating process the problematic situation first had to be defined in terms that both sides could understand and agree to. Secondly, an agreement about the correct solution was necessary. The character of this negotiation differed among participants. For instance, it could go very smoothly, as in the case of Gustav. Gustav described how an occupational therapist from a rehabilitation clinic made a home visit and asked many questions about what activities he used to perform. Those questions and answers resulted in an agreement on a stair lift and an electric wheelchair as solutions to his problems. In contrast, Anders described how he struggled to convince the professionals about his definitions of problems and solutions.

> And they had the idea that I would not remain in my home because I could not manage the stairs, and I could not manage to get to the toilet, and I could hardly manage to get between the rooms, and then of course, if you have that attitude it is not possible. …They had to give up because I, I was the one who was going to make the decision. …No, there's got to be a limit to this nonsense.

The case of Greta provides another example of how the negotiation process could continue after the modification was installed, and how it could involve various actors. After falling when opening the building door, Greta received an automatic door opener. The automatic door helped Greta to get in and out, but she still felt unsafe because the landing was narrow. She asked the home modification officer if it was possible to receive a grant to widen the landing or install a ramp. The officer told her that such modifications were limited to people who used wheeled walkers. Greta instead decided to solve the problem by informing residents who used walkers about their ability to apply for a HMG to widen the landing, and by asking them to do so.

The outcomes of negotiations influenced the older persons' strategies to create situations where they could perform activities, as they wanted, and also their expectations of future activity performance. For example, the smooth negotiation process between Gustav and the occupational therapist seemed to confirm Gustav's positive expectations of the home modification, even though the installation was repeatedly delayed.

9.5.4 A Continuous Process

Our findings demonstrate how the strategies to regain or create possibilities for action changed through the service process in response to sometimes unpredictable events or actions taken by different people involved. This evolution of struggle was best exemplified by the case of Maria. Maria had applied for a stair lift so that she could leave the house by herself (she could not negotiate the stairs). She also had applied to have a standing shower installed so that she could shower on her own. Maria was determined to escape the rigidity of her daughter's schedule and shower when she wanted to, for hygienic reasons and to be flexible and take advantage of the shower when her energy level was high. Likewise, she emphasized her need to spontaneously move about in the local community, to get a pizza at the neighborhood pizzeria instead of cooking, for instance. Even though Maria's application was approved by the HM administration, her landlord was not supportive of the modifications.

Maria's initial response to this emerging situation was to attempt to change the landlord's stance on the matter. When that proved unsuccessful, Maria developed a creative way to take care of her hygiene without showering. She used bowls placed in the bathroom so that she could take care of personal hygiene by herself. In addition, Maria began intense practice in using the stairs by herself. Because the new strategies took a lot of physical effort, Maria restricted those activities to times when she felt more energetic. In sum, Maria's changed her original strategy to obtain home modifications into a strategy based in novel activity performance. As suggested in the transactional literature (Cutchin et al. 2008; Heatwole Shank and Cutchin 2010), the change of goal in this case is a type of creativity used to recreate the situation and attain possibilities for future action. However, the situation created in Maria's case still included large restrictions in possibilities for action, illustrating an ongoing process of struggle.

When the older person and professionals had similar understandings of the responsibilities and eligibility in the service process, we found that professionals responded to the older persons' strategies in line with the older person's expectations. In contrast, different understandings led to situations where the older persons tried to adjust their actions to the unexpected actions taken by the professionals, often leading to frustration.

9.6 Conclusion

The questions developed on basis of the concept of place integration generated a different framework for developing knowledge about older people and the home modification process. It helped us focus on central driving forces and relationships as part of the active process involving the provision of home modifications. Moreover, it brought the situational whole to the forefront as the condition and consequence of action by older participants and providers. Applying place integration as a conceptual tool helped us see the problems and challenges that older participants were facing. It also directed our attention to the logics behind older participants' actions taken to handle such problems and challenges, whether they succeeded or failed in the process. The study presented in this chapter methodologically focused on situations since the conceptual tools applied were based on place integration. This methodological choice made it possible to capture important driving forces and relationships at play in the arena defined by the home modification process.

The research presented in this chapter shows how needs and expectations, as well as outcomes of home modification interventions, were developed in relationship to older persons' primary concerns. Those primary concerns emerged as being in situations where they had possibilities to perform various activities in accordance with their overriding values and preferences. This knowledge potentially informs the design of interventions such as home modifications, pointing to the importance of addressing older persons' preferences and values, rather than specific tasks. This also pertains to a larger variety of interventions that can target older persons' needs and expectations, such as access to food and services outside of the home. The research presented in this chapter also shows that interventions not matched to older persons' own strategies to handle everyday problems might result in increased disability and restricted activity performance. By extension, redefining the concept of efficiency in service provision, to include the fulfillment of needs and expectations in the context of the ongoing process of place integration is a worthwhile insight.

References

Ahacic, K., Kareholt, I., Thorslund, M., & Parker, M. G. (2007). Relationships between symptoms, physical capacity and activity limitations in 1992 and 2002. *Aging Clinical and Experimental Research, 19*(3), 187–193.

Alsaker, S., Bongaardt, R., & Josephsson, S. (2009). Studying narrative-in-action in women with chronic rheumatic conditions. *Qualitative Health Research, 19*(8), 1154–1161.

Cutchin, M. P. (1999). Qualitative explorations in health geography: Using pragmatism and related concepts as guides. *The Professional Geographer, 51*(12), 265–274.

Cutchin, M. P. (2001). Deweyan integration: Moving beyond place attachment in elderly migration theory. *International Journal of Aging & Human Development, 52*, 29–44.

Cutchin, M. P. (2003). The process of mediated aging-in-place: A theoretically and empirically based model. *Social Science & Medicine, 57*(6), 1077–1090.

Cutchin, M. P. (2004). Using Deweyan philosophy to rename and reframe adaptation-to-environment. *American Journal of Occupational Therapy, 58*(3), 303–312. discussion 313–306.
Cutchin, M. P. (2007). From society to self (and back) through place: Habit in transactional context. *OTJR: Occupation, Participation, and Health, 27*, 50S–59S.
Cutchin, M. P. (2008). John Dewey's metaphysical ground-map and its implications for geographical inquiry. *Geoforum, 39*(4), 1555–1569.
Cutchin, M. P., Owen, S. V., & Chang, P. F. (2003). Becoming"at-home" in assisted living residences: Xploring place integration processes. *Journal of Gerontology: Social Sciences, 58B*, S234–S243.
Cutchin, M. P., Aldrich, R. M., Bailliard, A., & Coppola, S. (2008). Action theories for occupational science: The contributions of Dewey and Bourdieu. *Journal of Occupational Science, 15*, 157–165.
Dewey, J. (1998). Common sense and scientific inquiry (from *Logic: The theory of inquiry*). In L. Hickman & T. Alexander (Eds.), *The essential Dewey* (Vol. 1, pp. 380–390). Bloomington: Indiana University Press (Original work published in 1938).
Dickie, V., Cutchin, M. P., & Humphry, R. (2006). Occupation as transactional experience: A critique of individualism in occupational science. *Journal of Occupational Science, 13*(1), 83–93.
Fischer, F. (2003). *Reframing public policy*. Oxford: Oxford University Press.
Gitlin, L. N. (2003). Conducting research on home environments: Lessons learned and new directions. *Gerontologist, 43*(5), 628–637.
Grape, O., Blom, B., Johansson, R. (Eds.). (2006). *Organisation och omvärld-nyinstitutionell analys av människobehandlande organisationer* [Organisation and society – Neoinstituional analysis of human treatment organisations] (in Swedish). Lund: Studentlitteratur.
Griffiths, L. (2001). Categorising to exclude: The discursive construction of cases in community mental health teams. *Sociology of Health & Illness, 23*(5), 678–700.
Gustavsson, A. (2000). *Tolkning och tolkningsteori 1. Introduktion* [Interpretation and interpretation theory 1. Introduction.] (in Swedish). Stockholm: Pedagogiska Institutionen, Stockholms Universitet.
Heatwole Shank, K., & Cutchin, M. P. (2010). Transactional occupations of older women aging in place: Negotiating change and meaning. *Journal of Occupational Science, 17*, 4–13.
Iwarsson, S. (2005). A long-term perspective on person-environment fit and ADL dependence among older Swedish adults. *Gerontologist, 45*(3), 327–336.
Jagger, C., Arthur, A. J., Spiers, N. A., & Clarke, M. (2001). Patterns of onset of disability in activities of daily living with age. *Journal of the American Geriatric Society, 49*(4), 404–409.
Johansson, K., Lilja, M., Petersson, I., & Borell, L. (2007). Performance of activities of daily living in a sample of applicants for home modification services. *Scandinavian Journal of Occupational Therapy, 14*(1), 44–53.
Johansson, K., Borell, L., & Lilja, M. (2009a). Older persons' navigation through the service system towards home modification resources. *Scandinavian Journal of Occupational Therapy, 16*, 227–237.
Johansson, K., Lilja, M., & Josephsson, S. (2009b). Creating possibilities for action in the presence of environmental barriers, in the process of ageing in place. *Ageing and Society, 29*(1), 49–70.
Law, M., Cooper, B., Strong, S., Stewart, D., Rigby, P., & Letts, L. (1996). The person-environment-occupation model: A transactive approach to occupational performance. *Canadian Journal of Occupational Therapy, 63*(1), 9–23.
Ministry of Health and Social Affairs. (1992). *Lag om Bostadsanpassning* [The home modification legislation] (in Swedish). Stockholm.
Vik, K. (2008). *Older adults' participation in occupation in the context of home-based rehabilitation*. Thesis, Karolinska Institutet, Stockholm.
Wahl, H. W., Fange, A., Oswald, F., Gitlin, L. N., & Iwarsson, S. (2009). The home environment and disability-related outcomes in aging individuals: What is the empirical evidence? *Gerontologist, 49*(3), 355–367.
Wiles, J. (2005). Conceptualizing place in the care of older people: The contributions of geographical gerontology. *Journal of Clinical Nursing, 14*(8B), 100–108.

Chapter 10
A Transactional View of Shedding at the Berry Men's Shed

Alison Wicks

10.1 Introduction

Shedding encapsulates the totality of occupation that occurs within a men's shed program. The unique men's shed program in Australia is community-based and occupation-focused, providing male-friendly spaces for men to engage in personally meaningful occupations, enjoy each other's company and make a contribution to their local community. The recent proliferation throughout Australia of the men's sheds program is remarkable. Moreover, the transformations of materials, people and communities that are outcomes of the transactional nature of shedding are significant in terms of the production of goods, development of personal capacities and increased participation, as well as enhanced social capital within the community that supports and is supported by the program. This chapter explores the transactional aspects of shedding by using the Berry Men's Shed as an exemplar, and by sharing my observations and insights of shedding from the perspective of an occupational scientist, an occupational therapist, and an active men's shed member.

Before contextualizing the discussion on the transactional nature of shedding at the Berry Men's Shed with an overview of the history and benefits of the men's shed movement in Australia, it is important to clarify what a shed is, because the word shed, though used widely in the Australian vernacular, may have different meanings in other countries. Essentially, in this chapter, a shed refers to anything used for storage, shelter, or as a workshop. A shed can vary in size and layout, from a small, rough lean-to with open front or sides to a very large, strongly built and sophisticated building. But, according to at least one shedder, "What makes a shed a shed, is the value placed on it by its owner" (Thomson 2002, p. 5). Although sheds are not unique to Australia, the Australian shed is usually separate from domestic buildings,

A. Wicks (✉)
Discipline of Occupational Therapy and Public Health, University of Canberra, Bruce, ACT, Australia
e-mail: alison.wicks@canberra.edu.au

M.P. Cutchin and V.A. Dickie (eds.), *Transactional Perspectives on Occupation*,
DOI 10.1007/978-94-007-4429-5_10, © Springer Science+Business Media B.V. 2013

perhaps due to the fact there is space for a shed on the average Australian house block (Thomson 2002).

Although there is currently no definitive history of the Australian men's shed movement, Golding (2006) believes it originates from the early craft and trade-based organizations such as farm machinery preservation societies and wood turning guilds. These early organizations, however, were not promoted as being for men only and focused on a specific craft or trade related activity. It was in the 1970s, at Broken Hill in outback western New South Wales (NSW), that community sheds first became accessible to male members of the community. Various types of sheds were established throughout Australia during the 1990s, their spread attributed to grass root popularization by Thomson (1995). By the end of 2011, there were approximately 730 member sheds of the Australian Men's Shed Association, representing almost 100,000 men (David Helmers personal communication 2012). Research on the benefits of men's sheds for individuals and communities is gradually increasing. Earle et al. (1995) found that in Australia community-based sheds play an important role for retired men, providing them with a place to go to participate in accepted activities that reinforce identity, facilitate creativity and foster social interaction. A later study (Golding et al. 2007) examined the effectiveness and importance of community-based men's sheds in Australia, and explored how the nature of such sheds affect informal learning experiences and the lives of men who use them. That study found sheds provide

> a connection to other men in a safe, mutually supportive and inclusive environment where learning and health are fostered informally, without subverting the main reason for men coming to the shed. Men's sheds essentially have to do with men's happiness, connection to community, and social and emotional wellbeing (Golding et al. 2007, p. 40).

A case study of a men's shed in rural Victoria, Australia, undertaken to reveal what the shed meant to the shedders, identified five interrelated themes from analysis of semi structured interviews with shed members: having a sense of purpose and feeling useful; having a place to go and do things; experiencing a sense of pride and accomplishment related to doing work; having a sense of belonging and connection to the shed; and, enjoying the companionship and camaraderie of the shed (Ballinger et al. 2009).

While there has been research into the benefits of the men's shed movement, there also has been discussion on why and how the men's shed phenomenon is becoming so popular. For example, it has been suggested by Golding (2008) that community-based sheds provide a critically important "third place" (Oldenburg 2001, p. 2) offering a neutral public space where men can participate in regular activities for social well-being and psychological health. More specifically, a third place is a setting beyond home (the first place) and work (the second place) where people share good company in a relaxed setting on a regular basis (Oldenburg 2001). Hayes and Williamson (2005) maintained men's sheds have developed in response to a growing awareness that many men are left without a space or place to safely meet. Golding (2008) identified that partnered older men who were retired from paid employment were attracted to the sheds as a means of getting out of the house and having an opportunity to socialize with other older men. Hence there seems to be a push from home, and a pull to the shed. It has also been found that shed participation is most enjoyable and positive when it is discretionary, supervised but non-hierarchical and underpinned by trusting relationships, social ritual and activities (Golding 2008).

As a shed observer and a shed member, I agree with Golding's (2008) findings about the factors that underpin an enjoyable shed experience. I also believe there are two more key factors that have influenced the acceptance of men's sheds in a diverse set of communities and attributed to the rapid spread of sheds around the country. The first is that they began, and many continue to be developed, as grass roots organizations. Their establishment is natural and spontaneous, driven by the politics of the local community, as opposed to being orchestrated by traditional power structures, and they are developed using locally available human and material resources. The second factor is that they are developed to meet the particular needs of the men in a community. These two factors consequently account for the wide diversity among sheds, not only in terms of the shed's physical structure but also in terms of the shed's mission and the program of activities that is developed to achieve the mission. Hayes and Williamson (2006) acknowledged such diversity in their typology which describes five types of men's shed based on ethos: occupational, clinical, recreational, educational, and social, and they maintained there are a number of models for each type.

10.2 Berry Men's Shed

The Berry Men's Shed is in Berry, a small rural community in the City of Shoalhaven on the south coast of NSW, Australia. In the past Shoalhaven was primarily a dairy farming area, but today, tourism is the main source of revenue (Shoalhaven City Council nd). Close to the sea and nestled below the escarpment of the Cambewarra Range, Berry is a popular destination for day visitors from urban areas. It also is an increasingly popular destination of retirees making "the big shift" and relocating to coastal communities or rural environments in search of a relaxed lifestyle (Salt 2001).

According to the Berry Men's Shed inaugural coordinator, Tom Darby (2007), there was never a grand plan for the Shed, an issue which has since created some problems but also contributed to its success in some ways. Tom has recounted how the Shed came to fruition almost by accident. In November 2004, a parishioner of the Uniting Church in Berry was moving into a retirement village, and having to dispose of the entire contents of his personal shed. He enquired if the church could benefit from the sale of his shed belongings. It was duly collected and stored in a container. A chance reply to the question "what next?" was "we could start a men's shed in the old church hall." This answer prompted a public meeting held in April 2005. Although only a few people attended, the local members for the Federal and State government did and both offered support. Word spread quickly that "a husband day care" was being set up. Within a month the church was inundated with donations of tools, timber and equipment, some necessary minor modifications to the 110 year old church hall had been undertaken, 25 members had joined, and six community projects had been commissioned (Berry Men's Shed nd).

Since opening its doors, the Berry Men's Shed has adopted a non-discrimination policy. Anyone can join the Shed, regardless of gender, age or physical and mental health status, and the Shed has taken great care not to, or be seen to, compete with local tradesmen or businesses. Initially, there was no joining fee or membership subscription, just a request for a weekly donation of $2.00 to cover morning and afternoon teas (Darby 2007).

And so the Berry Men's Shed evolved. Within 2 years of operation, 100 projects had been completed. By May 2012, 300 community projects had been completed and membership had reached 65 (Richard Wiseman personal communication 2012) (Tom Darby personal communication 2010). In November 2011, a new, customized designed shed was officially opened. Community grants, the sale of their products, and the recent introduction of a $10.00 annual membership fee have helped to keep the Shed financially afloat. The Berry Uniting Church has provided the old hall rent free and the seed funding from the church to update the electrical fittings has since been repaid. The Shed has devised a way to cost its community projects: the client pays for materials before work commences, the Shed charges a flat fee $50.00 per day, regardless of the number of members working on the project, and 5% of the total materials to cover operation costs such as expendable materials and machinery maintenance (Darby 2007). In 2010, the Berry Men's Shed revised its organizational structure by creating some new positions as a means of sharing the workload. The seven positions are: Chairperson, Finance Officer, Fundraising Officer, Shed Manager, Supervisor, Deputy Supervisor, and Information Officer (Wiseman 2010).

10.2.1 Activities at the Shed

The Shed is open for 7 h a day, 2 days a week. Woodworking is the primary occupation undertaken. Although it was originally thought that members would want to work on personal projects, most choose to work on either community projects or fittings for the shed such as additional shelving or cupboards for tools. The community projects are commissions from individuals, local schools, and organizations. Projects range from very small items such as mahjong racks and bread boards to larger items such as picnic tables. Occasionally a request to make something unusual is received. For example, the Shed members were very surprised to receive an order for a full sized Tardis, a replica of a telephone box that serves as a time machine for Dr. Who, the main character in a popular British television series. The Tardis aroused much interest within the community when it was completed and then transported down the main street of Berry. Although woodworking consumes most of the shed time of regular members, non-woodworking activities are organized by members on a regular and irregular basis for the general public. Interestingly, these activities which are wide ranging in their aims and target various age groups are undertaken by the Shed members, known as Shedders, as their contribution to local community development.

The *Gateway Garden* has been established by the Berry Men's Shed and is open for all members of the community. The garden consists of a one acre area donated by a local family specifically for a community garden. The garden has been designed to encourage the use of permaculture, organic, and traditional gardening principles. There are raised garden beds to accommodate people with mobility problems. The garden is open all the time. There is no membership fee, but users are asked to donate either a one or two dollar coin for each day they attend.

The *Men's Heath Half Hour* is held bi-monthly at the Shed and is all open to all. Invited speakers address a range of issues, from prostate cancer to depression and eye health. Lunch is provided after the talk, encouraging socialization and dialogue. The *Kids in the Shed* program runs in the school holidays and teaches woodworking skills to primary aged children. It has become a very valuable experience for local children, especially those from single mother families as they are given the opportunity to work with men, who consider themselves honorary grandfathers, in a workshop setting. Similarly, *The Kids in the Kitchen* program in which children are supervised by Shed members in the preparation of a luncheon which is then served to their parents or care givers, has been a popular activity offered by the Shed.

An annual excursion to the State Woodworking Exhibition in Sydney is organized for Shed members, enabling them to see some examples of fine craftsmanship, purchase new equipment and enjoy a day out together. Occasionally, members of the Berry Men's Shed visit other Sheds, to share ideas and talk about shedding. Sometimes, members of other Sheds visit Berry and there is always a regular stream of visitors and prospective members wanting to know more about the shed program. One particular activity which benefits both the Shed and the Berry community is the biannual street stall where members display and sell products made in the Shed. This activity has proven to be an effective means of promoting the Shed to the general public, gaining new members, and acquiring commissions as well as receiving revenue.

10.3 A Transactional View of Shedding

From my understanding of the transactional perspective as described in the occupational science literature (Cutchin 2004; Aldrich 2008; Cutchin et al. 2006, 2008; Dickie et al. 2006), this view has relevance to those interested in occupation, since it encourages consideration beyond the personal experience of the doing and the contextual influences that shape the doing, and focuses on "the transaction—the active relation—that integrates person and situation" (Dickie et al. 2006, p. 91). Such a holistic view enables us to see how occupation transforms the situation and the person "in ongoing and emergent ways" (p. 91). Based on the literature, shedding, as exemplified by the Berry Men's Shed program, is an occupation involving shedders, their shed, the materials they use, and the local community. Given all these elements, shedding can viewed as a transactional experience.

10.3.1 Elements of the Shedding Experience

In exploring shedding at the Berry Men's Shed as a transactional experience, I begin by identifying various elements of the experience, which are either person or situation based, and then consider their contribution to transformations of people and contexts.

10.3.1.1 Space

The hub of shedding at the Berry Men's Shed is clearly the shed itself. The shed is divided into two main spaces: the workshop and the meeting room. The two spaces contrast with each other in form and function. The workshop is where all the woodworking activity occurs. It is filled with equipment, tools, work benches, timber, and shedders who sometimes have to jostle to find space to work. The meeting room is relatively quieter, a no-work space. It is the dust free place where the shedders gather three times a day; half an hour for morning tea, 1 hour for lunch and half an hour for afternoon tea. Here the men discuss a wide range of topics, from politics to recipes, as they sit around the table. Information about the Shed and future projects is also shared at these times.

Sometimes, the shed space is temporarily extended. In order to avoid congestion in the workshop space or to dissipate noise and unpleasant smells, or simply to enjoy the sunshine and fresh air, shedders set up their equipment outside in the church grounds. Painting is usually done on trestles erected on the grass. Occasionally, when a project needs to be installed, shedding extends to a customer's home or to a building in the community.

When adopting a transactional perspective, it becomes apparent that spaces within the shed are flexible. They are modified to accommodate the diverse activities that take place within the shed on any given day. As a consequence, the shed spaces are continually transforming to provide for maximal experience in terms of comfort, meaning or effectiveness.

10.3.1.2 Sensations

On entering the shed, various senses are simultaneously stimulated, immediately engaging you in the shedding experience, whether you are a shedder or not. Most of the sensory stimulants are created by a transaction between person and object, so are only present when the shedders are active, indicating industriousness and productivity. Collectively, these sensations could be considered characteristic of shedding and are essential to the experience of being a shedder. The noise, smells and textures experienced within the shed contribute to the uniqueness of shedding.

First, there is a cacophony of sounds: the screech of the thicknesser[1] when a shedder pushes through a length of timber to be thinned and smoothed; the shrill of the drills as someone bores a hole in a piece of timber or metal. In fact, due to the volume of sounds created, shedders are required by Shed policy to wear their ear muffs. Sounds emanating from the shed are constant on work days, though they vary at different times. At meal breaks, when the woodworking sounds stop, new sounds of constant laughter and loud voices resonate from the meeting room as the members tell their stories and swap jokes.

Second, there are distinctive smells that pervade the shed: the sweet smell of freshly sawn timber; the acrid smells of newly applied paint, varnish or kerosene. Members of the Shed frequently comment how the smells and sounds of the shed transport them back to other places in other times, such as their previous workplaces, or stimulate memories of their involvement in other projects.

A third and seemingly critical sense is touch. You can regularly observe shedders running their hands over the surface of the wood to determine the direction of the grain or check the effectiveness of their sanding, or touching the blade of the plane with their fingertips to decide if it requires re-sharpening. The tactile sense is well developed in experienced shedders. Years of practice are required to hone this particular sense in shedding. Interestingly, visitors to the Shed frequently pick up items to feel them and look more closely.

10.3.1.3 Time

The Berry Men's Shed is open on Tuesday and Thursday every week, except for the holiday period over Christmas and New Year. The advertised opening hours are from 9:00 a.m. to 4:00 p.m. Some shedders come and go throughout the day, according to their shed needs or their other commitments, while the executive members or duty officers are usually onsite from 8:00 a.m. to 5:00 p.m. Some members attend the Shed every day it is open, some adopt a once weekly attendance pattern. There are some members who only attend occasionally.

Deadlines are generally avoided at the Shed. Given that a Shed credo is "It will be ready when it is finished," customers are rarely given a completion date for a project. Time frames are largely irrelevant at the Shed as the emphasis is on the process rather than the finished product. Also, it takes time to repair mistakes or modify designs. Mistakes and modifications are frequent at the Shed because different shedders can be involved in a project on different days, depending on the allocation of tasks by the Shed Supervisor. The Supervisor allocates according to the requirements of the task, skills of the shedder, and/or the desire for a shedder to

[1] A thicknesser is also known as a thickness planer used to create boards that are of an even thickness throughout their length and flat on both surfaces.

develop a new skill. Although sometimes frustrating, mistakes and modifications are generally accepted as an important part of the learning process that is embedded in shedding.

It appears that the time element at the Shed contributes to the members' enjoyment of their involvement in Shed activities in several ways. First, as the Shed is only open two days a week, members can participate in their hobbies or other community programs as well. Second, many members have retired from full-time employment and appreciate having part-time commitments and the opportunity to have no commitments. And third, it is less stressful for all when there is no requirement to meet strict deadlines, possibly a common occurrence for many members when they were employees. The time element at the Shed fits well with the retirement tradition.

10.3.1.4 Relationships

Shedding at the Berry Men's Shed involves a range of different relationships. First, there are the relationships between the shedders. Most shedders relate to other shedders only during their time spent at the Shed, however, some share similar interests and hobbies and so relate with each other outside of time spent at the Shed, for example at church or at Rotary Club meetings. There have been strong friendships forged between shedders, while differences of opinions have caused other relationships to fracture. Some shedders choose to remain solo players. Others maintain that the support and friendship of fellow shedders have enabled them to cope with personal stressors such as bereavement, illness or loss of identity resulting from retirement. An interview with some of the shed members revealed some interesting insights (Malpage et al. 2008). Gordon stated that one of the benefits of the shed program is that it "gives us purpose" (p. 195). For Robert, the shed has been very important as he made the transition from full time work as a dairy farmer to retirement. "When you retire, you wonder what you are going to do. The opportunity of coming here and meeting people I otherwise wouldn't, fills my day" (p. 194–5). Membership of the Shed has helped some newcomers to Berry more readily adjust to their new home environment. Several of the shedders now advocate that the support of Shed members, like a family, and their participation in the Shed program, have helped them avoid depression.

There also are relationships between shedders and certain tools, person to object relationships. Some shedders enjoy using a particular tool because they have acquired a high degree of competency with that tool. For example, one shedder will be requested to do most of the wood turning as he is the most skillful on the lathe. Others avoid using certain tools, perhaps because of previous bad experiences. Some are instructed by the supervisor not to use a particular tool as they have inadequate skill to use it safely. Several of the men prefer to use their personal tools for certain jobs, knowing that they keep their own tools well maintained and in correct working order. Rather than getting frustrated if someone has not sharpened a tool before putting it away, as is the expectation, or stopping to sharpen the tool himself, a member can continue uninterrupted by using his personal tool. Such strategies employed by the shed supervisor and individual members help to maintain harmonious dynamics for the group as a whole, and keep members happy and willing to participate in the program as individuals who are also fully part of-the-Shed.

Organization to organization relationships have developed since the Shed has been operating in Berry. For example, Berry Men's Shed has an account with the local hardware store which supplies stock as required. This relationship keeps the financial transactions local and supports a local business. As expected, there is a close relationship between the Shed and the Berry Uniting Church which is the Shed's primary benefactor. Several large projects for the church have been completed by Shed members, either at the request of the church or as a gift from the Shed. In addition, there are organization-to-people relationships between the Berry Men's Shed and people in the community, such as those who regularly attend the Health Half Hour or who tend a plot in the Gateway Garden. These people are interested in and support the Shed, though they choose not to become shedders. In effect, the Shed has been essential in building and tightening intra-community relationships that benefit many.

This exploration from a transactional perspective of different elements in shedding highlights the complexity of this particular occupation, reinforcing the stance that such an occupation is an "important mode through which human beings, as organisms-in-environment-as-a-whole, function in their complex totality" (Dickie et al. 2006, p. 91). In addition, when a transactional perspective is adopted and core person and situation based elements of shedding at the Berry Men's Shed are identified, such as space and place, time, sensations, and relationships, we can begin to understand how transformations occur. Not only do the core elements interact, but they also integrate synergistically. The outcome of the synergistic transaction of the elements is transformation of objects, people, and contexts.

10.3.2 Transformations as a Result of Shedding

Perhaps the most obvious transformations that occur in shedding are material ones. At the hands of a skilled shedder, a piece of roughly hewn timber becomes transformed into a smooth, highly polished piece of fine art or a functional item that can be used in everyday living. Objects such as old fence posts donated by someone in the local community are recycled and transformed into new items such as luggage racks which can be sold at the stall to generate income for the Shed. Waste becomes revenue. Such transformation of material results from processes involving time, place, materials, tools, action, people, and relationships among them.

People are also transformed at the Shed over time. As a consequence of shedding some individuals have acquired a new or renewed sense of self-worth. Developing new skills, forming new relationships, being accepted, and gaining an identity as a shedder can be some of the significant outcomes of Shed membership for someone who has not experienced a personally satisfying transition from the paid workforce to retirement. An engaging occupation (Jonsson 2000) such as shedding, which can involve intense participation, be infused with meaning, and involve a community of people who share the same commitment to the Shed, may be a critical factor for a person seeking a satisfying life in retirement. Shedding can also enable someone recently retired to transform from an active employee to mentor and educator as there are opportunities to share work skills with others in the Shed. For some older and retired shedders, their need for generativity (Erikson 1981) may be met through shedding.

Spaces and places have also been transformed through shedding. Although the outside appearance and actual size of the church hall, which has now become known as "the Shed," have not changed over the past 4 years, the layout and use of this space have changed significantly. Some of the equipment in the workshop area has been moved around to facilitate work on a particular project, accommodate new equipment or to create a more efficient, tidier and safer place in which to work. The meeting room, however, has not changed in layout although photos of projects once they are completed are added to the display already on the wall, and the commissions accepted by the Shed are updated on the white board. A donated air conditioner has been installed for the comfort of the shedders. Hence, as an outcome of shedding, the church hall has metamorphosed and on any Shed day it serves multiple functions, demonstrating how transformations occur through the remaking of intra-situational relationships.

The new shed, much of which was built by the shedders, has been designed to meet the specific needs of shedding and will accommodate new machines and tools and provide opportunity for additional activities, such as metal work, to be undertaken. There are plans to move the church hall to a new site on the church grounds and it will become available for use by other members of the community.

10.4 Conclusion

Whether wearing a hat as an academic exploring the complex and ubiquitous nature of occupation, a practitioner enabling health and wellbeing through occupation, or as a Berry Men's Shed member who chooses to occupy my non-work time in an enjoyable and productive way, it is easy for me to appreciate the value of shedding not only for the members but also for the local community. As an occupational perspective already pervades my world view, I can see that when the shedders are making things with their hands, they are using their time productively, enjoying each other's company, learning new skills, sharing knowledge, feeling needed, having fun, and making a contribution. Moreover, people in the community and community organizations are obviously benefitting from the products of the Berry Men's Shed. For example, some of the commissioned work includes computer desks for the primary school, a letter box for the pre-school, display cabinets for the museum, and bench seats for the park. The Berry economy also is influenced by Shed activity.

Adopting a transactional view of the occupation of shedding and thereby exploring the relations between the transactional elements and the resultant transformations have provided new insights to the complexity of the whole shedding experience. Shedding is more than just doing. It is doing *in the Shed.* It is doing *with other shedders.* It is *doing for others* (Wicks 2010). Shedding demonstrates the transactional principles of "interpenetrating natures of the real world" (Aldrich 2008, p. 151) and the "co- constitutive relationships" (p. 155) generated by doing. The transactional view has revealed that the occupation of shedding is a process not merely located at the level of the individual shedder, but rather at the Shed level and at the community level, of which the shedder is an integral part (Dickie et al. 2006, p. 91). Such an understanding is not gained when a view of occupation is too individualistic or when interrelations between person and context rather than transactions between them are studied.

Indeed, my understandings of shedding from a transactional perspective have motivated me to consider other community-based occupations in a similar way. Consequently, I am now strengthened in my resolve to continue to advocate at local, national and international levels for people and communities to have opportunities and choices for participating in community-based programs that meet their needs. In particular, I am determined to lobby for continued support of grass-roots organizations which establish occupation-focused programs for any age group, by calling for material, personnel and financial resources and encouraging appropriate policy development to enable their continued existence.

Conducting this assessment of shedding at the Berry Men's Shed from a transactional perspective has been a worthwhile exercise, in several respects. Personally, my time spent being a shedder has become even more meaningful and enjoyable, as I now recognize how my relation with the Shed has many positive repercussions for the other shedders and the local community and how I am contributing to the social capital of my own community. With regard to my future practice, I will be even more determined to *work with* people and their communities rather than for them and my support will go first and foremost to grass roots organizations rather than to programs that have been established by practitioners in isolation from their individual and community clients. My research on and advocacy for policies at all levels of government for participation for all people and communities, will continue in a more determined manner.

Finally, a transactional perspective of shedding has revealed how the human and material transformations that have occurred in and around the Berry Men's Shed have contributed to the growth of a local community as well as the growth of individuals within that community. As someone who considers herself a pracademic,[2] endeavoring to translate research to practice and policy to increase individual and community participation, the pragmatism underpinning the transactional

---

[2] A pracademic is someone who is both an academic and an active practitioner in their subject area.

perspective is personally meaningful. For those interested in exploring occupation, how context and occupation mutually influence each other and are concerned with issues "that speak to making a better world, such as social justice, inclusion and participation" (Cutchin and Dickie 2012, p. 24), the pragmatic attitude of transactionalism is very relevant.

References

Aldrich, R. (2008). From complexity theory to transactionalism: Moving occupational science forward in theorizing the complexities of behaviors. *Journal of Occupational Science, 15*, 147–156.

Ballinger, M., Talbot, L., & Verrinder, G. (2009). More than a place to do woodwork: A case study of a community-based men's shed. *Journal of Men's Health, 6*(1), 20–27.

Berry Men's Shed. (nd). http://www.berrymensshed.com.au/. Accessed 31 Dec 2010.

Cutchin, M. (2004). Using Deweyan philosophy to rename and reframe adaptation –to-environment. *American Journal of Occupational Therapy, 58*, 303–312.

Cutchin, M., & Dickie, V. (2012). Transactionalism: Occupational science and the pragmatic attitude. In C. Hocking & G. Whiteford (Eds.), *Critical perspectives on occupational science: Society, inclusion, participation* (pp. 23–37). London: Wiley.

Cutchin, M., Dickie, V., & Humphry, R. (2006). Transaction versus interpretation, or transaction and interpretation? A response to Michael Barber. *Journal of Occupational Science, 13*, 97–99.

Cutchin, M., Aldrich, R., Bailliard, A., & Coppola, S. (2008). Action theories for occupational science: The contributions of Dewy and Bourdieu. *Journal of Occupational Science, 15*, 157–165.

Darby, T. (2007, September 7). *Berry Men's Shed.* Paper presented at 2nd Men's Shed conference, Manly, Australia.

Dickie, V., Cutchin, M., & Humphry, R. (2006). Occupation as transactional experience: A critique of individualism in occupational science. *Journal of Occupational Science, 13*, 83–93.

Earle, L., Earle, T., & Von Mering, O. (1995). Sheds and male retirement: The place to go. *Australasian Leisure for Pleasure Journal, 1*(1), 5–19.

Erikson, E. (1981). On generativity and identity. *Harvard Educational Review, 51*, 249–269.

Golding, B. (2006, April 19–21). *A profile of men's sheds in Australia: patterns, purposes, profiles and experiences of participants: Some implications for ACE and VET about engaging older men.* Paper presented at Australian Vocational Educational and Training Research Association conference, University of Wollongong, Wollongong.

Golding, B. (2008, July 14–17). *Common wealth through community men's sheds: Lives and learning networks beyond work.* Paper presented at Pan Commonwealth Forum on Open Learning, University of London, England.

Golding, B., Brown, M., Foley, A., Harvey, J., & Gleeson, L. (2007). Men's sheds in Australia: learning through community contexts, NCVER, Adelaide, South Australia, 2007. www.ncver.edu.au/publications/1780.html. Accessed 31 Dec 2010.

Hayes, R., & Williamson, M. (2005, November 10–11). *Preliminary evidence-based, best-practice guidelines for Victorian Men's Sheds.* Paper presented to Men's Shed conference, Lakes Entrance, VIC.

Hayes, R., & Williamson, M. (2006). *Evidence-based, best-practice guidelines for Victorian Men's Sheds.* Prepared for the Office of Senior Victorians, the School of Public Health, La Trobe University, Bundoora, VIC.

Jonsson, H. (2000). *Anticipating, experiencing and valuing the transition from worker to retiree: A longitudinal study of retirement as an occupational transition.* Stockholm: Karolinska Institute.

Malpage, J., Wicks, A., & Martin, K. (2008). Photo essay: Meaningful occupation at the Berry Men's Shed. *Journal of Occupational Science, 15*, 194–195.
Oldenburg, R. (2001). *Celebrating the third place*. New York: Marlowe & Company.
Salt, B. (2001). *The big shift: Welcome to the third Australian culture*. South Yarra: Hardie Grant.
Shoalhaven City Council. (nd). http://www.shoalhaven.nsw.gov.au/region/econodev/geninfo.htm. Accessed 31 Dec 2010.
Thomson, M. (1995). *Blokes and sheds*. Sydney: Angus & Robertson.
Thomson, M. (2002). *The complete blokes and sheds*. Pymble: HarperCollins.
Wicks, A. (2010, May 4–7). *Doing things for others with others: How the Berry Men's Shed promotes social participation of older men and social capital in a rural community.* Paper presented at the World Federation of Occupational Therapists Congress, Santiago, Chile.
Wiseman, R. (2010). *Berry Men's Shed Newsletter: February*. Berry: Berry Men's Shed.

Chapter 11
A Transactional Perspective on a Consulting Practice

Lauren Holahan, Laurie Ray, and Virginia A. Dickie

11.1 Introduction

We arrive in a rural town to conduct a regional day-long IEP goal-writing workshop for related service providers, EC administrators, and special educators. Although we have conducted this workshop several times previously, we are somewhat anxious, given a special education professor from UNC Chapel Hill is bringing visiting scholars from Portugal to experience, firsthand, what US educators and therapists are grappling with in serving students with disabilities. We know the meeting address and both Google maps and GPS lead to a run-down shopping center, anchored by a large local country buffet restaurant. There are no cars in the parking lot and the restaurant is closed, but we pull in to wait and consider our options. About 20 minutes before the workshop is to begin, the hosting LEA Exceptional Children Director arrives and ushers us into the dimly lit restaurant, which is decorated in deep red velvet brocade wall paper and dark paneling. We are shown to a banquet hall where the set-up from a gospel-sing the night before remains; the song list and dates for upcoming performances are posted at the front of the room. The smell of fried chicken hangs in the air. The sound system buzzes. As participants begin to arrive (looking confused as they squint across the tenebrous room), we go about arranging chairs and tables, setting up an ancient portable projector screen, and inquiring about the handouts the EC Director was to bring. He says he did not make the copies, because "there were just so many of them and I could not imagine you needed them all and I didn't know which ones were important." The UNC professor and his Portuguese guests arrive.

In the midst of these circumstances, we forge ahead with the training. We convince the Exceptional Children Director to contact his office to get the handouts produced and delivered by lunch time. We raise our voices and turn off the static-prone PA system. We shift the order of content to accommodate the handout issue.

L. Holahan (✉) • V.A. Dickie
Department of Allied Health Sciences, Division of Occupational Science and Occupational Therapy, University of North Carolina at Chapel Hill, Chapel Hill, NC, USA
e-mail: lauren_holahan@med.unc.edu

L. Ray
Department of Allied Health Sciences, Division of Physical Therapy, University of North Carolina at Chapel Hill, Chapel Hill, NC, USA

M.P. Cutchin and V.A. Dickie (eds.), *Transactional Perspectives on Occupation*,
DOI 10.1007/978-94-007-4429-5_11, © Springer Science+Business Media B.V. 2013

> We create lightness in interactions with the audience and each other, moving about the room as we speak, so those at the back can see and hear. We call on participants' memories and imagination to reflect on their practice rather than focus on the strange environs. We have them work in small groups and experience the immediacy of each other, rather than foggy images on the screen. Most of this problem-solving happens without a huddle. Confident in one another's perceptions and skills, we engage embodied habits of interaction (Holahan and Ray, 2011).

This not atypical event in the work of North Carolina Department of Public Instruction (NCDPI) occupational therapy (OT) and physical therapy (PT) consultants Lauren Holahan and Laurie Ray can be described with a transactional perspective as the functional coordination of problematic situations (Cutchin and Dickie 2012; Dickie et al. 2006). The account is rife with suggestions of a much bigger picture—acronyms such as EC and IEP that imply well-established sociopolitical structures, technology (GPS, PowerPoint and Google maps), economics (the run down shopping center and inadequate meeting room), a relationship with a university as well as a global flavor, personalities such as that of the EC Director, and the skills and mutual understandings of the consultants as they go about the occupation of conducting the training. With embodied habits of working together, they engage in a ballet combining their typical and practiced ways of doing (they have conducted the workshop several times) with creative improvisations to incorporate the immediate demands of a decidedly problematic environment (Cutchin et al. 2008). Invisible but part of this account of the activities of two individuals on a single day, is a rich history of advocacy, legislation, economics, professional education, policy, and negotiation. The day itself, the workshop in a rural part of the state, is one of many varied occupations carried out by Holahan and Ray in the context of their practice as consultants. The concept of *functional coordination* (Garrison 2001; Cutchin and Dickie 2012) describes much of their work, which is embedded in a history of advocacy and policy and the groundwork of the visionary practitioners who developed these positions.

The transactional perspective provides a means of describing and understanding occupation from narrow to wide angle, and near to far depth of field. As Rosenberg and Johansson point out (see Chap. 12), because the transactional situation is a somewhat vague construct, it can be challenging to determine where to focus attention. Often occupation is studied from a close-up perspective, at the level of the here and now activity, while other aspects of the occupational situation are unacknowledged or out of focus. In contrast, in this chapter we examine the occupation (in this case synonymous with job) of the two consultants with a wide-angle perspective, explicating the transactional nature of their work. In doing so, we hope to demonstrate the manner in which a transactional perspective on practice provides a rich and holistic understanding of its totality.

The work of Holahan and Ray exemplifies what Sullivan called the "activity of engagement in the world" (2002, p. 209). As consultants to NCDPI they must use a wide range of knowledge and skills in order to understand and influence policy as well as understand and affect what goes on in the day to day classroom experiences of students with disabilities, their teachers, and the therapists who work with them. Their roles are positioned within both a university and a state educational agency, with expectations to promote best practice, support practitioners and administrators in schools, respond to budget and policy imperatives, and engage as members of their various work and professional communities. Similarly, their work acts as "relational glue" (Cutchin et al. 2008) helping all parties merge the occupational subcultures (Trice 1993) of therapy and education. Without direct authority over those whose work is their focus, they use information, education, advocacy, problem solving, and moral persuasion to improve and maintain quality education for children with disabilities in the state-wide educational system.

We begin this case study with the history of the consultants' positions, followed by a brief overview of some of the many federal and state laws that regulate delivery of educational services for children with disabilities and professional practice. It should begin to be apparent that in many respects the consultants, the statutes, and the educational system of North Carolina co-constitute the situation of school-based therapy services.

11.2 History and Evolution of the Consultant Positions

North Carolina has a strong tradition of providing guidance, consultation, and technical assistance to school-based related service providers and administrators. The state enacted one of the first comprehensive special education laws in the nation in 1974 (North Carolina State Board of Education 2009). At the same time, a burgeoning early childhood evaluation initiative was fueled by state dollars and pediatric experts in the state university system. With the advent of federal Public Law (PL) 94–142 in 1975, North Carolina legislators and North Carolina Department of Public Instruction (NCDPI) leaders recognized the need for specific expertise in the provision of related services, such as occupational and physical therapy, as did scholars in those disciplines at the University of North Carolina, Chapel Hill (UNC-CH), who approached NCDPI with a plan to collaborate on program development and recruitment (Lindsey, personal communication, 2011).

A 6-month pilot project with physical therapy and occupational therapy consultants to NCDPI was established in 1977 to educate local education administrators, recruit occupational and physical therapists to work in schools, and develop programs consistent with both the law and then-current research/theory in each discipline. NCDPI contracted with UNC-CH to provide the consultants, and the contracts were renewed for another year. According to Jane Rourk, the OT Consultant from 1978 to 2007, "there was a sense back then that the positions would be temporary, that once therapists were hired by the LEAs [Local Education Agencies], the need for the state consultants would decline" (personal communication, 2011).

That sense of a temporary effort was, over time, replaced by a long-term commitment to the quality of school-based practice. Diane Lindsey, who served as the PT Consultant to DPI from 1977 to 2005, reported that after the early organizational years, the work turned to creating a community of practitioners with a shared vision for best practice in schools guided by current research and statute (personal communication, 2011). New knowledge, new and changing laws, and the day-to-day successes and challenges of therapists working in schools quickly found common ground with the consultants serving as arbitrators and coordinators at policy, administration, and practice levels. Today the consultants continue to hold faculty appointments in the Department of Allied Health Sciences at UNC Chapel Hill where they have office space and technological supports. Their roles are to provide direct assistance to the Exceptional Children (EC) Division of the Department of Public Instruction (DPI) in the areas of occupational therapy and physical therapy as a part of the total effort on behalf of students with disabilities. This entails a wide variety of responsibilities including direct consultation to therapists, teachers, and administrators; development and maintenance of a website; interpretation of state and national regulations, policy influence, recommendations on personnel issues; training; and more.

The larger situation of school systems, required by law to provide education to children with disabilities, generated the need for assistance and the temporary solution to provide consultation. As implementation of the statutes took place and changed over the years, shifting problematic situations arose and were addressed by the consultants. More than 30 years later, this continues to be the case. This case study of the OT and PT consultants' positions illustrates the concept of functional coordination in the world of special education. As such, it provides an example of a holistic and transactional practice.

11.3 Policy Aspects of the Consultants' Situation

A vast number of federal and state laws and regulations govern schools and the provision of education to children with disabilities. The Individuals with Disabilities Education Act (PL 101–146) (IDEA) is the primary federal law mandating and governing special education and early intervention for children with disabilities. This law, and accompanying regulations, has continued to evolve from the original 1975 statute. Though IDEA's purpose has always been to ensure access to education for students with disabilities, the most recent reauthorization of the law has an increased emphasis on outcomes and educational achievement (Swinth et al. 2007).

Occupational and physical therapists in school systems must adjust to working within an educational context governed by complex rules emanating from legislation. For therapists trained or experienced with a medically oriented practice model this is often a problematic situation, requiring both attention to the details of a different set of rules and regulations and a shift in personal and professional philosophy. To address this, the PT and OT Consultants help orient practitioners new to school-based practice regarding this IDEA governance through state-wide "boot camps" held each summer as well as providing ongoing training for all practitioners in focused areas such as service delivery models in the least restrictive environment, team writing of integrated IEPs, transition services, providing modifications and accommodations in regular education, and progress monitoring. Further, the consultants help IEP teams (which include parents, family members and students), individual practitioners, and administrators problem-solve in individual cases, particularly when IEP team members have different views of what therapy is required to meet educational goals.

In most respects, schools are governed by state laws, and all of the laws, regulations, and policies governing non-disabled students apply to students with disabilities. The PT and OT consultant are heavily involved in crafting, monitoring, and providing training and technical assistance on the particular policies affecting related service (OT and PT) providers and programs. Other laws such as Section 504 of the Rehabilitation Act of 1973 which insures students will not be discriminated against because of disability and the Americans with Disabilities Act of 1990 (ADA) apply to educational processes. The PT and OT consultants have contributed to state- and LEA-level school planning and facilities guidance in light of ADA requirements of accessible buildings, playgrounds, campus routes, and buses/transportation.

In transactional terms, when school-based practitioners or their administrators encounter problematic situations because their habitual ways of working are challenged by changes in laws and regulations, the consultants reframe the issues, interpret laws and policies, and arrive at solutions that encompass varied needs of students, teachers, and OT and PT practitioners, while incorporating legal and management demands. This work requires a level of understanding encompassing all aspects of the situation from the laws created in Washington, DC to the needs of the individual child receiving special education services.

Practice laws are another issue the consultants address. All OT and PT practitioners working in North Carolina must be licensed by and adhere to the rules of their respective state regulatory boards. The consultants have addressed the application of those rules to school-based practice and worked to modify the rules when needed. An example of the rules' impact on school practice, and the consultants' mediation therein, has been with the emerging role of practitioners in regular education "interventions" amid changing educational approaches. The consultants conduct statewide training on the benefit of related services providers in these regular education initiatives and strongly encourage OT and PT involvement. However, licensure standards for both professions require an evaluation prior to treatment by any licensee. Practitioners have been reluctant to provide support in regular education because no formalized evaluation process precedes the classroom intervention. The consultants' work with other DPI Exceptional Children experts has informed the growing understanding that the focus of OT and PT practitioners in these programs is on high-quality instruction—rather than on individual student deficit—and the teacher is the client. The OT and PT practitioners act as educational supporters or enhancers and are free to share their expertise with educational partners. By giving therapists and policy makers the perspective and language to address this apparent conflict in rule and practice, the consultants opened up innovative "interventions" in NC schools. The consultants conducted research and arrived at interpretations and language to support the school practitioners. This is similar to Coppola's point (see Chap. 16) that Dewey argued teachers should be facilitators, not didactics. Ultimately, all such efforts are directed toward enhancing learning for all children, certainly in keeping with Dewey's concern for creating citizens who can more fully engage in a democratic society.

Another example illustrates how consultants are more than a conduit to reach school-based therapists with license-related information: they also work with the licensure boards and advocate for interpretation and implementation of rules in a manner consistent with the roles of school-based therapists. In 2006, the NC Board of Physical Therapy Examiners added a continuing competency requirement to licensure for North Carolina. While working to gain "approved provider status" for all continuing education programming sponsored by the NC Department of Public Instruction, the PT consultant also discussed implementation of various rules with this new policy. Additionally, she was able to advocate for the definition of "professional development" to include continuing education frequently utilized by school-based PTs and PT Assistants (PTAs). Further, she responded to the Board regarding questions raised by school-based PTs and PTAs during the roll-out of this new policy requirement and assisted with dissemination of requirements, resources and practitioner responsibilities to the school system.

The previous examples illustrate how the OT and PT consultants functionally coordinate the problematic situations arising from state practice regulations. In doing so, the consultants' work is clearly transactional, moving among the various elements of the provision of related services in the school system. But that is not the end of the story. School-based therapists' work is fraught with even more discrepant regulations and expectations than we have already addressed. Different federal laws govern disclosure of educational information (FERPA) and disclosure of health care information (HIPAA). Habits necessary for working within the educational system are not always sufficient when therapists' work bridges into the health care system. This is most evident in providing services paid for by Medicaid, where, if certain qualifications are met, schools can recover costs for specific medically necessary services including physical and occupational therapy.

Two examples will serve to illustrate the interwoven and transactional nature of the consultants' activity with respect to Medicaid. First, under HIPAA policy, parental consent for release of personally identifiable information to outside agencies—the state Medicaid agency being one—is required for all schools. In August, 2006, IDEA regulations added language indicating parental consent must be obtained "each time" access to public benefits or public insurance is sought, an administrative burden on schools that would have essentially shut down school-based Medicaid claiming across the nation. The consultants actively advocated for clarity from the U.S. Office of Special Education Programs (OSEP) on the regulations through the National Alliance for Medicaid in Education and through the NC Director of Exceptional Children office. Within 7 months, OSEP provided interpretation of the regulation allowing schools to seek parental consent for "bundled" disclosures of student information to state Medicaid agencies. In response, within weeks the consultants revised sample parent consent forms available to NC LEAs and essential Medicaid dollars continued to flow through to schools. This situation demonstrates the national, state, and local linkages and intertwining of the consultant roles, and how knowledge and activity at each level affects services to public school students with disabilities.

Secondly, Medicaid cost recovery in schools presents practitioners with a number of ethical and clinical dilemmas that routinely shape assistance and training provided by the consultants. Under IDEA, a student receives PT or OT under the educationally relevant mandate to support the student's progress in his or her educational program. Under Medicaid law, however, a service is reimbursable in schools under the medical necessity mandate—to prevent, diagnose or treat medical conditions. School-based practitioners require constant support to negotiate these two mandates. External pressure to generate funds for the LEA (which may cause ethical stress when the therapist does not perceive medical necessity exists) and to provide clinical-model services (which may cause ethical stress when the therapist does not perceive educational relevance exists) fuel many conversations among consultants and constituents by phone and email, at regional meetings, and at state-wide institutes. Further, many LEAs must use contracted therapists whose income is often directly related to services provided to Medicaid-eligible students with IEPs. Here again, the consultants are in constant contact with local Exceptional Children administrators as they write contracts, monitor contracted staff performance, read invoices, and manage morale when a combination of directly-hired and contracted staff are used. The experience and relationships of both the PT and OT consultant as school-based practitioners and administrators has proven invaluable in this area. They understand the seemingly disparate foci of the educational and Medicaid systems from different vantage points, and keeping in mind the ends-in-view[1] of providing education for all children, integrate these perspectives into their collaborations with practitioners and administrators.

11.4 Key Perspectives of the Consultant Roles

11.4.1 School-Based Therapist Perspective

Therapists currently working in NC schools see the consultants as resources for support, advocacy, information, guidance, policy-making and interpretation, education, and mediation. In terms of support, guidance, and advocacy, OT and PT practitioners rely on the state consultants to work through policy and personal interaction to:

- Create agreeable working conditions (e.g., by conducting workload analyses)
- Serve as sounding board in difficult work situations (e.g., when an IEP team and practitioner disagree on service delivery)

[1] Garrison (2001, p. 280) explained that "Dewey spoke of intentional "ends-in-view" that serve to guide inquiry at every stage of the process; it is a means to its own realization. Ends-in-view are constantly adjustable."

- Provide clinical guidance (e.g., clarifying scope of educationally relevant practice)
- Clarify local understanding and implementation of policy and procedure (e.g., identifying data required to exit a student from PT)
- Provide resources for practice (e.g., forms and templates on consultant website), and
- Provide a "sense of belonging" for itinerant practitioners (e.g., via listserv communication, meetings and peer groups).

The consultants are expected to keep abreast of policy changes at federal and state levels, both within education and the disciplines, and to proactively communicate updates to their varied constituents. Practitioners rely on consultant listservs, websites, meetings, and on-site trainings for this type of information flow.

From the therapists' perspectives, consultants have a two-fold role as educators. First, they are charged with providing relevant, timely, engaging, and evidence-based continuing education through annual OT and PT Institutes, Related Service Summits, Summer Institutes, regional trainings, invited presentations, and talks at professional association meetings. Secondly, the consultants are seen as the therapists' voices with parents, educators, other specialists, and administrators who need to be educated about what school-based OTs and PTs do and why it matters in educating students. The consultants are expected to either provide that training directly, or provide resources for practitioners to use in their own local training.

Therapists also expect the consultants to bring consistency to practice across the state, not only within the discipline across county lines, but across related service disciplines within any given LEA. The consultants create and sustain linkages for therapists working in schools. For example, a therapist interested in developing a stronger OT presence in his LEA's high school-to-community transition program can contact the consultant to find out if there are other LEAs doing this sort of work, what AOTA offers in this area, if there are any related journal articles, and who else to contact at NCDPI for training. The consultant would then investigate and provide relevant contacts and resources. A school-based PT with concerns about transportation procedures in their school system may have little recourse to address problematic issues directly given a limited knowledge base. The consultant can provide the local practitioner with current law and regulation, verify best practice and suggest similar LEAs that are handling like concerns in an appropriate manner. On the other end of this issue, the consultant can network with DPI transportation staff at the state level to determine how to improve the implementation of transportation policy. Similarly, school-based practitioners look to the NCDPI consultants for language and support in linking with community therapists and those who provide services to children and youth in clinics and home health particularly when a student's needs must be addressed both at home and at school, as in the case of obtaining and maintaining an appropriate wheelchair. A related role as seen by constituents is that of mediator. The consultants are routinely invited to a LEA to meet with the therapy team and the Exceptional Children Director to facilitate common understanding of workload/therapist allocation, educationally relevant services, and/or program strengths and needs.

Perhaps the most pervasive, but difficult to define, role assumed of the consultants is that of best practice guide. Therapists report the consultants are central in providing structure (e.g., intervention plan template), content (e.g., study skills curriculum for an after school club), support (e.g., guidance regarding ethical issues when utilizing public funding of equipment and Medicaid cost recovery for schools) and encouragement (e.g., availability for case-specific phone consultation) for imagining and implementing best practices. The existence of the consultant positions create prospective/proactive standard setting, rather than a retrospective/reactive monitoring; indeed, practitioners see the consultants as scouts who are "looking out for us" and "keeping us out of trouble." Thus from the perspective of practitioners, consultants are advocates and resources to provide needed support in problematic situations. The consultants' skills reside in their ability to assess these situations and draw on their resources and knowledge to help practitioners develop the skills and behaviors to address these situations constructively. The ends-in-view is best practice of OT and PT within the context of the educational system.

11.4.2 Administrator Perspective

Local education administrators, particularly in special education and human resources, see the consultants as experts in their disciplines within the public education context and rely on them to provide accurate interpretations and ensure LEA compliance with discipline-specific and Medicaid policies. It is important they receive these services *before*, or at least concurrently, with the practitioners they employ. Administrators, who are almost always educators by training, lean on consultants to give them the "inside story" on how therapists think, how to recruit, retain, manage, and appraise therapy staff, how to reward them for work well done, and how to correct them when they err. What is incentive for a teacher may not inspire a therapist, and those educators-turned-administrators who want to grow quality related service programs often count on the consultants for insight into the differences. Additionally, administrators expect the consultants to be knowledgeable about funding streams, especially Medicaid, for therapy services, positions, programs, and supplies.

Administrators also desire consultants' help with therapist recruitment. NC is in the midst of an allied health care provider shortage in all practice settings, and none are harder hit than public schools where salaries are lower than the private sector. The consultants are seen as "in touch with the therapy world" and knowledgeable about details of recruitment and contacts. The consultants have produced guidance documents on contracting and retention, created web pages posting LEA therapy vacancies, developed training and pursued funding to implement clinical affiliations/fieldwork in schools, and advocated for a DPI-funded tuition-reimbursement program.

Like practitioners, administrators see the consultants as mediators between themselves and therapists. Administrators rely heavily on statewide data the consultants gather—such as average number of contact hours per therapist or percentage of students in special education who receive PT—to guide decision-making. If the administrator initiates contact with the consultant, the administrator tends to view the consultant as a resource and support. If a therapist initiates contact with the consultant, administrators tend to be somewhat less invested and somewhat more suspicious of the consultant's role and purpose. The converse is true for therapists in both situations. Thus the seeming dualism of therapists-administrators changes with the situation, and the consultants work is less between the parties and more within the problematic situation of the moment.

11.4.3 Consultant Perspective

The theme of the consultants' work, from their own perspective, is all about "making *you* look good" and the nature of such a commission is *every day different*. The OT and PT consultants are dedicated to helping best practice get better and good practitioners, parents, administrators, and colleagues get great, to the end result that all students in North Carolina public schools thrive. Pursuit of that vision, or ends-in view, is a transaction of seemingly miscellaneous occupations: look at any week from the consultants' calendars and you might find visiting local school systems, participating in division meetings and committee work at UNC-CH and NCDPI, preparation for Summer Institute sessions, conducting an out-of-state workshop, designing a grant program for clinical education in schools, or a day in the office, culling recent relevant research, and responding to e-mails and phone calls. In any one of these tasks, the consultants may play a variety of roles. This diversity in workload is stimulating, expansive, challenging, and rewarding. The consultants are always *on*. The required levels of alertness, environmental scanning, and ability to think on one's feet—be it in negotiations between a team of practitioners and administrators or in front of room full of parents—create an invigorating experience. The variability in work type, work setting, schedule, people encountered, and even dress code, affects the consultant's perception of time, distance, and productivity. More often than not, several projects and tasks need simultaneous attention—meeting participants are registering as the website is updated as handouts for an upcoming presentation are emailed to the sponsoring agency as applications to the graduate program at the university are reviewed.

An important contributing factor in the consultants' ever-new experience—and success—is the considerable degree of autonomy afforded in setting work agendas, schedules, project selection, and time lines. In many ways, NCDPI and UNC-CH leave the work to the consultants and operate on a subtle no-news-is-good-news basis. The absence of complaint, the pursuit of projects that do not require too many resources (especially time from those higher on the chain of command), and the perception that the consultants are busy are some of the unspoken keys to maintaining stasis. And, it is in the midst of this somewhat unexamined freedom, the consultants are compelled to flourish and pursue something more than stasis, for in the context of two enormous institutions in work that covers an entire state, invisibility is combated with excellence.

11.5 Conclusion

The consultants have to perpetually coordinate elements of a situation through different tasks within complex, problematic situations. While habits established over time guide the consultants in many of their activities, novel situations frequently arise where these habits are not adequate (Garrison 2002; Cutchin et al. 2008). At these moments, consultants engage in what Dewey called "dramatic rehearsal" (Fesmire 2003) both individually and together, to resolve the situation in the best possible manner. What will be the best solution for all parties, what will best meet the needs of the student(s), how are such possibilities constrained by law, economics, logistics, and personalities? The answers are discovered in an ongoing process of integrating situations through action and learning through the process—a key essence of transactional experience.

References

Cutchin, M., & Dickie, V. (2012). Transactionalism: Occupational science and the pragmatic attitude. In G. Whiteford & C. Hocking (Eds.), *Critical perspectives on occupational science: Society, inclusion, participation* (pp. 23–37). London: Wiley.

Cutchin, M., Aldrich, R., Bailliard, A., & Coppola, S. (2008). Action theories for occupational science: The contributions of Dewey and Bourdieu. *Journal of Occupational Science, 15*(3), 157–165.

Dickie, V., Cutchin, M., & Humphry, R. (2006). Occupation as transactional experience: A critique of individualism in occupational science. *Journal of Occupational Science, 13*(1), 83–93.

Fesmire, S. (2003). *John Dewey & moral imagination*. Bloomington: Indiana University Press.

Garrison, J. (2001). An introduction to Dewey's theory of functional "trans-action": An alternative paradigm for activity theory. *Mind, Culture, and Activity, 8*, 275–296.

Garrison, J. (2002). Habits as social tools in contest. *OTJR: Occupation, participation and health, 22*(supplement), 11S–17S.

North Carolina State Board of Education. (2009). *North Carolina Academically or Intellectually Gifted Program Standards*. NC Department of Public Instruction. http://www.ncpublicschools.org/docs/academicservices/gifted/aig-program-standards.pdf

Sullivan, S. (2002). Pragmatist feminism as ecological ontology: Reflections on living across and through skins. *Hypatia, 17*(4), 201–217.

Swinth, Y., Spencer, K. C., & Jackson, L. L. (2007). Occupational therapy: Effective school-based practices within a policy context (COPSSE Document Number OP-3). Gainesville: University of Florida, Center on Personnel Studies in Special Education.

Trice, H. M. (1993). *Occupational subcultures in the workplace*. Ithaca: ILR Press.

Part III
Methodological Implications

Chapter 12
Where the Transactions Happen: The Unit of Analysis When Applying a Transactional Perspective

Lena Rosenberg and Karin Johansson

12.1 Introduction

In this chapter, we discuss the methodological challenges associated with applying a transactional perspective in the context of occupational therapy research. We discuss in particular how a unit of analysis that focuses on *where and when the transactions happen* can be conceptualized and applied. Based on our experiences from clinical work and research with interventions in the home environment for older persons with functional limitations, we conclude that a transactional perspective contributes substantially to the understanding of how such interventions are integrated into everyday life. We suggest that *the situation* is an appropriate unit of analysis to grasp where and when transactions happen. To do this we present two different empirical studies that used the situation as the unit of analysis to research provision of interventions in the home environment (e.g., assistive technology and home modifications) to older persons with functional limitations (cognitive and physical). In addition, challenges and strengths of using a non-traditional unit of analysis will be discussed.

12.2 The Need for a Transactional Perspective

It is well known, from a theoretical as well as from a clinical standpoint, that interventions in the home environment interact with the older persons' everyday life through complex relationships involving factors like values, habits, preferences, emotional connections to the home, and social relations associated with the home

L. Rosenberg (✉) • K. Johansson
Department of Neurobiology, Care Sciences and Society,
Division of Occupational Therapy, Karolinska Institutet, Stockholm, Sweden
e-mail: lenarosenberg@bredband.net

M.P. Cutchin and V.A. Dickie (eds.), *Transactional Perspectives on Occupation*,
DOI 10.1007/978-94-007-4429-5_12, © Springer Science+Business Media B.V. 2013

(Gitlin 2003; Iwarsson 2005; Wahl et al. 2009). However, at present there is a lack of methods that allow researchers to grasp this complexity. Consequently, a risk exists that a large portion of what is important in the context of interventions (e.g., the prescription of assistive technology or the provision of home modifications) is missed. Additionally, research on and provision of health and social care service tends to ignore the emergent character of human life. The focus is often on definitions of problems and solutions directed at specific goals, as if those were static. However, in everyday problems, solutions and goals are continuously changing as life goes on. This is particularly ignored when it comes to older people living in the home environment (Cutchin 2003), and this dismissal can be attributed to ageist attitudes towards older persons, categorizing life at older ages as static and objectifying the older person (Richards 2000).

Recognition of the on-going, emergent character of older people's lives has implications for service provision to this group. A service organization that fails to recognize how problems, solutions, and goals are continuously redefined might encounter failed interventions as well as wasted efforts and resources (Heywood 2004). Accordingly, it has been argued that theories and methods that do not recognize this changing character of older people's lives fail both to generate theoretical understandings of human action and society and to critically contribute to the evaluation and design of social policies and service provision (Law et al. 1996; Cutchin 1999; Fischer 2003; Griffiths 2003; Rubinstein and de Medeiros 2003; Dickie et al. 2006). The transactional perspective is a promising approach to recognize the changing character of older people's lives. It brings to the forefront where and when transactions happen; that is, where, when and how actors and contexts are connected in an on-going process. The focus on such connections can be defined as a focus on the driving forces and relationships involved in changes of aspects relevant to the studied issue. To find a unit of analysis that can capture the on-going transactions of people's life is important in research and health care in general. This is of particular importance in relationship to interventions provided in the home since such interventions become interconnected to the everyday at home through complex relationships involving, for example, the physical environment, everyday habits, meanings and values of the home. This chapter takes up the challenge of capturing the on-going transactions of older people's life in relationship to interventions provided in the home through discussing methodological consequences of applying a transactional perspective.

12.3 Methodological Consequences of Applying a Transactional Perspective

When addressing where and when transactions happen, the focus is on driving forces and relationships that make changes in aspects relevant to the issue in focus. This requires a shift from traditional units of analysis applied in environmental gerontology and occupational therapy, such as distinct variables or phenomena, to an arena where variables and phenomena are integrated through a focus on their relationships. This arena has been conceptualized as an event (Law et al. 1996), occupational setting (Kielhofner 2008) or situation (Cutchin 1999, 2007). In the two studies discussed here, the term *situation* was chosen based on Deweyan pragmatism. According to John Dewey (1998), the classical philosopher of pragmatism, situations are the focal point of inquiry, and each comprises a number of transactional relationship of interest. Thus the situation defines where, when and which transactions happen, and therefore provides an adequate unit of analysis for research aiming to apply a transactional perspective. Moreover, pragmatism focuses on the ever-changing and integrated character of human experiences and action. The objects of inquiry are the time and place-specific contexts in which experiences and actions occur. These have been conceptualized by Dewey as unique situations that can never be repeated but are suggestive of similar situations (Cutchin 1999, 2007). Drawing on this philosophical resource, we discuss the possibilities and challenges with the application of situations as the unit of analysis for studies aiming to understand outcomes of services provided to older persons in their homes.

In order to understand how interventions in the home environment are integrated in people's everyday lives, it is crucial to identify a unit of analysis that can capture driving forces and relationships in older persons' everyday lives in their homes. By extension, knowledge derived from using situation as the unit of analysis contributes to an understanding of how interventions in the home can be designed and provided to adequately support older persons in their everyday lives.

12.3.1 Applying the Situation as a Unit of Analysis: Two Examples

In this section, we present and discuss two different empirical studies that used the situation as the unit of analysis to study provision of interventions in the home environments of older persons. One study focused on what happened when assistive technology (AT) was provided in the homes of people with dementia (Rosenberg and Nygård 2012), hereafter referred to as the AT study. The other study focused on provision of home modifications (HM) to older persons with physical functional limitations (Johansson et al. 2009), hereafter referred to as the HM study. Both studies were conducted in Sweden where HM and AT are provided as integral parts of health and social care. These services are prescribed, distributed and mostly financed through the national health care system. Besides being provided in the home environment, a shared characteristic of the two studied service processes is that they can involve a number of different actors, including the older person, his or her kin, and different professionals. All of these actors influence the process through their actions and experiences. In the following, we will first briefly present the methodologies used in the two studies, and then discuss how challenges of applying a transactional perspective were met in relation to the unit of analysis.

12.3.1.1 Assistive Technology for Persons with Dementia

Three persons with mild stage dementia who were about to receive AT were included in the study, one after the other. As the unit of analysis was the situation, persons and features of the physical environment were included as they appeared to be relevant to the situation through the research process. Each person with dementia together with other persons and physical features in that specific situation were considered as one case (Merriam 1998). The cases were followed from the time it was decided that AT should be prescribed to the person with dementia until the data described that the situation had become stable (i.e., no new events were occurring related to the use of the AT). Beside persons with dementia, family, friends, and health professionals were included as part of the situation. Situations were investigated through an ethnographic approach including open interviews (Kvale 1996; Nygård 2006) and participatory observations (Patton 2002; Nygård 2006). The major part of the data collection took place in the homes of the persons with dementia, and the period of data collection varied between cases from 3 weeks to 15 months. Initial data collection took place in three predetermined occasions: (a) 2–6 days before the person with dementia received the AT, (b) at the time when the person with dementia received the AT, and (c) when the person with dementia had lived with the AT for 1–2 weeks. Subsequent occasions of data collection were directed by questions raised in the on-going data analysis and by interactions or changes in each case. In order to identify such interactions or changes the researcher (LR) was in phone contact with the person with dementia, significant others, and the occupational therapist. Changes and interactions that called for new occasions of data collection could, for example, be new problems or possibilities mentioned by the person with dementia or the significant others. Problems or possibilities were, for example, expressed in the form of ideas of combining the AT with something else or using it for new purposes. Further, changes in the situation could also call for new participants to be included if they were shown to influence the process.

Altogether 35 occasions of data collection were conducted with a minimum of four occasions in each case. The open interviews and observations aimed at capturing actions, experiences, interpretations and ideas of the different actors involved in each particular case and how these were linked over time and with each other. Data analysis was continuously carried out throughout the data collection, following the recommendations of Charmaz (2006); with an emphasis on how situations emerged into new situations aiming to achieve a theoretical understanding of the AT process for people with mild stage dementia.

12.3.1.2 Home Modifications

Four older HM applicants were purposefully selected (Patton 2002) to include (a) different onset of functional limitations, for example chronic conditions or injuries and (b) variation in expected changes in performance of everyday activities with the applied HM. All participants had their applications of HM grants approved.

Data were collected with open interviews and focused participant observations (Patton 2002) in the participants' home environments on multiple occasions during a period lasting from before the HM had been installed until the data described some stability in the situation. Stability was identified as a situation where the participant had developed a way to perform the activity related to the applied HM that they could accept according to their preferences and values. This situation could include an installed HM or not. Cases were studied for a duration of 8–17 months. Data collection was originally scheduled before the HM was installed, as well as 2 and 6 months after inclusion. In addition, the four participants were contacted by telephone at intervals of 1 or 2 months between and after the scheduled occasions for data collection. If they described a change related to HM services or their way of performing the activity, time for a data collection occasion was booked. Altogether 16 occasions of data collection were conducted, with a minimum of three with each participant.

A semi-structured interview guide was used to allow the interviews to be shaped by the individual participants' situation. The interview guide covered the following areas: (a) how the participants managed everyday life and what problems they experienced, (b) expected or experienced changes in the everyday life situations related to the applied or installed modifications, and (c) actions taken to handle the situations and experiences of those actions. In addition the participants were asked to demonstrate how activities were performed relating to the applied or installed HM, which provided a concrete situation in which questions about immediate experiences and actions could be asked. The data analysis was based on a hermeneutic approach, meaning that dialectical relations between "experience-near" and "experience-distant" perspectives were interpreted, aiming to achieve a theoretical understanding of the participants' everyday experiences and actions (Geertz 1983; Gustavsson 2000).

12.4 Methodological Challenges and Recommendations for Studying Situations

One of the most challenging aspects of applying a transactional perspective in these studies was to balance openness to the entire situation with a focus on situational aspects relevant to the study. A strength of applying a transactional perspective is that it recognizes the messiness of human life, by allowing for the multifaceted aspects, variables, or phenomena to be included in our understanding of human actions and experiences. However, with this openness we risk ending up with the statement that everything is connected to everything, which does not generate any valuable knowledge about human actions and experiences in general, and certainly not about needs, provision and outcomes of services. On the other hand, the transactional perspective allows one to respond to criticisms of methods traditionally applied in occupational therapy and occupational science that only include predefined aspects, variables and phenomena. As such, the transactional perspective counters the problem of generating overly narrow and limited knowledge that does not recognize the multifaceted character of human life. Based on Deweyan philosophy, we have tried to meet this challenge through defining the situation as the unit of analysis. Still, the generic situation of Deweyan philosophical discourse remains too open a concept to serve as a unit of analysis that generates valuable knowledge. Therefore we want to emphasize the importance of defining the unit of analysis in relation to the research aim, which also requires that the research aim is carefully formulated. In the two studies discussed here, the unit of analysis was defined as "anything in the situation that appeared relevant in relationship to the research aim." This definition leaves the researchers with the challenge of defining what is relevant, which again requires careful balancing between total openness and strict adherence to definitions of what is relevant. To illustrate this in more concrete terms we need to present the specific aims of the two studies.

In the AT study the aim was to explore the actions and underlying driving forces in the process that started when an AT was brought into the situation where a person with dementia pursued their everyday lives. The specific interest was focused on the unfolding interactions in order to discover where they led, and how the AT intervention was coordinated with the situation of the person with dementia.

In the HM study the aim was to explore the process of aging in place, in relation to HM services. More specifically, the study aimed at increasing understanding of the transactions in everyday life relating to service delivery among some older individuals who have received approval of an application for HM services.

As described above, data for the HM study were collected through applying an interview guide and focused participant observation covering areas identified as relevant to the aim of the study. In the AT study, observation and interview data that captured actions, experiences, interpretations and ideas of the different actors were collected. This openness in data collection also requires a researcher's sensitivity in selecting data that appears to be relevant, without falling prey to prejudices and noting only expected elements of the situation. In the AT study an ethnographic approach was applied to openly explore what is happening, in terms of verbal as well as non-verbal action and interactions. This approach allowed for observing how the AT was used as well as the interactions between different involved actors and their verbal reflections on the situation. Similarly, the process related to HM services was followed in the HM study through a methodological approach where interviews were combined with focused participant observations. This allowed us to explore the participants' immediate experiences as well as their reflections regarding how an activity was performed and the motivations and actions behind the actual way of performing the activity.

One example in the AT study reflects how openness was connected to the research aim in data collection. The expected role of the occupational therapists was that of gatekeeper who would help the researchers to make contact with persons with dementia who were about to receive AT. When we started to collect and analyze data, it appeared that the occupational therapists were significant actors in the service process and hence they were included as participants in the study. In the HM study, the initial focus in data collection was on the older persons as receivers of HM.

At the first data collection occasions we realized that the particular actions the older persons took to handle the immediate situation largely influenced their broader transactions in everyday life. Subsequent data collection therefore also explored the reasons underlying those actions.

In both studies the focus was on *how* changes came about, rather than *what* changes had happened. To achieve this, data were collected during numerous occasions to allow a view of processes unfolding through time. We argue that a longitudinal, emergent methodological approach is essential to apply a transactional perspective. One example illustrating this is Harry's case in the AT study. Harry was a man with dementia who received AT to help him manage daily activities better at home, where he lived alone. He wanted to stay in his own home as long as possible and the occupational therapist wanted to support this. When the occupational therapist prescribed an electronic calendar she talked to Harry's daughter about combining it with a written schedule of his day care attendance in order to help Harry manage at home. The occupational therapist had the impression that the daughter was going to carry out the adaptation and therefore left the responsibility to her. As the case was followed over time by the researcher (LR), it became clear that the daughter never adapted the AT. The daughter was interviewed several times but it was only when Harry already had moved to a nursing home that she shared that such a move actually was her main goal during the whole process. This shed light on why she did not adapt the AT and the daughter's wish to get her father into a nursing home turned out to be a strong driving force in the case.

The following example from the HM study also illustrates the importance of following situations over time. Because Anders had been prescribed an electric wheelchair for outdoor use, a storing room was installed and a path was remodeled so that he could use the wheelchair. When the modification was installed, he still had to wait a number of months for the wheelchair to be delivered, and then data collection continued. When Anders started using the wheelchair, the home help officer decided that Anders was no longer allowed to receive his ready-made lunch at home (he was deemed able to get around outdoors by himself and pick it up). Anders was very upset about this, because he experienced it as unsafe and unpleasant to use the wheelchair in wintertime. After Anders had slipped once with the wheelchair outside the place where he picked up his lunch, he initiated a new negotiation about his need for lunch delivery. This resulted in an agreement that lunch would be delivered to Anders' home during wintertime. This example illustrates how the relationships between Anders, the physical environment and the social care system changed over time. If the data collection had ended when the modification was installed, those changing relationships would have never been recognized.

Both studies included participant observations as a method for data collection. Since participant observations generate real-time data on emerging situations they have a potential to identify aspects of relevance for the transactions that happen. It is not possible to predict when changes relevant to the focus of the research will happen. However, when conducting research that focuses on people's homes, it is not ethically or practically possible for the researcher to be present all the time. It is therefore crucial to apply methods that manage to grasp actions and relationships emerging between occasions for data collection. In the two studies presented here, this dilemma was solved by data collection methods that were sensitive to identifying traces of actions taken when researchers were not present. Traces of action included changes in the physical environment, placement of the AT, changes in the way an activity was performed, and changes in the equipment used to perform an activity, for example.

Questions that arose through observed traces of actions were asked in the interviews. One example came from a situation in the AT study where the AT, an electronic calendar, had been moved to another place in the home of one of the participants. During data collection, the researcher noticed that the AT had been moved and therefore asked the participant with dementia questions about the placement of the electronic calendar and his use of it. After that a telephone interview was conducted with his daughter to capture her ideas about moving the calendar. She explained that she had moved the calendar close to the telephone since her father often asked her about what day it was when they talked on the telephone. Since the kitchen (where the calendar was originally located) was the place where Harry planned his day, the new placement of the AT conflicted with the original idea that it would help Harry to plan his days. This information contributed to an understanding of how she viewed herself as an actor whose role was to train her father to use the AT.

Another example of how traces of actions informed the researcher in the AT study was the case of Karin, who had received a schedule to help her to remember events that were going to happen during the week. When visiting Karin for data collection the researcher observed traces in the form of written notes and decorations on the schedule, from Karin and others. Therefore, questions were asked about reasons behind what had been written and drawn on the schedule.

Both the AT and the HM studies applied a method for data collection that framed situations where the person with dementia or the HM applicant interacted with the home environment. By observing those interactions the researchers could identify changes, which served as clues to actions that had been taken between the data collection occasions. In the AT study the researcher attempted to create situations where the actors naturally would use the AT, as actions were considered important data. For example the researcher asked questions about what the actor with dementia, who had the schedule, was going to do the next day to see if she spontaneously used the scheme and if so, how. In the HM study the older persons were asked to perform the activity related to the applied or installed HM. Changes since the last data collection session were reflected upon in dialogue between the researcher and the older person, including questions and explanations of actions taken (by the older person or by others) leading to the observed changes.

We have described the methods for data collection applied in two studies with the ambition to achieve a transactional perspective. However, before data collection the *study object* must be carefully selected. In applying a transactional perspective, this is specifically challenging in light of the need to find a position between total openness and a narrowly focused perspective. The ultimate aim of the two studies presented was to understand how interventions in the home environment can support older persons in their everyday lives. We therefore chose study objects that bring the situation of one older person into focus. In the medical tradition the study object is often the individual or population. As we have attempted to illustrate above, there is a need to broaden the focus from the individual or groups of individuals to the situation of which individuals are a part. To include the perspectives of different actors involved in those situations is challenging but necessary to bring into further relief the primary position and experience of the older persons receiving AT or HMs.

As mentioned before, the two studies both continued data collection until the researcher judged that there was some stability in the situation. However, taking a transactional perspective seriously suggests recognition that there is no end to the processes under study. Yet with respect to practicalities such as resources, as well as ethics, data collection must be ceased at some point. To end data collection at a time point where there was some stability in the situation was a natural ending point for data collection because it signified the end of the specific problematic process under study. This is sometimes a difficult but necessary determination, and there is always the risk of missing important transactions by cutting data collection short before a good ending point has been reached in the situation.

12.5 Conclusion

Based on our experiences, we do not suggest that one method is more suitable than another for applying a transactional perspective, but we have raised some key methodological points from our studies that are important to consider. First, a clear aim is needed to allow openness in the data collection. Second, data should be collected over time and researcher flexibility is needed to capture good data about the transactions that take place. Third, a continuous data analysis parallel to the data collection is needed to sensitize the researchers to know what data, from whom or what, is needed as well as to know when to stop the data collection. We identified that real-time data were a strength in comparison with retrospective data and that participant observation could provide them. Another method to achieve real-time data is the use of diaries focusing on actions and experiences related to the studied topic. Still, methods for collecting real-time data on larger samples need to be developed.

We suggest that a transactional perspective is of specific importance in relation to research on service provision to older persons in the home environment. Not only does it bring attention to the how and why of processes that services address or create, but it also helps to overcome ageist perceptions of older persons as passive service receivers. Service organizations that recognize older people as agents and enhance their own efforts and problem-solving have been identified as tools of empowerment (Richards 2000). When older people's efforts at problem solving are not recognized in the service process, the result can be confusion, frustration and disempowering experiences for the older person (Heywood 2004; Richards 2000). This means that in order to provide services that efficiently meet older people's needs and support their efforts at problem solving, there is a need to recognize the ever-changing situation of older people's lives, and to recognize their agency.

References

Charmaz, K. (2006). *Constructing grounded theory: A practical guide through qualitative analysis*. London: Sage.
Cutchin, M. P. (1999). Qualitative explorations in health geography: Using pragmatism and related concepts as guides. *The Professional Geographer, 51*(12), 265–274.
Cutchin, M. P. (2003). The process of mediated aging-in-place: A theoretically and empirically based model. *Social Science & Medicine, 57*(6), 1077–1090.
Cutchin, M. P. (2007). John Dewey's metaphysical ground-map and its implications for geographical inquiry. *Geoforum*. doi:10.1016/j.geoforum.2007.01.014.
Dewey, J. (1998). *Experience and education: The 60th anniversary edition*. West Lafayette: Kappa Delta Pi, International Honor Society in Education.
Dickie, V., Cutchin, M. P., & Humphry, R. (2006). Occupation as transactional experience: A critique of individualism in occupational science. *Journal of Occupational Science, 13*(1), 83–93.
Fischer, F. (2003). *Reframing public policy*. Oxford: Oxford University Press.
Geertz, C. (1983). *Local knowledge: Further essays in interpretive anthropology*. New York: Basic Books.
Gitlin, L. N. (2003). Conducting research on home environments: Lessons learned and new directions. *The Gerontologist, 43*(5), 628–637.
Griffiths, L. (2003). Making connections: Studies of the social organization of healthcare. *Sociology of Health & Illness, 25*(2), 155–171.
Gustavsson, A. (2000). *Tolkning och tolkningsteori 1. Introduktion*. [Interpretation and interpretation theory. Introduction.] (In Swedish). Stockholm: Pedagogiska Institutionen, Stockholms Universitet.
Heywood, F. (2004). Understanding needs: A starting point for quality. *Housing Studies, 19*(5), 709–726.
Iwarsson, S. (2005). A long-term perspective on person-environment fit and ADL dependence among older Swedish adults. *The Gerontologist, 45*(3), 327–336.
Johansson, K., Josephsson, S., & Lilja, M. (2009). Creating possibilities for action in the presence of environmental barriers, in the process of ageing in place. *Ageing and Society, 29*, 49–70.
Kielhofner, G. (2008). *Model of human occupation* (4th ed.). Baltimore: Lippincott, Williams & Wilkins.
Kvale, S. (1996). *Interviews*. Thousand Oaks: Sage.
Law, M., Cooper, B., Strong, S., Stewart, D., Rigby, P., & Letts, L. (1996). The Person-Environment-Occupational model: A transactive approach to occupational performance. *Canadian Journal of Occupational Therapy, 63*(1), 9–23.
Merriam, S. B. (1998). *Qualitative research and case study applications in education* (Revth ed.). San Francisco: Jossey-Bass.
Nygård, L. (2006). How can we get access to the experiences of people with dementia? Suggestions and reflections. *Scandinavian Journal of Occupational Therapy, 13*(2), 101–112.
Patton, M. Q. (2002). *Qualitative research & evaluation methods*. London: Sage.
Richards, S. (2000). Bridging the divide: Elders and the assessment process. *British Journal of Social Work, 30*, 37–49.
Rosenberg, L., & Nygård, L. (2012). Persons with dementia become users of assistive technology: A study of the process. *Dementia, 11*(2), 135–154.
Rubinstein, R. L., & de Medeiros, K. (2003). Ecology and the aging self. In H.-W. Wahl, R. J. Scheidt, & P. G. Windley (Eds.), *Annual review of gerontology and geriatrics: Focus on aging in context: Socio-physical environment*. New York: Springer.
Wahl, H.-W., Fänge, A., Oswald, F., Gitlin, L., & Iwarsson, S. (2009). The home environment and disability-related outcomes in aging individuals: What is the empirical evidence? *The Gerontologist, 49*(3), 355–367.

Chapter 13
Ethnography and the Transactional Study of Occupation

Antoine L. Bailliard, Rebecca M. Aldrich, and Virginia A. Dickie

13.1 Introduction

The study of occupation from a transactional perspective calls for research methods that recognize and appreciate the entire situation of occupation(s). In addition to attending to the whole situation, such methods must also study specific elements of both occupations and situations. In this chapter, we examine the fit of ethnography and the transactional perspective for those dual purposes. The term ethnography refers to both a process of studying a culture or subculture and the written product of that process (the ethnographic text) (Schwandt 2007). In this chapter we focus on the ethnographic process. We characterize ethnography as both a process for studying the transactions that comprise an occupational situation and as a transactional enterprise in itself. We discuss how the marriage of ethnography and a transactional perspective offers a sophisticated understanding of the roles of *researchers* and their participants/*consultants* in the study *situation*. The chapter concludes with a discussion of future directions for the ethnography-transaction union with respect to development and enrichment of scholarship on occupation.

Ethnography is grounded within the natural and historical contexts of the daily happenings of a culture. The power of ethnography stems from its central feature of active engagement, through which the researcher *experiences with* study participants in addition to *observing* participants' occupations. In the role as *participant* observer, the ethnographer *lives* the events and circumstances that become the data for developing research findings.

Previous chapters have described what the transactional perspective offers to our understanding of occupation. We offer here a brief overview of the ideas from the transactional perspective and Deweyan philosophy that are central to this chapter.

A.L. Bailliard (✉) • R.M. Aldrich • V.A. Dickie
Department of Allied Health Sciences, Division of Occupational Science and Occupational Therapy, University of North Carolina at Chapel Hill, Chapel Hill, NC, USA
e-mail: antoine_bailliard@med.unc.edu

M.P. Cutchin and V.A. Dickie (eds.), *Transactional Perspectives on Occupation*,
DOI 10.1007/978-94-007-4429-5_13, © Springer Science+Business Media B.V. 2013

The transactional emphasis on *relationships* between all elements of a situation (Dewey 2000) is key to our view of ethnography, as is the notion that *situations* are ever-changing due to the fluctuating relationships that constitute them (Cutchin et al. 2008). In addition, our position is guided by the Deweyan philosophy that *knowledge* arises through experience in multiple forms and is developed through a *process of inquiry* (Dewey 2005; Hickman 1998). Finally, we take *uncertainty* as an inherent part of the research experience that should be embraced as a salient source of knowledge about a situation and not something to explain away (Dewey 2000, 2005). These understandings weave throughout the remainder of the chapter.

This chapter will explore the compatibility of ethnography with a transactional perspective of human occupation. We argue that ethnographic study reveals the transactional nature of occupation because it looks at whole situations; it foregrounds the innumerable influences interacting with occupations as well as the multiple occupations that constitute a situation or emerge in response to a situation. To support our position, we draw on examples from our work to highlight how *experiencing with* encompasses diverse features of situational transactions. Implicit in our argument is the assumption that occupational situations can be treated as if they are cultures or subcultures, thus making ethnography a suitable approach.

We ground our discussion in our experiences with ethnographic studies focused on particular occupations (Dickie) and situations that challenge occupational engagement (Bailliard and Aldrich). Authors Bailliard and Aldrich selected ethnography as their research method after immersion in Deweyan philosophy, while author Dickie adopted a transactional perspective as the result of her ethnographic studies of self-employed crafters and contemporary quilt making. Bailliard's work focused on exploring the experiences of Latino immigrants to a North Carolinian community, and Aldrich studied the situation of "discouraged" workers in a small factory town in rural North Carolina. Each of these examples will be used throughout the remainder of our discussion.

13.2 Ethnography

Ethnography has taken many forms over time in response to paradigmatic shifts in academia. The following description of ethnography reflects our experiences with ethnographic projects and is informed by an overview of the general principles from ethnographic literature. Ethnography as a process employs various research tools aimed at collecting and analyzing multiple forms of data in order to understand a culture (Marcus and Fischer 1986). The data collected with these tools elucidate the complex intricacies of a situation in a way that giving primacy to one source of data cannot accomplish. Participant observation is the heart of ethnographic fieldwork and is augmented by interviews, collections of documentary and historical evidence, mapping, researcher reflections, and various measurement tools. Ethnography is characterized by periods of *hanging out,* during which the researcher remains open to new avenues of inquiry and unanticipated sources of data. Data from these sources are recorded and collected in the form of field notes, audio and video recordings, transcriptions, printed documents, photographs, and artifacts.

Given the impossibility of predicting what will be revealed in a natural situation, hanging out—the vehicle through which the researcher aims to *experience with* study participants (or "consultants," as used in Lassiter 2005)—becomes a critical tool to ensure the researcher is present for those revelations. For example, in her study of discouraged workers, Aldrich (2011) spent time sitting in several social service agency lobbies to experience how waiting for services affected the formation of her consultants' daily routines. The experience of waiting was not outlined in Aldrich's original research plan, but its prominence in many discouraged workers' situations prompted her to build experiences of waiting into her study. Similarly, while spontaneously attending a church activity during his study of Latino immigrants, Bailliard (2011) noted subtle cultural clashes between the Hispanic and Anglo congregations who organized the event. Subsequently, Bailliard addressed the issue with consultants, who cited numerous other tensions that significantly affected their experiences of the church—a critical node of occupational opportunities in their daily living. This happenstance discovery prompted Bailliard to attend additional events and review church bulletins to explore how such divisions were evident and how they impacted his consultants' engagement in occupation. Both of these examples illustrate how the observant ethnographer gains understanding through *experiencing with* during study situations. Keen observation and recognition of what is not "expected" are essential to the research enterprise, as is careful attention to the nuances that deepen understanding of the "expected."

In order to remain open to unanticipated sources of knowledge and changes in the direction of inquiry, an ethnographer must plan broadly (Agar 1980). Developing an ethnographic research plan includes identifying a basic research question, delimiting a field (see, for example, Rosenberg and Johansson this book), a time frame, possible instruments, and a general strategy for gaining access to the situation. With a broad plan, the researcher can initiate the study and institute methodological changes that are attuned to his or her growing understanding of the situation (Whyte 1984). Often, these changes are precipitated by shared happenings with participants who guide the researcher through a cultural terrain. Some participants actively engage in the research process and have the power to fundamentally alter the direction of inquiry. These participants, better defined as *consultants* (Lassiter 2005), are experts with tacit understandings of their situations. The skilled researcher is sensitive to this expertise and invites the consultant to actively engage in the research process to promote a thorough understanding and representation of the situation. However, the researcher must be attuned to consultants' roles and status in the community and be aware of how those relationships position the researcher in the social fabric of the situation.

The uncertainty of the research process, and the sensitivity and attention it requires, may provoke anxiety for the researcher; early in our projects, each of us felt we were not making interesting or worthwhile discoveries, yet each of us has come to trust this process and its inherent uncertainty. On a related note, uncertainty often proves worrisome for the Institutional Review Boards (IRBs) tasked with ensuring that research is appropriate and ethical. Research plans that accommodate the uncertainty of situations clash with the specificity and objectivity sought by IRBs and funding sources both in and outside the university setting. For example, the IRB withheld initial approval of Aldrich's application until she described in detail how she would diminish participants' potential embarrassment when discussing their unemployment situation. Not having prior knowledge of *who* her participants were, Aldrich found it difficult to outline the precise strategies she would use if and when those situations arose. Furthermore, both Bailliard and Aldrich submitted IRB modifications several times as their research opened new avenues for inquiry and understanding. IRB oversight, though necessary and important, can complicate ethnographic pursuits and must be carefully negotiated, sometimes with review committees that are unfamiliar with ethnography.

The art of designing ethnography lies in a researcher's ability to create a *road map* with the specificity to satisfy IRB and funding criteria while also integrating sufficient flexibility to respond to unanticipated discoveries. These road maps are consistent with Dewey's notion of ends-in-view—the destination is a little unclear, the path has many possible routes, but there is a generalized direction and goal in mind. Though personally and institutionally challenging, it is necessary to remain open to changes in research plans that arise as the investigator becomes increasingly immersed in the research situation.

13.2.1 The Natural Fit of Ethnography and a Transactional Perspective

To a large extent, ethnography is atheoretical, and indeed as a method has been used within a number of theoretical frameworks. However, transactionalism and ethnography share many primary principles. Ethnography can ground the use of broad and flexible research plans consistent with a transactional theory of knowledge as an ever-unfinished outgrowth of experiential inquiry. The transactional perspective suggests that multifactorial influences on a situation are difficult to anticipate and thus defining the scope of inquiry with predetermined constructs or variables may limit what might be discovered. Similarly, when ethnographers enter the study of a situation with a general and broad focus, they often emerge with unanticipated findings that sprout directly from experience. For example, Dickie realized that women who were making crafts at home to sell in seasonal and weekend markets did not have young children, but over time her field notes contained many instances of these women providing support activities for extended families. This led to insight about the nature of households in the suburban areas she studied (Dickie 1998). Although all of the participants appeared to be living in nuclear households, in fact they were part of networks of kin who relied upon each other for multiple types of services such as dog sitting, caring for elders, childcare, and hosting holiday gatherings.

Consistent with the use of multiple tools for data collection in ethnography, the transactional perspective gives significance to the different types of knowledge in experience (Johnson and Onwuegbuzie 2004). The multiple relationships that constitute experience change with the situation, and certain relationships may, at times, be more salient than others (Aldrich 2008). Just as particular research methods must be matched with the research question, so must different tools accommodate the variety of relationships found in experience, including human relationships with objects and places. In the next sections, we will discuss implications of the alignment between ethnographic and transactional principles on the focus of research and relationships that enter into the research situation. Ultimately, we argue that ethnography itself can be understood as transaction: a transactional way of studying a situation.

13.2.2 Focus of Research/Scope of Inquiry

Earlier, we discussed the ethnographic tradition of broadly defining research plans in order to allow for unexpected encounters in experience. We also argued that the transactional view of uncertainty and knowledge serves as a sound theoretical basis for flexible and broad research plans. While a narrow scope of inquiry may impede the discovery of factors that are critical to a situation, a scope too broad can be risky. Echoing a concern by Garrison (2001), Dickie et al. (2006) acknowledged that unclear situational boundaries are a problematic feature of transactionalism (see Chap. 12). Likewise, ethnography has the potential to encompass too many details in pursuit of wholeness or, conversely, looking too broadly to be able to see the particular. The challenge of ethnography is to capture the situation "as a knowable, fully-probed micro-world with reference to an encompassing macro-world" (Marcus 1998, p. 33). Instead of complicating this enterprise, transactionalism acknowledges the process of inquiry itself as a vehicle for determining the boundaries of research by making indeterminate experience more determinate (Hickman 1998), so long as those boundaries do not create dualisms that mask the complexities of experience (Garrison and Watson 2005; Pappas 2008).

As an example of how the ethnographic process itself moves toward a determinate situation, Aldrich's study of discouraged workers focused on the experiences of five people in rural North Carolina. Concerned with what influenced their occupations, Aldrich cast a wide net to understand the situations through which they engaged in occupation. Beginning with an expansive set of research questions addressing "what discouraged workers *do*," Aldrich refined her study throughout the research process as situational elements directed her inquiry toward more specific questions; in turn, she discovered the extent of interconnection joining these elements. By beginning with a focused but flexible inquiry, Aldrich was able to delve deeply into the many factors that influenced the occupations of these particular discouraged workers. This allowed her to consider wider issues related to money, social services, and transportation, and while her study was ostensibly concerned about occupational engagement, it also became about the cultural values and moral judgments associated with particular occupations in consultants' daily lives. In a similar vein, Bailliard's broad approach to studying the occupational transformations of Latino immigrants allowed him to consider how political rhetoric in states over 1,500 miles from the study situation had a major impact on the occupations of Latinos in North Carolina. Likewise, Dickie (2003, 2010) discovered the importance of historical events (e.g., the US bicentennial), invention of tools (e.g., the rotary cutter), and the Internet (e.g., multiple quilting websites and on-line groups) as she interacted with quilt making communities across North Carolina.

Put simply, our inquiries were focused on situations of experience, and the process of exploring those situations through ethnography led to considerations that defined the nature and boundaries of those situations. Delimiting the focus of ethnographic research via a transactional perspective allowed us to see our inquiries in the whole context of complex experiences. Ethnographic researchers know that their slice of experience is rich with relationships of many sorts, giving it a complexity that is manageable in light of the boundaries created by researchers for analytical purposes. It is to those relationships that we now turn.

13.3 The Importance of Relationships

Ethnographers aim to explore culture through experiencing a situation with people. People are not usually conscious of the culture to which they belong; rather, awareness happens when people encounter cultural differences (Agar 2002). Thus, culture *happens* to the ethnographer through experiencing situational relationships with which they are unfamiliar. Of all situational relationships, the one of researcher and study participant(s) is most often discussed in the literature. Each person plays different roles in establishing and influencing relationships that constitute the situation. However, ethnographic understandings are not the sole possession of the researcher, but are a co-created product of the time spent with study participants. We will also discuss the nature of relationships of non-human transactional elements, emphasizing that ethnographic researchers and participants discover culture and knowledge through non-human situational elements as much as human ones.

13.3.1 Role of the Researcher

Because ethnography depends on the researcher's relationships with participants in shared activities, conversations, and experiences, the personal characteristics and interests of the researcher directly affect what information is conveyed, gathered, and prioritized. The nature of these relationships shapes what is experienced and collected as data in a situation. Ethnography is a form of "witnessing," and the research process imparts responsibility on the researcher to be faithful to the happenings and relationships that he or she experienced (Behar 1996). But because "we cannot represent others in any other terms but our own" (Van Maanen 1988), ethnographic researchers must recognize and value their places and perspectives in the research situation. Researchers are active participants in their studies with an influence on the situations and what is discovered. A researcher's very act of noticing and labeling an observation as important "influences the course of the observed event as radically as "inspection" influences ("disturbs") the behavior of an electron" (Devereux, as cited in Behar 1996). Likewise, Wolcott (1995) argued that decisions to collect particular information as data are themselves an early analytical step in the research process.

As a part of the situation being studied, the researcher's actions affect subsequent actions of participants. Therefore, the researcher and participant co-create the data such that their *relationship* is part of the study situation. It is not only natural but crucial that this relationship enters into analyses of research data. For example, Aldrich formed different relationships with each of her participants. She felt underdressed and yet culturally similar to a woman who wore a business suit to each research encounter, and worlds apart from a young man whose brief life already contained more violence and money than Aldrich had ever seen herself. When crafting her study narrative, Aldrich made certain to include elements of these relationships and her position, not only to give ethnographic depth to her communications but also to acknowledge her presence in the situations she described. Bailliard's personal history also entered into his relationships with Latino consultants. As an ethnic and cultural outsider in the study situation, at times he was greeted with significant hesitation and fear. For example, one of Bailliard's consultants was an undocumented immigrant who admitted that his wife had pleaded for him not to meet Bailliard because she feared that her husband risked detention and deportation. The woman called her husband several times during the interview to verify that he was safe. To be viewed with such suspicion was itself a revelation of the anxieties and stress experienced by Bailliard's study participants. As an alternative example of his position and its effect on the research situation, Bailliard's fluency with Spanish made him an insider in some respects because it enabled him to communicate with consultants in their primary language. Moreover, Bailliard's fluency provided insight about language differences among Spanish speakers of different nationalities. The impact of these variations was significant to study participants and was experienced by Bailliard himself.

13.3.2 Role of the Study Participant

The co-creation of knowledge in ethnographic work implies an active role of study participants in shaping the final product. Participants lead the ethnographer through the situation by suggesting avenues of inquiry or potential networking with additional participants. Viewed this way, consultants are expert guides who contribute far more than data to be analyzed; they influence *what* and *how* research data are collected. The skilled ethnographer confers with consultants in a manner that acknowledges their expertise in understanding their situation. Indeed, some ethnographers have capitalized on this understanding to involve consultants in written products of the research (e.g., Aldrich and Callanan 2011). The co-constructed product is considered a holistic representation of a situation that includes both ethnographer and consultant.

The active role of participants in collaborative ethnography reflects a transactional perspective on the relationships comprising the situation. Consultants influence the direction of inquiry, analyses, and the way the ethnographer relates to the study situation. For example, extensive interaction with consultants helped Aldrich shift her methods away from the use of focus groups toward a more naturalistic ethnographic approach (Aldrich and Callanan 2011). In Bailliard's study, his consultants' references to specific legal issues prompted him to shift his document reviews beyond local media to incorporate legal texts at the state and federal levels. In all of our studies, consultants recommended other individuals who should be interviewed, and in doing so revealed what they thought should be attended to in the research. Dickie even had the experience of quilters telling her what she needed to tell the rest of the world about what they did.

As a transactional relationship, both participants/consultants and the ethnographer are changed by transactions during the study. Conversations and interviews can prompt novel reflections about issues or reframe participants' perceptions of past events, in both positive and negative ways. For example, after attending a community event, Bailliard received a call from a consultant thanking him for an interview that took place months before. His consultant explained that the interview had prompted him to reconsider and reframe his immigration in a manner that he found enlightening and reassuring. In this case, the transactions joining researcher and consultant provoked a change in the consultant's conceptualization of his past experiences and self. This is just one example of why an ethnographer must be attentive to the power and persisting effect of research based transactions. The power of transactional relationships joining researcher and consultant illustrate the co-creative nature of ethnographies. As a shared inquiry, the consultant does more than affect what the ethnographer studies, directly influencing how the researcher relates to the situation itself. Indeed, consultants can facilitate personal changes in the ethnographer beyond the focus of the study itself. For instance, Bailliard's transactions with consultants encouraged him to reconsider his own immigration, highlighting the impact of certain experiences in his personal development. These personal changes affected Bailliard's reflections on the study, including subsequent data collection, inferences, and analyses. As an illustration of the power of consultants, Bailliard was forever transformed by the transactional relationships in his study.

In a similar way, Dickie joined with quilt makers in sorting through fabric at a seminar and began to acquire her own "stash" of fabric. This experience led her to examine the phenomenon of fabric accumulation, and to begin to understand the significance of a storehouse of raw materials for people engaging in craftwork, hobbies and leisure pastimes. What began as a study of an unfamiliar occupation has also led to her becoming a quilt maker, which has, in turn, led to an embodied understanding both of the process of being a quilt maker and of the quilts themselves.

Although these two examples highlight positive outcomes from the transactional nature of ethnography, the potential for doing harm is equally real and unpredictable. Because ethnographic relationships between researcher and consultant develop over long periods of time, the individuals involved may encounter damaging study situations. For instance, while the researcher-consultant relationship can be a source of profound and unexpected understandings, a deep attachment may encourage the researcher to avoid unfavorable representations of the consultant in the final ethnographic product. Similarly, the consultant may also have expectations about how he or she should be represented, especially when his or her relationship with the researcher yielded sensitive or important revelations. This, in turn, can complicate representations of the study situation and leave both the researcher and the consultant open to negative post-study feelings. For instance, in her study of discouraged workers, Aldrich developed a close relationship with the director of a community outreach organization. Although this provided her with essential connections, it also challenged her ability to protect her participants' anonymity and forced her to negotiate politically charged issues surrounding the outreach organization, causing some discomfort for Aldrich and her consultant. The depth of interpersonal relationships forged during ethnographic encounters transforms researchers, consultants, and the study situation they co-create. The final ethnographic product, as a representation of those encounters, is a co-creation between researchers and consultants emerging through a prolonged transactional relationship.

13.3.3 Beyond Interpersonal Elements of Relational Situations

Ethnography encourages consideration of the many relationships of a situation: place, objects, environmental features, traditions, history, politics, culture, economics, and so forth. For example, Dickie found that the rotary cutter, invented by a Japanese engineer in the 1980s, played an important role in the revival and ongoing interest in quilt making, the techniques people use to make quilts, and creation of new designs that are only possible with the tool. Bailliard's study location had a history of White supremacy activities that were still palpable in the community, as expressed by one of Bailliard's consultants who described feelings of alienation and fear in response to a Ku Klux Klan sign she noticed upon moving to the area in 2006. In addition, post 9/11 political rhetoric in the United States often links terrorism and immigration, something consultants cited as a constant backdrop to their everyday experience. Aldrich's study of discouraged workers occurred in a town that lost most of its manufacturing activity to off-shore locales over an extended time, just as northern states lost that activity to the South a century earlier. Thus the unemployment the town was experiencing was linked to historical labor patterns in a capitalist system. In each of these studies, the factors that influenced occupations stretched across time into present situations.

Transactionalism emphasizes the importance of all relationships in a situation and does not prioritize one over the other, though some may be more relevant than others depending on the focus of the researcher. For instance Bailliard's consultants frequently mentioned the sensory qualities of past transactions with their places of origin. Their relationship with these qualities continued to play an important part in their everyday experiences in the form of memories of smells, sights, sounds, and physical characteristics of those places. These memories framed experiences in the present by highlighting differences and often engendering a sense of what people had lost as a result of their move.

13.4 Conclusion

Ethnographic enterprises focus on understanding problematic situations by emphasizing the relationships of their constitutive elements. Thus, various aspects of ethnographic studies of occupation can be analyzed as transactions in their own right. For example, interviews are a transactional experience in that the researcher and participant co-create the knowledge gleaned from the interview situation. The researcher's body language and verbal responses and prompts for elaboration prioritize types of information or categories of conversation. The participant, by responding to the researcher, alters what would have been said in the absence of that response, but in turn suggests further directions in the questioning. Ethnographic interviews are commonly semi-structured, leaving space for the development of ideas, exploration of new topics, and discovery of information that might help resolve the problematic situation but that the researcher may not have anticipated prior to the study. Furthermore, each interview provides the researcher with feedback regarding the utility and effectiveness of the interview process that influences the course of further interviews.

The transactional perspective on occupation suggests focusing on occupation as the *relational glue* (Cutchin et al. 2008) of a situation; at the same time, occupations and situations should be studied holistically rather than circumscribing a predetermined set of phenomena. Ethnography provides a methodology appropriate to such study. Such an approach calls for being with those engaged in occupation, participating in the occupation, and being open to all of the elements of that occupation. It calls for looking beyond occupation as an individual endeavor in order to understand the myriad factors that are part of occupational situations.

Looking at occupation as part of situations challenges us to think about the boundaries we create as we delimit and define our studies. Are these boundaries theoretically sound as well as practical? Is the method an appropriate fit for the study aims? Does the method match one's epistemological stance? What types of assumptions are made during our methodological choices? What role is a researcher playing during data collection and analysis? How does the targeted audience for the research impact what is studied, how the study is designed, what are identified as data, and how findings are framed? A careful and critical reflection on such questions throughout the research process helps to ensure that methods are rigorous, transparent, and honest.

Applying a transactional perspective to ethnographic inquiry does engender a challenge for researchers in academia. The necessary plasticity and emergent design (Schwandt 2007) in ethnography may be difficult to justify to institutional review boards and funding sources that are more familiar with detailed plans for data collection and analysis. Herein lies the art of designing a transactional ethnography. The researcher must develop a methodological road map that is open to the emergent and uncertain nature of situations while sufficiently detailed to satisfy IRB and funding requirements. The potential for ethnographic work from a transactional perspective to clarify many mysteries of occupation for researchers makes this a worthy endeavor.

References

Agar, M. H. (1980). *The professional stranger: An informal introduction the ethnography*. San Diego: Academic.

Agar, M. H. (2002). *Language shock: Understanding the culture of conversation*. New York: HarperCollins.

Aldrich, R. (2008). From complexity theory to transactionalism: Moving occupational science forward in theorizing the complexities of behavior. *Journal of Occupational Science, 15*(3), 147–156.

Aldrich, R. (2011). *Discouraged workers' daily occupations: Exploring complex transactions in the experience of unemployment*. Dissertation, University of North Carolina at Chapel Hill.

Aldrich, R., & Callanan, Y. (2011). "We disappear off the planet": Insights about studying discouraged workers. *Journal of Occupational Science, 18*, 153–166.

Bailliard, A. (2011). *An ethnographic exploration of Latino Immigration to Smalltown, NC: Transformations in El Nuevo South*. Dissertation, University of North Carolina at Chapel Hill.

Behar, R. (1996). *The vulnerable observer: Anthropology that breaks your heart*. Boston: Beacon.

Cutchin, M. P., Aldrich, R. M., Bailliard, A. L., & Coppola, S. (2008). Action theories for occupational science: The contributions of Dewey and Bourdieu. *Journal of Occupational Science, 15*(3), 157–165.

Dewey, J. (2000). *Experience and nature*. New York: Dover (Original work published in 1925).

Dewey, J. (2005). *The quest for certainty: A study of the relation between knowledge and action*. Whitefish: Kessinger (Original work published in 1929).

Dickie, V. (1998). Households, multiple livelihoods, and the informal economy: A study of American crafters. *Scandinavian Journal of Occupational Therapy, 5*, 109–118.

Dickie, V. (2003). The role of learning in quilt making. *Journal of Occupational Science, 10*, 120–129.

Dickie, V. (2010). Are occupations 'processes too complicated to explain'? What we can learn from trying. *Journal of Occupational Science, 17*, 195–203.

Dickie, V., Cutchin, M., & Humphry, R. (2006). Occupation as transactional experience: A critique of individualism in occupational science. *Journal of Occupational Science, 13*, 83–93.

Garrison, J. (2001). An introduction to Dewey's theory of functional "trans-action": An alternative paradigm for activity theory. *Mind, Culture, & Activity, 8*(4), 275–296.

Garrison, J., & Watson, B. W. (2005). Food from thought. *The Journal of Speculative Philosophy, 19*(4), 242–256.

Hickman, L. A. (1998). *Reading Dewey: Interpretations for a postmodern generation*. Bloomington: Indiana University Press.

Johnson, R. B., & Onwuegbuzie, A. J. (2004). Mixed methods research: A research paradigm whose time has come. *Educational Research, 33*(7), 14–26.

Lassiter, L. E. (2005). *The Chicago guide to collaborative ethnography*. Chicago: The University of Chicago Press.

Marcus, G. E. (1998). *Ethnography through thick and thin*. Princeton: Princeton University Press.

Marcus, G. E., & Fischer, M. M. J. (1986). *Anthropology as culture critique: An experimental moment in the human sciences*. Chicago: University of Chicago Press.

Pappas, G. F. (2008). *John Dewey's ethics: Democracy as experience*. Bloomington: Indiana University Press.

Schwandt, T. (2007). *Dictionary of qualitative inquiry* (3rd ed.). Los Angeles: Sage.

Van Maanen, J. (1988). *Tales of the field: On writing ethnography*. Chicago: The University of Chicago Press.

Whyte, W. F. (1984). *Learning from the field: A guide from experience*. Newbury Park: Sage.

Wolcott, H. F. (1995). *The art of fieldwork*. Walnut Creek: AltaMira Press.

Chapter 14
Critical Discourse Analysis: Adding a Political Dimension to Inquiry

Debbie Laliberte Rudman

14.1 Introduction

Building on arguments outlined by Laliberte Rudman and Huot (see Chap. 5) regarding the need for greater attention to ways relations of power impact on how situations are constructed and the possibilities for action shaped for various actors within situations, this chapter aims to demonstrate the utility of critical discourse analysis as a methodology to examine the situated nature of occupation. According to Stuhr (2003), critical work informed by Dewey requires the addition of a genealogical dimension; that is, a dimension that deconstructs the present situation to understand how it has come to be associated with particular values, assumptions, practices and interests (Kendall and Wickham 2003; Powell and Biggs 2003). In this chapter, it is argued that critical discourse analysis can enable occupational scientists to add a genealogical dimension to the action-focused orientation of transactional perspectives on occupation, as well as consider power when examining the transactional relations of people and contexts.

In addressing a "problem" related to occupation in the present, or within a situational whole, it is vital to consider how the problem (and related proposed solutions), has come to be defined, as well as who has had the power to define it and whose interests are best supported. Understanding how problems and solutions related to the occupations of individuals and collectives have come to be socially constructed and enacted requires considerations of the "political." Within this chapter, the term "political" is used broadly to refer to the ways power relations are embedded in the "truths" and taken-for-granted assumptions that circulate through society, differentially shaping possibilities for being and doing within situations.

D.L. Rudman (✉)
School of Occupational Therapy, and Occupational Science Field, Health and Rehabilitation Sciences Graduate Program, Western University, London, ON, Canada
e-mail: drudman@uwo.ca

M.P. Cutchin and V.A. Dickie (eds.), *Transactional Perspectives on Occupation*,
DOI 10.1007/978-94-007-4429-5_14, © Springer Science+Business Media B.V. 2013

Although consideration of this political dimension does not provide a lens to examine all aspects of a transactional whole, it does provide a means to bring to awareness a dimension of the transactional whole that is often neglected in the study of occupation (Kronenberg and Pollard 2006; Laliberte Rudman 2010).

While acknowledging that a diversity of definitions of discourse and approaches to its analysis exist, this chapter, predicated upon an interest in understanding how power relations influence possibilities for occupation, focuses on critical discourse analysis (CDA) as a broad methodology. Throughout the chapter, examples of CDA work relevant to the study of occupation are integrated to illustrate its potential contributions to occupational science. While the deconstructive act involved in CDA itself has been critiqued as insufficient to address social inequities and injustices (Sayer 2009), it is proposed that it can contribute to occupational science by fostering a critical stance towards the "way things are" and opening up spaces for different ways of researching, addressing and enacting occupation.

14.2 Defining Discourse from a Critical Location

The key focus of critical discourse analysis is discourse. This raises the question of how to define discourse. As noted by Cheek (2004) and Wodak and Meyer (2009), although discourse is a term that is frequently and increasingly used with academic and popular texts it is often misused and authors rarely specify how they are defining it within a specific study. Such specification is important as a diversity of definitions, which embed varying epistemological assumptions, exist; for example, discourse has been defined as: any instance of communication; a patterned way of thinking evident in communication; the language associated with a particular social field; a system of statements that constructs an object; or a set of social practices that involves meaning making (Ainsworth and Hardy 2004b; Cheek 2004; Fairclough 2009). This diversity of definitions is not necessarily problematic, but rather is reflective of the varying theoretical perspectives that attend to discourse and can be drawn upon to conduct discourse analysis (Wodak and Meyer 2009).

Consistent with a critical ontological and epistemological position (Guba and Lincoln 1994; Labonte et al. 2005), definitions of discourse taken up in critical discourse analysis emphasize the productive nature of language and the ways in which social reality is constructed through language within relations of power tied to political, economic, cultural, gender and other influences. Thus, discourses are not understood as just ways of textually, visually or verbally describing a phenomenon as "it really is," but rather as a form of social action that shapes how phenomenon, such as addictions, disability or gender, are understood within particular socio-historical contexts. Consistent with a critical perspective, Jager and Maier (2009) proposed that "discourses are not 'mere ideology'; they produce subjects and reality" (p. 37), and Hardy and Phillips (2004) stated that "discourses do not simply describe the social world; they constitute it by bringing certain phenomenon into being through the way in which they categorize and make sense of an otherwise meaningless reality"

(p. 301). For example, discourses addressing addictions mark out particular types of habits and dependencies as problematic within a specific socio-historical context, and construct particular types of "addicts" through marking out specific characteristics and behaviors as non-normative and unhealthy.

Furthermore, as a form of social action, discourses are conceptualized as having practical or material effects in the world (Hacking 1986; Ainsworth and Hardy 2004b). In other words, discourses have effects on how people and collectives act in the world. As Hardy and Phillips (2004) propose, discourses are imprinted on the world through the social practices that flow from the meanings shaped and circulated through discourses. For example, Cheek (2004) contends that the "truth" status accorded to biomedical discourses of health and illness in health care have shaped dominant, taken-for-granted ways that health practices occur and do not occur, including which health professionals are able to speak about particular issues and what activities are taken-for-granted as legitimate for health care professionals and clients. Another example is provided by Ainsworth and Hardy (2004b) whose work focuses on the subject positions, or identity possibilities, constructed through discourse, and the effects of such subject positions on individual experiences and social practices. These authors provide the example of the discursive shaping of the category of refugee, illustrating how this category influences how an individual attempting to migrate to a new country can and should present themselves to others and the work and other occupations they are allowed to engage in. In addition, the ways in which the category of refugee is discursively shaped within various types of policy, organizational and media texts shapes how other social actors (such as immigration officers, service providers) "process" and interact with individuals who are categorized as refugees and what services they view as ideal and possible for such individuals.

In relation to power, the dominant ways a phenomenon comes to be shaped within and through discourse bounds possibilities for thought and action in ways consistent with the aims and beliefs of social actors and groups with the means to contribute to the construction and circulation of dominant discourses (Ainsworth and Hardy 2004b; Cheek 2004; Hardy and Phillips 2004). Although multiple, competing discourses exist about a phenomenon within a context, particular dominant discourses, shaped in ways consistent with larger power relations, come to be taken-for-granted as "truths" by many individuals and collectives within that context, while other discourses are marginalized and excluded (Cheek 2004). Thus, discourses are produced within and constitute power relations by holding in place meanings associated with concepts, objects and subject positions, which distribute power and privileges among actors.

14.3 Linking Discourse and Occupation

Of particular relevance to occupational science, discourses are conceptualized as structuring spaces for individual and collective action (Foucault 1982; Hardy and Phillips 2004). Although discourses are not proposed to determine how people will think and act, due to their embeddedness within broader power relations, they often bound what come to be viewed as ideal, ethical, and "right" ways to act within particular contexts or situations (Hardy and Phillips 2004; Mumby 2004). Thus, discourses simultaneously promote opportunities and constraints on occupation, and critical examination of discourses at play in a situational whole can provide insight into the occupational possibilities shaped for various actors within situations.

For example, the reality of what aging is within a particular socio-historical context does not exist apart from language; rather, through discourse, ways of thinking about and understanding aging, as an individual and collective phenomenon, are shaped. In turn, such discursive constructions create both possibilities and boundaries for how individuals and collectives can talk about and act in relation to aging, including what occupations are seen as appropriate and healthy for aging individuals and how policy makers, researchers and clinicians act in relation to aging (Laws 1996; Katz 2000; Laliberte Rudman 2006). Specifically examining how cognitive impairment in later life has come to be discursively constructed, George and Whitehouse (2010) have argued that the current dominance of molecular-reductionist and neuropsychological discourses of cognitive impairment and dementia with aging shape understandings of the aging brain as a disease that is to be overcome through medical curative advances. In turn, these dominant discourses often serve "to limit the potential of aging persons to contribute to society in the last stages of their lives by isolating them, and thus depriving them of the benefits of social participation and precluding the possibility that they might help build social capital through their efforts" (p. 343). At other levels, dominant discourses on cognitive impairment promote a focus on curative interventions and biomedical research, as well as contribute to a relative neglect of care-based interventions or research on the everyday experience and negotiation of cognitive impairment and dementia.

Thinking about the links between discourse and occupation thus raises questions related to the subtle ways discourses come to influence how individuals and collectives think about what they themselves, and others, can and should do in their occupational lives. It also highlights questions related to how social policies, health care practices and other types of social practices are framed within particular discursive constructions (Laliberte Rudman 2006, 2010). Placing these considerations within the larger political context in which power relations influence how discourses are shaped, who is involved in producing and circulating discourses, and what discourses come to be taken-for-granted as "truths," provides a way to explicitly attend to a political dimension in understanding occupation as a transactional whole and enact the critical dimensions of Dewey's work.

14.4 Key Elements of Critical Discourse Analysis

Within this chapter, the term critical discourse analysis (CDA) is used to encompass work which "involves the use of discourse analytic techniques, combined with a critical perspective, to interrogate social phenomena" (Ainsworth and Hardy 2004a, p. 236).

CDA is constituted by a diversity of methodological approaches that go beyond analysis of linguistic structure and content of discourse to examine its productive effects and the ways in which it relates to broader power relations (Ainsworth and Hardy 2004b; Cheek 2004; Grant et al. 2004). Thus, CDA is neither a singular methodology nor a fixed method. Rather, each methodological approach to CDA is grounded within a theoretical framework regarding the nature of discourse and the relationships between discourse, knowledge, and power (Potter and Wetherell 1987; Wodak and Meyer 2009). Thus, in this section, a detailed description of how to do CDA is not provided, but rather key features and principles that characterize and tie together varying approaches to CDA are outlined and illustrated.

In essence, most of the key features and principles that characterize CDA are associated with its location within a critical social paradigm and its use of critical social theory. While critical social theory itself encompasses a range of perspectives, theories identified as critical share a concern with issues of power and justice and attend to how injustices are socially shaped, perpetuated and enacted (Kincheloe and McLaren 2005; Carpenter and Suto 2008; Fairclough 2009; Sayer 2009). The use of critical social theory has numerous implications for how CDA studies are carried out, ranging from the types of questions asked to the approaches to analysis used. As summarized by van Dijk (2009),

> The critical approach of CDS [critical discourse studies] characterizes scholars rather than their methods: CDS scholars are socio-politically committed to social equality and justice. They also show this in their scientific research, for instance by the formulation of their specific goals, the selection and construction of theories, the use and development of methods of analysis and especially in the application of such research in the study of important social problems and political issues (p. 63).

More specifically, a variety of critical social theorists whose work addresses the productive power of language in the construction of reality, such as Foucault, Bourdieu, Giddens, Gramsci, Marx, Derrida, Habermas, have been taken up to inform CDA (Ainsworth and Hardy 2004b; Grant et al. 2004; Mumby 2004; Wodak and Meyer 2009). As these theorists provide differing conceptualizations regarding the role of language, as well as the social and political dynamics of power, it is essential that the theoretical underpinnings taken up in a particular CDA study are transparent (Cheek 2004; Wodak and Meyer 2009). For example, Smith (2007) drawing upon Fairclough's approach to CDA, informed by neo-Marxist scholars as well as Bourdieu and Foucault, outlined an approach involving three levels of discourse analysis: sociocultural practice, discourse practice, and text analysis. Tuen van Dijk (2009) has proposed a sociocognitive approach to CDA which also involves a focus on social dimensions of discourse, but adds analytical dimensions that attend to mental representations and cognitive processes of language users as they produce and interact with discourse. Thus, there is no one right way to do CDA, but it is key in relation to ensuring rigor and quality that it is theoretically informed by critically-based work (Parker 1992; Wodak and Meyer 2009).

CDA is often classified as a qualitative methodology, in that it focuses on language and looks at how and what meanings are constructed through language. However, as CDA is theoretically framed, it does not employ a purely inductive approach to analysis. In disciplines in which inductive analysis has often been marked out as an essential defining feature of qualitative work, the lack of an inductive, open-ended approach to analysis in CDA may be critiqued as "biased" or as leading to researchers only reading what they want to find within texts (Smith 2007). However, within various forms of qualitative research informed by critical social theory, the possibility of a pure inductive approach to analysis from "no-where" is critiqued, as it is assumed that a researcher always approaches a text with particular disciplinary, theoretical and other understandings (Kincheloe and McLaren 2005; Carpenter and Suto 2008). Thus, it is assumed that analysis is always theoretically informed, and it is acknowledged that the particular theoretical perspectives employed will lead to a particular reading of a text, rather than to a singular authoritative reading. This acknowledgement of the perspective-based nature of analysis also underlies the need for transparency in CDA:

> Naming oneself 'critical' only implies specific ethical standards: an intention to make their position, research interests and values explicit and their criteria as transparent as possible, without feeling the need to apologize for the critical stance of their work (Wodak and Meyer 2009, p. 7).

Rather than seeing theory as a source of bias, it is seen as enhancing the depth of analysis and as enabling the analyst to connect analysis and interpretation to broader social issues and concerns (Lather 2006; Frank and Polkinghorne 2010). Thus, the analysis approach shifts in CDA from inductive reasoning to abductive reasoning, in which there is constant back and forth between theory and data (Wodak and Meyer 2009).

CDA involves taking on a suspicious or questioning stance regarding the forms of knowledge and realities shaped through discourse, starting with an assumption that "any particular version of reality is not natural or inevitable and, in fact, may serve the political aims of specific interest groups" (Ainsworth and Hardy 2004a, p. 237). Following from such a critical stance towards discourse, CDA focuses on problematizing taken-for-granted aspects of reality and social practices that are viewed as producing, sustaining or reproducing social domination or privilege of one group over another and as leading to situations of injustice, marginalization, exclusion and inequity (Fairclough 2009; van Dijk 2009; Wodak and Meyer 2009). Such problematization, in turn, requires that CDA studies attend to the dynamics of social relations of power in the production and circulation of discourses within specific historical, political, cultural, economic and social contexts (Ainsworth and Hardy 2004b; Cheek 2004; Jager and Maier 2009). Potential foci of analysis can include the ways in which power is exercised by producing and sustaining particular discourses that articulate versions of the "ways things are," that link the desires and actions of actors to broader political interests, and that make socially constructed structures and practices appear as neutral and objective (Hardy and Phillips 2004).

For example, McGrath (2009), drawing primarily on Fairclough's methodological approach to CDA, conceptualized local government sport and recreation plans addressing people with disabilities "as a site of knowledge production, and reproduction" (p. 483) which, although framed as objective and non-discriminatory, embed and sustain "ideological assumptions that enable particular positions to dominate over other views" (p. 483). McGrath's analysis of 31 government authorities' sports and recreation plans revealed the ways in which people with disabilities were constructed within the documents as a homogenous group characterized by physical impairments and as in need of help, as well as how the "problem" of provision of recreation and sport for people with disabilities was framed in ways that led to a narrow focus on ensuring accessibility and suitability of the built environment. McGrath raised concerns regarding how "this homogenizing of people with disabilities as physically immobile disenfranchises many other impaired groups" (p. 492) in ways that those with hearing, vision, intellectual or mental illnesses of disabilities remain hidden and unheard and their opportunities for sport and recreation are not addressed. McGrath connected this narrow definition of the problem of access to persons with disabilities to sport and recreation, as well as the proposed solutions, to broader political changes in Australia, including the increasing use of a laissez-faire governance strategy, the rise of a public choice ideology, and the continued dominance of a medical model view of dependency and disability.

Another key feature of CDA is that it involves conceptualizing and analyzing discourses as social practices (Ainsworth and Hardy 2004a; Mumby 2004). Thus, it is vital for CDA to go beyond what a particular text says or does not say, and to consider what forms of knowledge are shaped through language and how such forms are enacted and embodied in everyday practices of individuals and collectives (Mumby 2004). For example, in a CDA study informed by Foucauldian theory and the methodological work of Cheek, MacEachen et al. (2008) problematized taken-for-granted understandings of the positivity of flexible work and work flexibility. These authors used a CDA approach to analyze in-depth interviews conducted with a sample of 30 individuals who were primarily in management positions in computer software firms. MacEachen et al. found that these managers drew upon dominant discourses of flexible work and work flexibility to promote its inherent goodness and benefits, but simultaneously described enacting these discourses in workplace management practices that promoted and sustained an intense, inescapable work life that was controlled by industry interests in sustaining productivity and competitive advantage in a global economy. These authors pointed to the types of workers excluded from this discourse, such as persons with disabilities and women with childrearing responsibilities, as well as the ways in which this discourse obscures work-related health problems by characterizing worker health as a matter of individual resilience. As such, this study questioned taken-for-granted beliefs regarding the benefits of workplace flexibility and whose interests it serves, pointing to ways flexible work discourses created "conditions and possibility for unlimited work hours" (p. 1023) and blurred the boundaries between home and work.

Drawing on Bourdieu and conducting a CDA study, Lee and MacDonald (2010) also examined links between dominant discourses and how people act in everyday life, specifically investigating how the healthism discourse within the sport and physical activity field was taken up by young, rural Australian women. The healthism discourse was described as a dominant discourse that conveys a central message that health can be achieved through individual effort and disciplined activity aimed at regulating body size and shape. Although Lee and MacDonald found instances when young women resisted the healthism discourse, they concluded that this discourse functioned as a moral imperative drawn upon by the women to judge their own bodies and to shape their approaches to health and fitness. These authors highlighted the marginalizing effects of the healthism discourses for young, rural women who often have a lack of formal exercise options in their environments, whose participation in some forms of exercise and farm labor is at odds with their gendered habitus, and whose participation in forms of physical activity other than exercise is unacknowledged.

Overall, CDA provides a methodological approach to examine the ways relations of power impact on how situations are constructed, including the possibilities for action shaped for various actors within situations. CDA links the linguistic to the social context (Mumby 2004; Smith 2007), by paying close attention to the ways in which discourses have been constructed and circulated through texts in ways that are embedded within existing social relations and function in "organizing social institutions or in exercising power" (Wodak and Meyer 2009, p. 7). CDA involves analyzing texts in relation to the conditions of possibility that are created for what can be said, thought and done by whom, to whom and in what contexts (Grant et al. 2004). Moreover, it seeks to connect such conditions of possibility to interests, assumptions and ways of thinking that align with broader relations of power operating within particular sociohistorical contexts.

For example, in my analysis of contemporary productive aging discourses as shaped and circulated within Canadian newspapers, the possibilities for work constructed as ideal for later life workers were examined (Laliberte Rudman and Molke 2009). Drawing on a governmentality perspective, productive aging discourses were conceptualized as a "modality of government that sets boundaries on what come to be seen as ethical, responsible, and ideal ways to be and do in later life, and what ways of aging, in turn, are supported through policies and programs" (p. 380). In this analysis, the ways in which productive aging discourses narrowly equate productivity with work were highlighted. Concerns regarding how this emphasis involved the simultaneous exclusion and devaluing of other forms of productive occupation, such as caregiving, as well as obscured the need for policies and programs to support a diversity of forms of productive occupations in later life, were raised. Moreover, this analysis attended to the ways in which particular outcomes were connected up with work in later life, such as age defiance, flexibility, and social connectedness, while other types of outcomes, particularly financial remuneration and job stability, were downplayed. The ways in which these outcomes align with business interests in creating a surplus, low-paid workforce of aging workers was critically considered, as well as the differential resources available to aging individuals to choose to work or not in later life. Another example of how this CDA study linked discursive emphases with broader power relations was in highlighting how a common discursive feature of the texts involved framing social problems, such as poverty, ageism, and later life unemployment, as personal risks and challenges to be overcome through responsible action aimed at altering one's self or one's work. This "individualizing of the social" was analytically connected to the rise of neoliberal approaches to governing which negate or minimize the role of state via shifting responsibility for personal and societal security and well-being to individuals.

A final key characteristic of CDA studies is a shared critical intent to enhance awareness of the constructed nature of phenomenon and the inequities that are shaped and promoted through particular constructions (Wodak and Meyer 2009). Parallel to the intent of Dewey's work to enhance the human condition, CDA aims to foster transformation based on the assumption that "…as soon as one can no longer think things as one formerly thought them, transformation becomes both very urgent, very difficult and quite possible" (Foucault 1988, p. 156). In other words, showing how discourses shape conditions of possibility that promote inequities creates the possibility for discursive and practical change (Cheek 2004; Jager and Maier 2009).

14.5 The Process of Doing CDA

Both Cheek (2004) and Smith (2007) have critiqued the ways in which CDA has been enacted in health-related research, pointing to how there is frequently a lack of attention to how discourse is conceptualized and a lack of articulation of the theoretical frameworks informing analysis and interpretation. Within the diversity of approaches to CDA, several authors have attempted to map out processes for doing CDA (see, for example, Kendall and Wickham 2003; Fairclough 2009; Jager and Maier 2009). Although such processes can be helpful guiding frameworks, it is essential that they are not used as 'recipes' that lead one to conduct CDA as a "thoughtless empirical technique" (Parker 1992, p. 122). Rather, it is crucial that decisions about how methods are designed and enacted in a CDA study are coherent with one's theoretical framework, research questions, substantive topic and the type of text or texts being analyzed (Smith 2007; Wodak and Meyer 2009). Thus, rather than outline "the" process for doing CDA, this section points to some key starting considerations and addresses deconstruction as a central aspect of the CDA process.

CDA studies involve a critical reading of texts to uncover the discourses that are drawn upon to produce and sustain taken-for-granted ways of understanding and acting in relation to a particular phenomenon. It is important to consider what problem is to be focused on within a CDA study, what theoretical underpinnings will be drawn upon, and what types of texts are relevant to include. Consistent with the key characteristics and principles of CDA noted above, the problem that is the focus of a CDA study should align with an interest in uncovering how taken-for-granted ways of understanding and acting in relation to a particular social issue or phenomenon create inequities and injustices. The theoretical framework or frameworks selected should be consistent with a critical social paradigm, and provide a means to conceptualize the inter-relationships between language, knowledge and power. A variety of types of texts are possible including those that pre-exist the research and those created within the process of research, such as newspaper articles, brochures, visual images, policy documents, government or organizational reports, advertisements, or transcribed interviews. The selection of texts for any particular study should suit the research problem and the theoretical framework, and should enable the researcher to generate a corpus of texts that allows for in-depth consideration of the discourses being drawn upon, shaped and circulated (Cheek 2004; Jager and Maier 2009).

CDA can involve a variety of forms of textual analysis, and can involve attending to a variety of features of texts, such as the forms of argumentation used, the metaphors and idioms drawn upon, and the types of knowledge and experts drawn upon (Wodak and Meyer 2009). Across various forms of CDA, a process of deconstruction is often a central feature of the analysis process. Deconstruction describes the ways an analyst seeks to break apart texts to "render problematic the assumptions, tenets and fabric of everyday life" (Ballinger and Cheek 2006, p. 216) and thereby "'defamiliarize' and 'de-naturalize' taken for granted assumptions about social reality" (Ainsworth and Hardy 2004a, p. 238). The process of deconstruction involves interrogating texts to break them apart in ways that uncover the assumptions that circulate within and through them (Cheek 2004). It is these assumptions that enable the analyst to question the taken-for-granted nature of discourses and to connect discourses to the broader social, cultural, political and historical context. Moreover, it is essential to deconstruct the texts, getting beyond the stories they seek to construct, in order to re-construct the discursive patterns that exist within texts and across a body of texts.

In my experience, the most challenging aspect of doing CDA is adopting an analytical attitude in which one continually attempts to suspend one's belief in the taken-for-granted, as one is always embedded within the discourses one is seeking to question and deconstruct. This act of attempting to step outside the discourses within which the researcher exists, which is central to the process of deconstruction, demands continual self-reflexivity and self-questioning of one's assumptions, beliefs and values (Finlay 2002; Cheek 2004). For example, contemporary texts addressing retirement planning and living often embed an assumption that is it is inherently good to be active in later life, connecting staying active to individual and societal benefits. This assumption fits well within the constellation of disciplinary influences that have shaped me as an occupational therapist and scientist; indeed, why should I question this assumption given that I am part of a profession and discipline which is dedicated to understanding and promoting the health and societal benefits of occupation? However, rather than take this apparent commensurability in assumptions at face value, what CDA has challenged me to do is to deconstruct how this assumption is being shaped within contemporary discourses pertaining to aging and retirement. This involves engaging with texts using questions such as: what types of occupational engagement are promoted as "good," possible and ideal, and which are shaped as "bad," not possible, and non-ideal?; who is given the authority to decide what occupations are appropriate for whom?; what resources are required to engage in idealized occupations?; what types of outcomes are constructed as ideals and desires to be worked towards through occupation?; who is able and not able to engage in idealized occupations?; and, how do idealized outcomes connect up with broader political systems of thought?

14.6 Conclusion

As stressed throughout this chapter, there are multiple ways CDA studies can be conceptualized and enacted within occupational science. As a broad methodological approach, CDA can be taken up within occupational science to further understanding of the "politics" of occupation; that is, how possibilities for occupation are differentially created within situations through the shaping and circulation of "truths" or taken-for-granted assumptions that themselves are shaped within power relations. Through fostering a critical stance about the taken-for-granted assumptions regarding what occupations are ideal, possible and healthy for whom within particular contexts, CDA can contribute to work based in a transactional perspective by raising awareness of how possibilities for action are constructed within a particular situation and the ways in which such possibilities are constructed differentially for varying actors.

As shown in the examples integrated within this chapter, CDA studies address not only how discourses appear within texts, but also how such discourses are taken up, negotiated and enacted in everyday practices and occupations. As such, CDA provides a methodological approach that can provide insight into the relational dynamics between contextual elements and people in situations, thereby contributing to work based in transactional perspectives (Cutchin and Dickie 2012). Moreover, CDA provides a means to shift the study of the "meaning" of occupation from an individualistic phenomenon, to an approach that considers how meanings associated with occupation are shaped by interactions between people within contexts (Chap. 4 by Reed and Hocking, this volume).

References

Ainsworth, S., & Hardy, C. (2004a). Critical discourse analysis and identity: Why bother? *Critical Discourse Studies, 1*(2), 225–259.

Ainsworth, S., & Hardy, C. (2004b). Discourse and identities. In D. Grant, C. Hardy, C. Oswick, & L. Putnam (Eds.), *The Sage handbook of organizational discourse* (pp. 153–174). Thousand Oaks: Sage.

Ballinger, C., & Cheek, J. (2006). Discourse analysis in action: The construction of risk in a community day hospital. In L. Finlay & C. Ballinger (Eds.), *Qualitative research for allied health professionals: Challenging choices* (pp. 200–217). Chichester: Wiley.

Carpenter, C., & Suto, M. (2008). *Qualitative research for occupational and physical therapists: A practical guide*. Oxford: Blackwell Publishing.

Cheek, J. (2004). At the margins? Discourse analysis and qualitative research. *Qualitative Health Research, 14*, 1140–1150.

Cutchin, M. P., & Dickie, V. A. (2012). Transactionalism: Occupational science and the pragmatic attitude. In G. Whiteford & C. Hocking (Eds.), *Critical perspectives on occupational science: Society, inclusion, participation* (pp. 23–37). London: Wiley.

Fairclough, N. (2009). A dialectical-relational approach to critical discourse analysis in social research. In R. Wodak & M. Meyer (Eds.), *Methods of critical discourse analysis* (2nd ed., pp. 87–121). London: Sage.

Finlay, L. (2002). “Outing” the researcher: The provenance, process and practice of reflexivity. *Qualitative Health Research, 12*(4), 531–545.

Foucault, M. (1982). The subject and power. *Critical Inquiry, 8*(4), 777–795.

Foucault, M. (1988). In L. D. Kritzman, L. D. Kritzman, & L. D. Kritzman (Eds.), *Politics, philosophy, culture: Interviews and other writing 1977–1984*. New York: Routledge/Chapman & Hall.

Frank, G., & Polkinghorne, D. (2010). Qualitative research in occupational therapy: From the first to the second generation. *OTJR: Occupation, participation and health, 30*(2), 51–57.

George, D., & Whitehouse, P. (2010). Dementia and mild cognitive impairment in social and cultural context. In D. Dannefer & C. Phillipson (Eds.), *The Sage handbook of social gerontology* (pp. 343–356). Thousand Oaks: Sage.

Grant, D., Hardy, C., Oswick, C., & Putnam, L. (2004). Organizational discourse: Exploring the field. In D. Grant, C. Hardy, C. Oswick, & L. Putnam (Eds.), *The Sage handbook of organizational discourse* (pp. 1–36). Thousand Oaks: Sage.

Guba, E. G., & Lincoln, Y. S. (1994). Competing paradigms in qualitative research. In N. K. Denzin & Y. S. Lincoln (Eds.), *Handbook of qualitative research* (1st ed., pp. 105–117). Thousand Oaks: Sage.

Hacking, I. (1986). Making up people. In T. C. Heller et al. (Eds.), *Reconstructing individualism* (pp. 222–236). Stanford: Stanford University Press.

Hardy, C., & Phillips, N. (2004). Discourse and power. In D. Grant, C. Hardy, C. Oswick, & L. Putnam (Eds.), *The Sage handbook of organizational discourse* (pp. 299–316). Thousand Oaks: Sage.

Jager, S., & Maier, F. (2009). Theoretical and methodological aspects of Foucauldian critical discourse analysis and dispositive analysis. In R. Wodak & M. Meyer (Eds.), *Methods of critical discourse analysis* (2nd ed., pp. 87–121). London: Sage.

Katz, S. (2000). Busy bodies: Activity, aging and the management of everyday life. *Journal of Aging Studies, 14*, 135–152.

Kendall, G., & Wickham, G. (2003). *Using Foucault's methods*. London: Sage.

Kincheloe, J. L., & McLaren, P. (2005). Rethinking critical theory and qualitative research. In M. K. Denzin & Y. S. Lincoln (Eds.), *Handbook of qualitative research* (3rd ed., pp. 303–342). Thousand Oaks: Sage.

Kronenberg, F., & Pollard, N. (2006). Political dimensions of occupation and the roles of occupational therapy. *American Journal of Occupational Therapy, 60*, 617–625.

Labonte, R., Polanyi, M., Muhajarine, N., McIntosh, T., & Williams, A. (2005). Beyond the divides. Towards critical population health research. *Critical Public Health, 15*(1), 5–17.

Laliberte Rudman, D. (2006). ‘Positive aging’ and its implications for occupational possibilities in later life. *Canadian Journal of Occupational Therapy, 73*(3), 188–192.

Laliberte Rudman, D. (2010). Occupational possibilities. *Journal of Occupational Science, 17*, 55–59.

Laliberte Rudman, D., & Molke, D. (2009). Forever productive: The discursive shaping of later life workers in contemporary Canadian media. *Work, 32*, 377–389.

Lather, P. (2006). Paradigm proliferation as a good thing to think with. *International Journal of Qualitative Studies in Education, 19*, 33–59.

Laws, G. (1996). ‘A shot of economic adrenalin’: Reconstructing ‘the elderly’ in the retiree-based economic development literature. *Journal of Aging Studies, 10*, 171–188.

Lee, J., & Macdonald, D. (2010). ‘Are they just checking our obesity or what?’: The healthism discourse and rural young women. *Sport, Education and Society, 15*, 203–219.

MacEachen, E., Polzer, J., & Clarke, J. (2008). ‘You are free to set your own hours’: Governing worker productivity and health through flexibility and resilience. *Social Science & Medicine, 66*, 1019–1033.

McGrath, R. (2009). A discourse analysis of Australian local government recreation and sport plans provision for people with disabilities. *Public Management Review, 11*, 477–497.

Mumby, D. K. (2004). Discourse, power and ideology: Unpacking the critical approach. In D. Grant, C. Hardy, C. Oswick, & L. Putnam (Eds.), *The Sage handbook of organizational discourse* (pp. 237–258). Thousand Oaks: Sage.

Parker, I. (1992). *Discourse dynamics: Critical analysis for social and individual psychology*. London: Routledge.

Potter, J., & Wetherell, M. (1987). *Discourse and social psychology. Beyond attitudes and behavior*. London: Sage.

Powell, J. L., Biggs, S. (2003). Foucauldian gerontology: A methodology for understanding aging. *Electronic Journal of Sociology*, *7*(2). http://www.sociology.org/content/vol7.2/03_powell_biggs.html. Accessed 4 Aug 2006.

Sayer, A. (2009). Who's afraid of critical social science? *Current Sociology, 57*(6), 767–786.

Smith, J. L. (2007). Critical discourse analysis for nursing research. *Nursing Inquiry, 14*(1), 60–70.

Stuhr, J. J. (2003). *Pragmatism, postmodernism and the future of philosophy*. New York: Routledge.

van Dijk, T. (2009). Critical discourse studies: A sociocognitive approach. In R. Wodak & M. Meyer (Eds.), *Methods of critical discourse analysis* (2nd ed., pp. 62–86). London: Sage.

Wodak, R., & Meyer, M. (2009). Critical discourse analysis: History, agenda, theory and methodology. In R. Wodak & M. Meyer (Eds.), *Methods of critical discourse analysis* (2nd ed., pp. 1–33). Los Angeles: Sage.

Chapter 15
Mixed Methods and Pragmatism for Research on Occupation

Kendra Heatwole Shank

15.1 Introduction

Mixed methods research has been described as the "third methodological movement" (Tashakkori and Teddlie 2003, p. 697) in the social and behavioral sciences, diverging from both formal quantitative/post-positivist and qualitative/subjectivist research traditions. In making a case for the mixed methods approach, many early proponents argued that Pragmatist philosophers' views of inquiry and knowledge were particularly suited for (and supportive of) a mixed methods approach. Prominent mixed methods scholars who have staked this claim include Tashakkori and Teddlie (2003), Creswell (2003), Johnson and Onwuegbuzie (2004) and Morgan (2007). Their work has suggested that using mixed methods in research is supported by American Pragmatism. At the heart of this argument is the pragmatist belief that knowledge claims arise from a research *process* rather than from antecedent paradigmatic positions and beliefs. Instead of adhering to a predetermined set of assumptions and tools, pragmatist thought suggests that the researcher (and research) should be focused foremost on the whole problematic situation (Cutchin 2008), driven by the particular question at hand (Patton 1990), and disposed to use the methods that will best increase understanding (Morgan). All these priorities serve to foreground the problematic situation, and downplay the traditional emphasis on meta-epistemological positions. When the problem or question is the most important factor in designing and conducting research, these scholars have argued, then the use of pluralistic approaches to conduct inquiry and build knowledge is justified (Tashakkori and Teddlie 2003).

Pragmatism has thus been used as a way of ex post facto justification for the use of plural methods in research. There are, however, important points of alignment

K.H. Shank (✉)
Department of Allied Health Sciences, Division of Occupational Science and Occupational Therapy, University of North Carolina at Chapel Hill, Chapel Hill, NC, USA
e-mail: kendra.heatwoleshank@gmail.com

M.P. Cutchin and V.A. Dickie (eds.), *Transactional Perspectives on Occupation*,
DOI 10.1007/978-94-007-4429-5_15, © Springer Science+Business Media B.V. 2013

between pragmatic thought and the use of mixed methods that should be explored prospectively to inform how research questions are formed, studies are designed, and data are collected and interpreted. Specifically, John Dewey's[1] emphasis on *holism*, *provisionality of knowledge*, the *situatedness of inquiry*, and the *value-laden nature of research* are concepts that will help organize an examination of how both pragmatic thought and mixed methods may hold greater utility for transaction-focused research when they are considered together.

A transactional perspective on occupation suggests that occupation should be viewed as holistic, emergent, contextual and meaning-rich human action. The literature attempting to empirically build such an understanding of occupation is growing, and scholars have successfully used a range of (primarily qualitative) methods toward that end. I suggest here that using qualitative *and* quantitative methods may be a fruitful approach to studying occupations, particularly as we grapple with how to see the whole of a situation as well as the particularities of that whole (see Chap. 13). The transactions of everyday life through which occupations emerge have dimensions that can be accessed through both qualitative and quantitative methods, and, as Dewey and others have argued, aspects of a situation should not be teased apart for inquiry. Mixed methods are one way of integrating in research the holism that we experience in situations.

In this chapter I will first explore the idea of incommensurable paradigms and outline how Pragmatism has been used by mixed methods proponents to bridge the divide between qualitative and quantitative approaches to research. I will then suggest how we can move beyond this "justification" argument by examining several points of synergy between pragmatic thought and mixed methods that may be beneficial when employing a transactional perspective. Finally, I outline some implications for conducting mixed methods research about occupations and communities that are consistent with the transactional perspective.

15.2 Defining Mixed Methods

Before moving forward, the term *mixed methods* should be clarified. The term has been defined in several ways and has many different synonyms including blended research, multiple methods, triangulated studies, and mixed research (Johnson et al. 2007). The most common conceptualization connotes a mixing of qualitative and quantitative methods, data, and/or analyses within one research program. Johnson, Onweugbuzie and Turner collected and sifted definitions from leaders in this field to distill a general definition of mixed methods. They concluded that

> Mixed methods research is the type of research in which a researcher or team of researchers combines elements of qualitative and quantitative research approaches (e.g. use of

[1] My understanding of Pragmatism is informed primarily by the Deweyan version; other forms of the tradition vary somewhat, including with respect to these concepts.

qualitative and quantitative viewpoints, data collection, analysis, inference techniques) for the broad purposes of breadth and depth of understanding and corroboration (p. 123).

The general nature of mixed methods research is that it permits researchers to use diverse methods that have complementary strengths and non-overlapping weaknesses in order to gain a better, more comprehensive and reliable outcome (Johnson and Onwuegbuzie 2004).

There are two parts to the definition above: mixed methods research is defined by *what* is mixed, but also by the assertion that there is *something to be gained* by mixing. It is more common to think about mixed methods as qualitative + quantitative; however the second part of the definition—the purpose of mixing methods—is more ends-oriented and aligns with the broader concerns of the pragmatists. An early argument for using mixed methods was that it helped researchers avoid some types of bias by "triangulating"; that is, to more accurately understand something by approaching it from multiple angles (Johnson et al. 2007). While the idea of triangulating is not philosophically consistent with a belief in emerging and provisional understandings, it holds that multiple viewpoints can provide better inferences than a singular approach. Mixed methods research is not just–or even primarily–defined by its form; it should be defined by its function, which is that elements of "pure" research approaches are combined in non-traditional ways *in order to increase understanding and move scientific inquiry forward.*

For the purpose of this chapter, "mixed methods" does not refer to any specific design or pairing of methodologies, nor to specific types of data collected and used. Instead, the end-in-view of using plural methods—the desire to achieve a more comprehensive and complete understanding of whole situations—will be the characteristic in focus. Relative to pragmatism, the term mixed methods encompasses a spectrum of research that is not dictated by a particular scientific orthodoxy (Dean 2004) but rather is a flexible framework through which multiple vantages are brought to bear on a problematic situation.

15.3 The Incommensurability Thesis

Mixing methods is often taken to imply that two opposite, or at least quite different, things are being combined into a new whole. This combination is viewed by many as a strength of the approach for the reasons outlined above, yet it is also a criticism of mixed methods research. Mixed methods, the argument goes, yokes incommensurate assumptions about the world, the nature of knowledge, and ways of knowing (Johnson and Onwuegbuzie 2004; Morgan 2007).

The belief that qualitative and quantitative approaches to research are incommensurable is linked to Kuhn's concept of scientific paradigms (Morgan 2007), which suggests that groups of scholars share meanings about the nature of knowing and how research should be done to expand that knowing (Bishop 2007). Two epistemological paradigms that are broadly recognized are post-positivism and subjectivism.[2] Post-positivist epistemology (which underlies quantitative research) retains ontological realism and the existence of objective truth from its positivist roots, which translates in practice to an emphasis on discrete variables, controlled experiments, and confidence levels to explain and predict phenomena. A subjectivist epistemology (which supports much qualitative research) privileges understanding reality as it is experienced and interpreted by individuals, which can only be accessed via interviews, observations, and other first-person accounts. These epistemologies seem quite disparate—"cascades" of research that descend down different mountainsides and into different pools of knowledge (Daly 2007). This waterfall-like depiction of the scientific process is based on a linear understanding of research: a scholar has a certain epistemological stance, which spills into a corresponding paradigm of research; then theories and methodologies extend from that paradigm; and research methods and the data collected flow from the values of the tradition. Bishop described this linear perception succinctly, stating that natural sciences and social sciences are not different in *degree*, they are different in *kind*.

Morgan (2007) argued, however, that while qualitative and quantitative approaches have tendencies toward certain ways of asking questions (induction versus deduction) and certain ways of collecting and analyzing data (explaining versus understanding), that these are just tendencies; rarely, in real-world research, are the two as distinct and rigid as the cascade metaphor implies. This top-down metaphysical view that emphasizes differences can be a limitation in understanding the research process (and the real-world experiences social science deals with) by setting up a false dualism: the idea that qualitative and quantitative approaches are clearly bounded and non-overlapping. Research/researchers may have inductive-subjective-contextual or deductive-objective-generalizing tendencies, but rarely does research start in the top-down, absolutist way the cascade metaphor implies (Johnson and Onwuegbuzie 2004).

How can the dualistic framework of "pure qualitative" and "pure quantitative" research be reconciled for using mixed methods? Johnson and Onwuegbuzie (2004) pointed out that there are many points of agreement between the post-positivist and subjectivist epistemologies, such as an acknowledgement of the relativity of reason; recognizing that hypotheses are not testable in isolation; and a growing appreciation for the social and value-laden nature of scientific inquiry. They surmised that the two approaches share enough in common to be comingled. From the vantage of the Pragmatists, however, we would do better to move away from conceptualizing science and research as epistemology-driven altogether.

---

[2] Howe (1988) was an early voice in this debate; he wrote that "incompatibilists maintain that problems arise at the level of epistemological paradigms" (p. 10), and that the methods associated with each would therefore be incompatible. Also, I purposely leave constructivist epistemologies out of the discussion here to simplify the argument.

John Dewey, who offered the most cohesive version of American Pragmatism, eschewed the top-down privileging where a single "meta" epistemology dictates research practice (and the resulting knowledge) (Boisvert 1998). Incommensurability between paradigms depends on a top-down view (as in the stream of water that splits, taking different paths down a mountain). Dewey believed, conversely, that a process of inquiry arises from *experience* instead of from abstract philosophical positions (Cutchin 2008). In this view, the nature of the problematic situation drives inquiry: research questions and modes of inquiry (methods) must be coordinated together in a way that reflects and addresses real-world complexity.

Pragmatism, especially as it was espoused by Dewey, rejects all dualisms—dualisms of knower and known (Boisvert 1998), of individuals and their environments (Cutchin 2008), and of objectivism and subjectivism (Maxey 2003). This rejection would surely extend to the idea that quantitative and qualitative methodologies are distinctly separate, non-overlapping, antithetical approaches to inquiry. In both conceptualization and practice, there is complementarity and common ground for these research traditions. From a pragmatic stance diverse methods are not incompatible approaches, generating cascades from different starting points toward different ends. Such methods are instead valued tools for inquiry with their own particular strengths, like different lenses on a camera which add depth, focus, and new dimensions to the composition.

Pragmatism has thus provided the philosophic grounds for mixed methods researchers to reject the incommensurability thesis. Yet Pragmatism has more to offer for fitting the two traditions together. For example, pragmatists believe that ideas and methods have to fit their situations (Campbell 1995). Therefore it follows that the appropriate methods for a particular question *depend on* that question. Methodologically, Pragmatism suggests that there are no external measures for what is right or true in a situation (Fesmire 2003), and it emphasizes the *workability* (Morgan 2007) of a method to answer the question as the means for evaluation (Garrison 2001). This is illustrated by Kaplan's (1964) baseball metaphor. He explained that methods should not be equated to the writers of the rule book laying down concrete national guidelines; nor are methods like umpires, strictly regulating and enforcing those rules. Rather, methods can be best compared to the coaching, where recommendations for plays and strategies are based on the particularities of how a game is unfolding. The appropriateness of the recommendations should be evaluated by the play of the game. Means—or methods—are chosen based on the ends in view (Aldrich 2008), and are therefore not good or bad, just effective or ineffective (Garrison 2005).

Valuing a combination of methods coordinated for the question at hand over valuing a traditional mono-method is a logical extension of these pragmatic positions. For mixed methods researchers, pragmatism offers a bottom-up approach that counters the metaphysical epistemologies. Both emphasize the real-world usefulness of tailoring a combination of methods for a particular research inquiry that has breadth, depth, rigor, and that effectively increases understanding of the problem at hand.

15.4 Extending the Argument

Several concepts from a pragmatic theoretical orientation are embodied in mixed method research. Examining this congruence between pragmatism and mixed methods will help extend the argument beyond a philosophical rejection of incommensurability, toward a methodology characterized by real-world utility and application for research on occupation. A closer examination of some of the philosophic issues that American Pragmatism tackles will, in particular, help make the case for adopting a transactional perspective to understand occupation, and for using mixed methods to build that understanding.

15.4.1 Holism

First is the imperative for a *holistic* approach to research, related to Dewey's concept of transaction (Garrison 2001). The transactional perspective views the world as constituted of events, or emergent processes involving elements that change with and through each other, e.g., that co-constitute each other (Aldrich 2008). Transactions reflect an improvised and integrated relationship of person and place, and that relationship represents ongoing actions that maintain and reconstruct it (Cutchin 2001). Inquiry into action, therefore, has to take a broader view, addressing the intricacies and negotiations of the whole situation (Dickie et al. 2006). The "situation" is not neatly bounded and may be difficult to define, but it foregrounds the relational nature of a transaction: *all* elements are in relationship, shaping and being shaped by the situation. The key point for research is that any element of interest is in-relationship-with-the-whole. Elements cannot be studied in isolation, because they do not exist in isolation.

The methodological implications of a holistic, anti-dualistic theoretical approach are twofold: a transaction cannot be understood from a purely individualized, subjective stance (Dickie et al. 2006); nor can the emerging process be understood through methodological approaches that reduce a situation to discrete and separate parts (Garrison 2005). Instead, a methodological approach consistent with the transactional view would include tools to look at both the diverse elements of the situation and to address the relationships of those elements. A mixed methods approach allows the researcher to choose the methods particularly suited to examine aspects relevant to the situation, thus attending to both salient elements *and* their relationships. An understanding of the transactional whole emerges when these data are integrated in a cohesive analysis process.

15.4.2 Provisionality

A second relevant concept from Pragmatism is the idea that *knowledge is provisional*, and that a process of inquiry results in the making of "warranted assertions"

(Fesmire 2003, p. 35). Contrary to the intent to establish significance or causality (as in some quantitative approaches), or to essentialize phenomena (as in some qualitative approaches), Dewey believed that inquiry was a process that was never complete—knowledge is emergent, provisional, and always subject to revision (Boisvert 1998; Garrison 2005). He stressed that processes of inquiry had to be grounded in and justified by previous inquiry ("warranted"), and that the outcome was not a static truth, but rather the best judgment possible based on the evidence ("assertions") (Crick 2010).

Warranted assertions, by definition, are subject to revision. This is evidenced in many fields of inquiry, where the understandings of yesterday are not the same as those held today, nor will today's knowledge necessarily hold true in the future. Like an explorer making a map, we assert what we know based on what we see now; when others use the map it will be changed, corrected, expanded and refined, just as we and others will continue to test and refine understandings of occupation. Sullivan (2001) captured the provisional nature of knowledge when she described it as a "constant spiral" through time that is best characterized as "growth" in understanding (p. 49).

Since the transactional nature of situations and actions-in-situation are also being made and remade constantly, making warranted assertions that are evidence-based, relevant, and inform the community of scholars and practitioners interested in occupation is a challenge. Using multiple, mixed methods is one way to approach the task: while data and analyses could take either quantitative or qualitative form, when taken together they provide a stronger basis for warranted assertions. Just as diverse paths and experiences in a new physical location will improve the explorer's ability to make an accurate and useful representation for others, more ways of understanding occupation and the transactions through which occupations arise will improve the depth and breadth of inferences about occupation and engagement that are possible.

15.4.3 Situated Inquiry

Third, the pragmatists emphasized that *inquiry is situated* in particular social, historical, political and cultural contexts. Just as action is not isolated from all the elements in a situation, the research process cannot be isolated from the context in which it occurs. Using the language of Pragmatism, the relationship of knower and known is itself a transaction. Creswell (2003) stated that a theoretical lens that grants the interconnectedness of research and the context where it occurs is a lens disposed to address issues of social justice, to examine and weigh political aims, and to value and include various voices and perspectives in the research process. Dewey was very clear that the purpose of knowledge, or understanding, was to solve social problems and effect positive change—that is, to move toward the good (Campbell 1995)—which has been noted as a prominent feature of the transactional perspective (Cutchin and Dickie 2012). The best methods to answer a question ought to be used, since better understanding serves the betterment of humankind.

This purpose-orientation is an important point of congruence between the pragmatic understanding of situated inquiry and a mixed method approach. Both prioritize understanding the situation, via the most useful methods available, in order to gain a more complete understanding. Situated inquiry is a significant shift from the image of a "pure" scientific method which is conducted in a pre-determined, logical way that can be replicated by others. Using plural methods, especially in combinations that are not exclusively quantitative or qualitative, allows for the inclusion of many perspectives. Each perspective—whether discrete measurement, first-person account, historical narrative, material culture and discourse, or other method—is a situated tool applied to a situated problem.

15.4.4 Value-Laden Inquiry

Finally, a pragmatic approach to research recognizes that the process is *value-laden*. Central for pragmatists is the belief that knowledge is not gained abstractly, as an end in and of itself. Rather, increased understanding leads toward desired ends, and ends are desired because they are valued; thus the pragmatist's concern with the ethics of inquiry (Morgan 2007). Research is value-laden because the researcher discriminately focuses on what to ask, which problematic situation to address and in what way, because of personal experiences, priorities, and the circumstances under which the research is undertaken. Morgan argued that, as researchers, "values and our politics are always a part of who we are and how we act" (p. 70). These personal and socio-political values, including experience as well as the desired end of the research, are as important for shaping the inquiry process as pre-existing metaphysical positions. Dewey wrote that the knowing subject affects the object of knowledge (Maxey 2003). The implication of this belief is that the research process cannot be divorced from the values and experiences of the observer. Mixed methods research embodies this idea of valuation, since method selection by the researcher is definitional to the approach: some methods are chosen—valued over others—in order to best examine and understand the research problem. Both deductive and inductive methods come into play as researchers negotiate the process of asking and seeking to understand questions that are relevant, desired, and valued.

Once the value-laden nature of inquiry is acknowledged, formalism becomes a questionable approach to scholarship. Instead, we are better off allowing and selecting useful methods, which is more closely aligned with the common sense approach of Dewey's pragmatism. Thus a pragmatic conceptualization of research entails viewing inquiry as a holistic endeavor which is situated in a particular context, where the emergent knowledge is provisional and unfolding, and which is most successful in moving a community toward the good when scholars recognize that inquiry is value-laden. This conceptualization is embodied by the flexible, non-reductionist and integrative nature of mixed methods research which, as the final section explores, is particularly well-suited for studying occupation in communities.

15.5 Mixed Methods for Occupational Science: A Way to Study Community

The implications of pragmatism as it is extended through mixed methods for research on occupations and communities are numerous. In this final section, we will look at studying occupation as a "thing itself" and the nature of occupation-in-community as a *situational whole*. Both points serve to flesh out how a philosophic emphasis on the continuity and contingency of the world is instantiated in research methodology. This is an important step in moving from a theoretic valuing of occupation toward the actual work of studying the communal, social, shared experience from which participation cannot be teased (Cutchin and Dickie 2012). The discussion and examples that follow will highlight how mixed methodology is a strategic approach for developing the nuanced understanding of occupation that a transactional perspective calls for, particularly in relation to community.

15.5.1 Occupation as a Thing Itself

In Hocking's (2009) exploration of how to describe occupation, she urged us to study occupation "distinct from people's engagement in it" (p. 141). Occupation becomes the central construct of interest—not as a characteristic of human beings, but as an active phenomenon that represents the complex and emergent relationship of situations and people (Dickie et al. 2006). Understanding occupation as a transaction first requires that it be studied as a thing itself—not hitched to the interpreted experience of humans (Barber 2006) nor the meaning assigned by an individual (Yerxa et al. 1990). However this approach is still vulnerable to becoming circumscribed: bounding an occupation as a single experience or as what is immediately observable is far too tidy. To really understand occupation requires a level of complexity that makes us wonder whether occupations are actually "processes too complicated to explain" (Dickie 2010).

Occupation, even studied as a "thing" distinct from humans' engagement in it, cannot be understood in isolation. Focusing on the relationships among people and places is ideal for studying occupations—the action that unfolds in the context of these relationships—but it introduces the inherent complexity of experience. "Community" is an emerging topic for research in this vein. "Community" generally encompasses the social relationships, places, experiences, and patterns of participation that groups of people share, perpetuate, and change. This focus on relationships and action is consistent with pragmatic philosophy, and is at the heart of the idea of transaction. However this remains just an idea until woven into the questions, methods, and analysis processes of research.

There are very few examples of this type of research in the occupational therapy and science literature, but one worth highlighting is Hocking and colleagues' (2002) study of Thai recipe work. Hocking et al. studied the recipe work of older Thai women around the experiences of the Songkran holiday. They concluded that participation in this occupation is embedded in the context of particular histories and cultures, and continues to be socially meaningful while changing with technologies, material goods, geographic location and social norms.

Using multiple methods can paint an even clearer picture of action. For example, participant observations coupled with measures of frequency and duration of occupation; real-time spatial data of individuals or groups navigating place fleshed out with first-person accounts of the experience of inhabiting a particular place; visual media of an occupation juxtaposed with a quantification of the economic or historic elements; and both qualitative and quantitative approaches to understanding time could be employed. Occupation occurs as part of a community, and community is complicated. Employing a combination of qualitative and quantitative measures may be the most strategic way to build a corpus of knowledge about occupation *itself*.

15.5.2 Situational Whole

In any inquiry, addressing the *situational whole* within which the action of interest unfolds can be complicated to carry out in a meaningful way. To examine how it can be done, it may be helpful to begin with how it is *not* done. First, neither occupations, actions, variables, nor human beings should be conceptualized as lump things that can be atomistically delimited or essentialized. As Sullivan (2001) argued, this "neglect[s] the tremendous role that situations, physical surroundings, cultural meanings, and other seemingly non-bodily factors play" (p. 51). All elements of the situation are important to consider—not as a peripheral "setting the stage" for occupation, but rather as interwoven with and integral to the action. By reducing a situation or occupation into discrete elements for measurement alone, we produce a more limited understanding. A second limitation to avoid is privileging the subjective first-person experience as the primary–or even only–way of understanding occupation. If occupation is a relationship of person and situation characterized by complexity, creativity, and habit all organized toward a provisional and changing end (Cutchin et al. 2008), then it is *not* something understood simply through first-person accounts. As Dickie and colleagues (2006) succinctly pointed out, "an understanding of individual experience is *a necessary but insufficient condition* for understanding occupations that occur through complex contexts" (p. 83, emphasis added). Thus research approaches that are consistent with a theoretical interest in an inclusive view should, at their best, neither rely solely on the reduction of elements into discrete measureable units, nor privilege a subjective portrayal of knowing.

What does this look like in research practice? An emerging literature centered on occupation-in-community provides some examples. Several studies about older adults aging in place have used diverse methods in order to consider the many influences that shape occupational participation. The ENABLE Age project, conducted with European older adults to assess the relationship between "home" and health, is one example. Iwarsson and her colleagues employed semi-structured interviews (Fange and Ivanoff 2009), an observational assessment tool, self-report questionnaire and standardized function assessments (Wahl et al. 2009), and a systematic and critical analysis of the policy issues and housing policy trends in the selected countries (Iwarsson et al. 2007). While the authors cited the relatively dualistic *person-environment fit* conceptual framework, and acknowledged that the work is not comprehensive regarding some social aspects of participation such as caregivers' roles, they still effectively used multiple methods to address diverse aspects of the situation and to explore how those elements may relate to long-term wellbeing.

Another example is the Time Geographic Method, which originated in social geography but has found wider purchase. Kroksmark and colleagues (2006) outlined the diverse methods that may be used in a time-geographic study, which include (but are not limited to) questionnaires, yesterday interviews, participant observation, and time diaries. This grouping of methods is strategic for understanding "use of time and space throughout a day or days ..." and for analyzing "people's social networks as they move through their everyday lives" (p. 11). With the express purpose of contextualizing action, time use methodologies allow researchers to describe situations and their change as well as our experience of them. Mixed methods is practically suited to address the richness and complexity of occupation because it provides tools to look at the situational whole where occupation is contextualized and experienced by social actors. Additionally, methods appropriate for gathering and analyzing data about structural aspects of communities can be used towards this end, such as Laliberte Rudman's (2006) use of discourse analysis relative to neoliberalism and the media representation of retirees in Canada (see Chap. 14). Qualitative and quantitative methods can thus be integrated in the pursuit of a contextualized—and contextualizing—understanding of community and occupation.

15.6 Conclusion

The multiple methods employed in these examples enable the researchers to understand various facets of the problematic situation. The use of mixed methods also encourages the broader community of scholars on occupation to see previously-unnoticed relationships, to question existing assumptions, and to find new insights into occupation itself. In this ongoing process of inquiry, it is important to acknowledge our history and bias (Kantartzis and Molineux 2010). As a community of scholars, we have been and will continue to be concerned with maximizing function and wellbeing for individuals and communities, or what Dewey would call "the good." The disciplinary mandate for improving lives that is at the core of occupational therapy is both shared and acted on by researchers who seek to better understand the concerns of people in communities (Maxey 2003). For pragmatists, "research is driven by anticipated consequences. Pragmatic choices about what to research and how to go about it are conditioned by where we want to go in the broadest of senses" (Cherryholmes 1992, p. 13). In other words, research has direct implications for achieving the good.

Recognizing the transactive continuity in the world where we live and study makes us aware of the weightiness of action. Accepting the provisionality of knowledge that we have a hand in creating should keep us humble. Taking account of the particular (and complex) situation in which an inquiry unfolds requires that we cede some control of the research process. And acknowledging that we operate with values about what is worth studying, how, and to what ends keeps us honest. These are challenging provisions. Mixed methodology is suggested here as one way to carry out research with this pragmatic attitude, where a focus on the situation and the process of occupation predispose us to include–and be *in*–community. Methodology that is experience-driven, tailored to a problematic situation, and evaluated by its usefulness maximizes the potential for the resulting knowledge to be applied, returned to the community and refined in a continual process of growth.

References

Aldrich, R. (2008). From complexity theory to transactionalism: Moving occupational science forward in theorizing the complexities of behavior. *Journal of Occupational Science, 15*, 147–156.

Barber, M. D. (2006). Occupational science and the first-person perspective. *Journal of Occupational Science, 13*, 94–96.

Bishop, R. (2007). *The philosophy of the social sciences*. New York: Continuum International.

Boisvert, R. D. (1998). *John Dewey: Rethinking our time*. Albany: State University of New York.

Campbell, J. (1995). *Understanding John Dewey: Nature and cooperative intelligence*. Peru: Open Court Publishing.

Cherryholmes, C. C. (1992). Notes on pragmatism and scientific realism. *Educational Researcher, 21*, 13–17.

Creswell, J. W. (2003). *Research design: Qualitative, quantitative and mixed methods approaches* (2nd ed.). Thousand Oaks: Sage.

Crick, N. (2010). *Democracy & rhetoric: John Dewey on the arts of becoming*. Columbia: University of South Carolina Press.

Cutchin, M. P. (2001). Deweyan integration: Moving beyond place attachment in elderly migration theory. *International Journal of Aging & Human Development, 52*, 29–44.

Cutchin, M. P. (2008). John Dewey's metaphysical ground-map and its implications for geographical inquiry. *Geoforum, 39*, 1555–1569.

Cutchin, M. P., & Dickie, V. (2012). Transactionalism: Occupational science and the pragmatic attitude. In G. Whiteford & C. Hocking (Eds.), *Critical perspectives on occupational science: Society, inclusion, participation* (pp. 23–37). London: Wiley.

Cutchin, M. P., Aldrich, R., Bailliard, A., & Coppola, S. (2008). Action theories for occupational science: The contributions of Dewey and Bourdieu. *Journal of Occupational Science, 15*, 157–165.

Daly, K. (2007). *Qualitative methods for family studies & human development*. Thousand Oaks: Sage.

Dean, K. (2004). The role of methods in maintaining orthodox beliefs in health research. *Social Science & Medicine, 58*, 675–685.

Dickie, V. A. (2010). Are occupations "processes too complicated to explain"? What we can learn by trying. *Journal of Occupational Science, 17*, 195–203.

Dickie, V., Cutchin, M., & Humphry, R. (2006). Occupation as transactional experience: A critique of individualism in occupational science. *Journal of Occupational Science, 13*, 83–93.

Fange, A., & Ivanoff, S. D. (2009). The home is the hub of health in very old age: Findings from the ENABLE-AGE project. *Archives of Gerontology and Geriatrics, 48*, 340–345.
Fesmire, S. (2003). *John Dewey and moral imagination: Pragmatism in ethics*. Bloomington: Indiana University Press.
Garrison, J. (2001). An introduction to Dewey's theory of functional "trans-action": An alternative paradigm for activity theory. *Mind, Culture, and Activity, 8*, 275–296.
Garrison, J. (2005). Dewey on metaphysics, meaning making, and maps. *Transactions of the Charles S. Peirce Society: A Quarterly Journal in American Philosophy, 41*, 818–844.
Hocking, C. (2009). The challenge of occupation: Describing the things people do. *Journal of Occupational Science, 16*, 140–150.
Hocking, C., Wright-St. Clair, V., & Bunrayong, W. (2002). The meaning of cooking and recipe work for older Thai and New Zealand women. *Journal of Occupational Science, 9*, 117–127.
Howe, K. R. (1988). Against the quantitative-qualitative incompatibility thesis or dogmas die hard. *Education Researcher, 17*, 10–16.
Iwarsson, S., Wahl, H. W., Nygren, C., Oswald, F., Sixsmith, A., Sixsmith, J., et al. (2007). Importance of the home environment for healthy aging: Conceptual and methodological background of the European ENABLE-AGE Project. *The Gerontologist, 47*, 78–84.
Johnson, R., & Onwuegbuzie, A. J. (2004). Mixed methods research: A research paradigm whose time has come. *Educational Researcher, 33*, 14–26.
Johnson, R., Onwuegbuzie, A. J., & Turner, L. A. (2007). Toward a definition of mixed methods research. *Journal of Mixed Methods Research, 1*, 112–133.
Kantartzis, S., & Molineux, M. (2010). The influence of Western society's construction of a healthy daily life on the conceptualization of occupation. *Journal of Occupational Science, 18*, 62–80.
Kaplan, A. (1964). *The conduct of inquiry: Methodology for behavioral sciences*. San Francisco: Chandler.
Kroksmark, U., Mordell, K., Bendixen, H. J., Magnus, E., Jakobsen, K. A., & Alsaker, S. (2006). Time geographic method: Application to studying patterns of occupation in different contexts. *Journal of Occupational Science, 13*, 11–16.
Laliberte Rudman, D. (2006). Shaping the active, autonomous and responsible modern retiree: An analysis of discursive technologies and their links with neo-liberal political rationality. *Aging and Society, 26*, 181–201.
Maxey, S. J. (2003). Pragmatic threads in mixed methods research in the social sciences: The search for multiple modes of inquiry and the end of the philosophy of formalism. In A. Tashakkori & C. Teddlie (Eds.), *Handbook of mixed methods in social & behavioral research* (pp. 51–90). Thousand Oaks: Sage.
Morgan, D. L. (2007). Paradigms lost and pragmatism regained: Methodological implications of combining qualitative and quantitative methods. *Journal of Mixed Methods Research, 1*, 48–76.
Patton, M. W. (1990). *Qualitative and research methods* (2nd ed.). Newbury Park: Sage.
Sullivan, S. (2001). *Living across and through skins: Transactional bodies, pragmatism and feminism*. Bloomington: Indiana University Press.
Tashakkori, A., & Teddlie, C. (2003). *Handbook of mixed methods in social & behavioral research*. Thousand Oaks: Sage.
Wahl, H. W., Schilling, O., & Iwarsson, S. (2009). The home environment and quality of life-related outcomes in advanced old age: Findings of the ENABLE-AGE project. *European Journal of Ageing, 6*, 101–111.
Yerxa, E., Clark, F., Frank, G., Jackson, J., Parham, D., Peirce, D., et al. (1990). An introduction to occupational science, a foundation for occupational therapy in the 21st century. In J. Jackson & E. Yerxa (Eds.), *Occupational science: The foundation for new models of practice*. New York: The Haworth Press.

Part IV
Applications

Chapter 16
Deweyan Educational Philosophy in Occupation-Centered Curricula

Susan Coppola

16.1 Introduction

Just as theories of action inform our understanding of occupation, those theories can be applied to enlighten teaching processes in occupational therapy and occupational science. In this chapter, John Dewey's philosophy of experience as it relates to progressive education will serve as a pedagogical basis to interpret and inform an occupation-centered curriculum and significant learning experiences. The chapter will focus upon the concepts in Dewey's statement: Experience and Education (1963), and apply those ideas to occupational therapy and science curricula.

John Dewey's work covers a period from the 1880s to the early 1950s. In it, he addressed broad fields of study, from aesthetics to journalism and social sciences, using an internally cohesive pragmatist philosophy (Spadafora 2009). His influence on educational reform may be his most notable achievement. A good deal of today's cutting edge pedagogy evokes the philosophy of experience that Dewey developed a century ago (Jenlink 2009; Jones 2009; Hickman 2011). Thus much of what is in this chapter will not be new to teachers of all ages, but identification of Dewey as an inspiration for modern pedagogy may be novel. What distinguishes Dewey's pedagogical theory is that it is embedded in his metatheory of action, a version of the philosophy called pragmatism. His theory is about how individuals and groups work as part of the environment, through adaptive processes, and toward the good in their day to day lives. Critical of traditional education, Dewey set out to reform it (Dewey 1897, 1963, 2004). He put forward a view of education as an art and a science and an indirect practice of teaching that aligned with his pragmatist philosophy. His work is identified with the progressive education movement for children, yet the

S. Coppola (✉)
Department of Allied Health Sciences, Division of Occupational Science and Occupational Therapy, University of North Carolina at Chapel Hill, Chapel Hill, NC, USA
e-mail: sue_coppola@med.unc.edu

M.P. Cutchin and V.A. Dickie (eds.), *Transactional Perspectives on Occupation*, DOI 10.1007/978-94-007-4429-5_16, © Springer Science+Business Media B.V. 2013 principles of his educational philosophy translate to college education and life-long learning (Schell and Schell 2008; Fishman and McCarthy 1998).

At the heart of Dewey's progressive education work was his philosophy of experience (Dewey 1963). That philosophy is a holistic view that "every experience influences in some degree the objective conditions under which subsequent experiences are had" (p. 37). We live in a stream of time and situations that vary in quality for their educative value. He argues for educators to understand the "organic connection between education and personal experience"(p. 25) in order to create quality learning situations that "live fruitfully and creatively in subsequent experiences" (p. 28). This chapter will begin with Dewey's key concepts of learning as a social process involving habits and the conditions that optimize learning situations. A learning activity example will illustrate these concepts as well as Dewey's view of deliberation, creativity and problem solving. The final sections will discuss how these principles work together in a cohesive curriculum centered on occupation.

16.2 Education as a Social Process

For traditionalists, education is *socialization* into the norms, ideas and information held by elders (Dewey 1963). Dewey (2004) was critical of the traditional role of student as docile recipient of subject-matter determined by the teacher. In traditional education, the teacher gave little consideration to the experience of learning as central to what was learned (Dewey 1963). The traditional methods suited the learning objectives based on a constricted view of intelligence. Dewey (1963) stated that traditional education was guided by the objective of acquiring knowledge of a subject or application of a particular skill and thus a pedantic method was the corresponding way of teaching. In other words, *information* about a subject was a marker of learning rather than habits of problem solving and innovating in new situations. Traditional education philosophy is therefore based in a static worldview, which involves application of existing information, skills and cultural practices that could be learned as separate entities (Dewey 1963).

The progressive education movement of the twentieth century, in which John Dewey played a prominent role, viewed education as cooperative *social processes* of problem solving, reasoning and reflection on real-life experience. Progressive education was preparation for a future of changing circumstances by developing intelligence, individuality and creativity. Dewey's writings foreshadow post-positivist thinking that took hold more than half a century later (Cochran 2002). Dewey (1929) postulated the uncertainty of situations and the inextricable force of environmental contexts for action. At the same time he was putting forward an optimistic view of human creativity, freedom and morality (Fishman and McCarthy 2007). Accordingly, his view of education was not to perpetuate doctrine that exists in culture but to suggest that "education is decisive for *renewal* of human culture and society" (Hansen 2006, p. 10).

Dewey's educational reform writings were largely concerned with children, although he addressed learning in general as part of his worldview. The expression "active learning" described engaged learning with a reflective mind that can occur at any educational and age level. In his seminal essay, "My Pedagogic Creed," Dewey (1897) declared education a "process of living, not a preparation for living" (p. 78). Readers of this text will likely have encountered traditional and progressive education of varying quality and formed opinions about pedagogy that in turn influence teaching practices. Dewey claimed that dualisms, like progressive and traditional education, are not helpful; yet his writings about education are a reaction against conformity in traditional education and a call for a sound philosophy of education based on a theory of experience (Dewey 1963). That philosophy goes beyond current wisdom about using learning objectives to determine teaching methodology, to a more complex and nuanced exploration of learning situations.

Dewey's holistic way of thinking about learning situations is based upon his philosophy of experience (Dewey 1963). In this philosophy, each situation is a transaction, a dynamic, integrated process that is part of a continuous stream of time and experience. Learning occurs in the situation: the transaction is in the present but inextricably linked to the past and future experiences of the actors within evolving situations (1963). By nature of habits, imagination, and creativity, the transactional experience creates change (learning) in students, teachers and the environment. Each change is part of evolving relationships among the constituents of the situation, altered by each collective experience and its effect on what comes after it. As an example, an occupational therapy instructor might introduce the situation of a family that works together to have a sustainable farming business. After a car accident, one member uses a wheelchair and another has a cognitive impairment. The students, by thinking through situations of this family, envisioning and acting out possible scenarios engage in an imaginative process. This process shifts the attention of the group to create a new shared situation. At the same time this deliberative process enlists and also alters the students' habits of thinking and problem solving individually and collectively.

Dewey was an early theorist about the classroom as a learning community, and the value of collaborative and shared experiences for learning (Dewey 2004). Peer learning, common in current pedagogy, has important philosophical roots in Dewey's overall conception of human nature (Dewey 1963; Schell and Schell 2008). Social theorist Lave (1988) stressed Dewey's notion of learning *as part of* activity. The concept of "communities of practice" (Wenger 1999) puts learning communities into a modern context, applied to varied settings, including workplaces. Communities of practice are groups of people who share a concern or a passion for something they do and learn how to do it better as they interact regularly (Wenger 2006; Lave and Wenger 1996). In education it is useful then to consider the class, regardless of size, as a social group with the potential to function as an effective community of practice (Schell and Schell 2008).

Learning situations are constituted of and influenced by all things, by the natural and built environment, by time that has passed and the time that remains in class and beyond (Dewey 1963; Cutchin 2007). Each person (student and teacher) entering a classroom situation carries—in the form of their constellation of embodied habits—patterns of interacting with teachers and peers and ways to situate oneself in the classroom space. Each student has purposes and needs for how the experience will or should go based upon habits, and thus will experience the situation in a unique way (Dewey 1963).

Dewey's educational philosophy was tied to a social view of humans as actors in situations in which morality and inquiry were constituent parts. Dewey (1998) stated that "morals has to do with all activity into which alternative possibilities enter" (p. 321). Morality in his view resides within the ethical judgments that arise and are revised through ongoing inquiry. Morality is *part of* intelligent inquiry, and thus part of education that shapes individual conduct. Social values and judgments are tacitly conveyed to students, thus ethics is not a subject but embedded in all educational experiences (Garrison 1997).

Tenets of democracy are within Dewey's pedagogy, and like morality are not subjects taught, but experienced (Dewey 2004). Dewey argued that democracy in educational processes exercises—and therefore communicates and perpetuates—important values (Dewey 1963). Such values are recognizing the worth of each person and viewing the collective wisdom of the group as greater than that of any individual. In democratic contexts, rules of conduct are made by the group relative to the situation, resources (including time) are distributed fairly (not necessarily equally), and justice is the responsibility of each individual and the collective. For individual students, this type of experience can promote occupational therapy principles of valuing individuals, collaboration, and justice.

Dewey argued for education to be an integrated inquiry process that contains social and intellectual properties, art and science, discipline and imagination (Dewey 1963; Garrison 2009). The complexity of the learning situation belies the simplicity of his philosophy of education as based in authentic experience. He claimed an "intimate and necessary relation between the processes of actual experience and education" (Dewey 1963, p. 20). He poses a challenge to educators in his simple aim of education, to become a lifelong learner (Dewey 1963; 2004). What does it mean to be a lifelong learner? How does a person become open to new learning and use intelligence in situations? How can educational experience build those habits? In response to these questions, the concept of habit, as part of learning situations and also the outcome of educative experiences, becomes central to Dewey's view of education (Dewey 1963).

16.2.1 Habits of, by, and for Learning

Dewey (1963) drew upon Abraham Lincoln's democratic ideals to summarize his social view of "education as of, by, and for experience" (p. 29). In other words, education is comprised of experiences, it is through experiences that we learn, and the purpose of education is to create future experiences. In this we find a corollary of habits as of, by and for learning. Habits are particularly valuable in education because they can foster being open to new situations, using systematic inquiry processes, and employing imagination for problem solving.

Human behavior is comprised of habits that are in continuous states of modification and use, called forth by changing situations (Dewey 1998). "The essence of habit is an acquired predisposition to *ways* or modes of response, not to particular acts, except as, under special conditions, these express a way of behaving" (p. 33). These habits, learned through social transactions, are employed to coordinate action with existing circumstances and move toward a desired purpose. Cutchin (2007) extended Dewey's view of habits as being formed also through transactions with the physical and natural environment. In Dewey's view, "individuals function through habits operating as behaviors, desires, working capacities, morals and will" (Cutchin et al. 2008). Although the term "habit" conjures images of observable pre-determined behavior, habits instead are "ordering and systematizing minor elements of action…dynamic in quality…and operative…even when not obviously dominating activity"(Dewey 1998, p. 33). Habits also bring efficiency to action by freeing our conscious attention to coordinate within the unique circumstances of the present situation. Even the "possibility of being in a situation rests upon the possibility of having habits" (Kestenbaum 1977, p. 19).

In the education of occupational therapists, Dewey's work guides us to consider students' habits in learning situations and the "formation of attitudes that are emotional and intellectual" (Dewey 1963, p. 35). He broadly conceived character as the "working interaction of habits" (Dewey 1998, p. 33). "Learning style" inventories, for example, appear to draw on this conceptualization and address certain habits of learning such as holistic versus sequential thinking. These are not the only habits at play in learning, of course. The use of the imagination, creativity, self-control, emotional responses and mental rehearsal are constituents of habits and habits themselves. Habits are not always observable by others, nor apparent to the individual, yet are embodied in physiology and mental processes (James 1890; Dewey 1998). Where students place themselves in the classroom, what tends to draw or elude their attention and their relationships to teachers and peers are some of the elements of habit commonly discussed in education. An important insight, however, is that habits are under constant revision as each moment calls for subtle change in habits to better coordinate with the evolving situation (Dewey 1998).

It is impossible to consider all aspects of learning situations, including the perspective of each student. Teachers must rely upon their own habits formed through experience to pay attention to select aspects of the learning situation, and respond in particular ways toward a purpose (Dewey 1963). Habits, imagination and creativity guide the teacher to structure activities, engage with the students in particular ways, and adapt (or not adapt) to the responses of the students within the situation. The teacher's objective in progressive education is to create *quality* learning situations. To this end, Dewey (1963) proposed that the teacher's overarching problem to be solved is a "well thought out philosophy of the social factors that operate in the constitution of individual experience" (p. 21).

In his theory of experience, Dewey (1963) stated that some experiences are "mis-educative" (p. 25). Experiences that close students' minds to new ideas, that create lazy attitudes, or produce disjointed thinking can foster habits that are mis-educative because they limit future learning. Current examples of mis-educative habits in occupational therapy education might include: when students adopt narrow habits of thought, such as a belief that people with particular medical conditions have the same personality; trust that a quick internet search is always sufficient to research a topic; and, thinking that teamwork is important but other disciplines should not influence occupational therapy practice. Such habits limit future learning, but fortunately they may be un-learned through subsequent experience.

Mis-education in the form of unexamined assumptions and over-generalizations by students could be used as one measure of effectiveness of teachers. Moreover, curricula could be evaluated by graduates' openness to growth and new learning. At present, scores on national certification exams and employment history serve as markers of quality for OT education programs. Instead, imagine how graduates might be assessed on their habits when they are in practice situations. An additional assessment might seek to determine if graduates take the time to reflect upon experiences, change their practice patterns over the years, employ sound inquiry processes to improve services, and pursue further formal or informal education.

16.3 Conditions that Optimize Learning Situations for Students

Education comes from experience, but not all experiences are equal in their learning potential (Dewey 1963). *Interaction and continuity* are core concepts in Dewey's pedagogy (p. 51). The significance of learning experiences, in his view, are determined by the extent to which they are both interactive and offer continuity of experience. While inseparable in the educational process, it is worthwhile to explore each aspect, beginning with views of continuity.

Continuity encompasses the experiences of actors (students and teachers) in the form of habits learned in past situations that can be used for understanding and acting upon a new situation (Dewey 1963). Thinking of students as whole people does not mean that the teacher can or should tend to all aspects of the student's past and present experience. At the college level, it is not possible to know students' histories, yet appreciating what they bring to the learning situation can guide the teacher to build continuity and the optimal challenge in the learning situation.

A Russian contemporary of Dewey, Lev Vygotsky (1978), developed the concept of the "zone of proximal development"—a concept akin to Dewey's notion of continuity—that emphasizes how the teacher structures and supports learning in context. Dewey and Vygotsky (who never met) shared the notion that learning occurs during participation in an activity and that development is not required for activity participation but is rather the outcome. As a matter of continuity, the teacher structures the situation, including her or his part in it, with a dynamic and nuanced approach to how the student participates rather than a broad concept of "readiness" to participate. In occupation therapy, the "just-right challenge," explicated by Lorna Jean King (1978) is a related intervention strategy for progressing clients toward goals in light of their current abilities. In the immediate learning situation, continuity is found in the flow and cohesiveness of ideas, physical environment and materials, social relationships, and all aspects within and outside the control of the teacher. These elements are objective aspects of the learning situation that themselves are changing. The experience has a "moving force" which all actors (students and teacher) are part of and adapting to (Dewey 1963, p. 38). In Dewey's philosophy, the teacher moves with the force of the group, and progresses the subject matter forward by measured challenges for the students. The teacher strives for coordination with the students while creating deliberate gaps or problems for the students to take on. As Dewey (1963) states, "growth depends upon the presence of difficulty to be overcome by the exercise of intelligence" (p. 79). Continuity arises by means of the careful sequencing and highlighting of concepts, problems and solutions, as the learning situation evolves and constituent parts change (Dewey 1963).

With each person having their own habits of thinking, imaginative processes, and history of learning, the learning situation has infinite possibilities. The goals of the learning situation, although formally defined as the teacher's objectives are not everyone's purposes. In OT education, students' hopes range from becoming a competent OT to getting through a particular lab activity without embarrassment. For the teacher, sites may be set on a wide range of future purposes for ourselves and our students. Dewey (1963) uses the phrase *end-in-view* to refer to a purpose that "involves foresight of the consequences which will result from acting" (p. 67). These are ends in the individual's foreseeable future, and those ends serve as means to other future ends, which move forward with time and action. The concept of end-in-view is helpful in thinking about the match or mismatch of what teacher or student seek from the learning situation. During the situation, the students' "ends-in-view" may be influenced by a problematic clinical situation from fieldwork, an idea from readings in another course or whether class will end on time. These "internal factors… also decide what type of experience is had" (Dewey 1963, p. 42). The teacher has ends-in-view that are also changing as the transaction evolves, and ideally becomes coordinated around more shared aims. Given the varied aspirations of actors, in a dynamic situation, collateral and unexpected learning are givens (Dewey 1963). He thus proposed "perhaps the greatest of pedagogical fallacies is the notion that a person learns only the particular thing he is studying at the time" (p. 48).

Continuity of the current learning situation also is in relation to future profound situations that students will encounter. Curricula centered only on current practice are therefore not fulfilling their obligation to students, and instead should focus on preparing students to respond to future needs of society. In occupational therapy the ongoing debate about the place and substance of technical skill as part of curricula creates a tension. On this matter, Dewey (1963) wrote, "Almost everyone has had occasion to look back upon his school days and wonder … why it is that the technical skills he acquired have to be learned over again in changed form in order to stand him in good stead" (p. 47). This is not to say there is no place for technical skills and knowledge in preparing professional occupational therapists, but rather that the skills and knowledge become outdated and are therefore insufficient for future practice. Instead, Dewey would argue that the focus be on the practical intelligence of practitioners, in particular the ability to identify, reason thorough, and resolve professional problems. For each learning experience the students should at some point see how that experience contributes to their lives as occupational therapists and the social contributions made by their work (Dewey 1963). Students who are in accord with the philosophy of the curriculum will be better able to participate and learn from it. This aspect of continuity calls for attention to the admissions process when selecting students for a program, recognizing that students with strongly held habits of learning that align with traditional education may struggle to adapt to a progressive model of learning.

Dewey's focus was on learners as objects of education (Fenstermacher 2006), with less attention to what the teacher brings to the situation. His focus was relational, as he identified the essential reciprocity in education, "in such shared activity, the teacher is a learner and the learner is, without knowing it, a teacher" (Dewey 2004, p. 160). Habits of faculty, influenced by their past experiences, or biographies, are part of learning situations, yet they have, to date, been under-theorized in occupational therapy education (Hooper 2008). The teacher in the learning situation has a particular teaching style, even when using progressive education principles of Dewey. With increasing social diversity, classrooms have indeed become places of cross-cultural communication. Self-awareness as a teacher is necessary to consciously bridge gaps in learning and teaching approaches between teacher and learner, and to prepare for the evolving cohorts of students.

Presently in college in the USA are the Millennial and Net Generations, who are known to be tech savvy, resourceful, and used to success (Oblinger and Oblinger 2005). These students' habits of learning are shaped by virtual worlds, multitasking, and on-demand access to vast information resources. Faculty may feel challenged to connect with students when syllabi, learning assignments and course preparation are not in keeping with students' high tech habits. Despite these trends, face-to-face experiences cannot all be replaced with virtual transactions. Students will primarily practice occupational therapy in the physical world with clients and colleagues, and educational experiences should resemble those worlds. Yet, technology opens up vast possibilities for participatory learning with diverse topics and individuals (Cunningham 2009), and virtual exchanges will increasingly be a practice context in the future (AOTA 2010).

Dewey's pedagogic principles can be helpful in navigating and evaluating the quality of learning experiences as well as advancing participatory learning. In Dewey's (1963) words, "it is part of the educator's responsibility to see equally … that the problem grows out of the conditions of the experience being had in the present, and that it is within the range of capacity of students; and…that it is such that it arouses in the learner an active quest for information and for production of new ideas" (p. 79). The teacher's role in virtual or face-to-face situations is to create learning situations. Fundamentally the conditions of Deweyan learning situations are that students engage actively, collaboratively, and successfully in meaningful problem solving, and that situation inspires further learning (Dewey 1963).

16.4 Progressive Education Principles in a Classroom Experience

> We always live at the time we live and not some other time, and only by extracting at each present time the full meaning of each present experience are we prepared for doing the same thing in the future. This is the only preparation which in the long run amounts to anything (Dewey 1963, p. 49)

Deweyan pedagogy can enrich teaching and learning in the lived moment of the classroom. The following classroom example will offer instances of Deweyan principles in a learning experience. The classroom session is about occupational therapy evaluation, using a video interview of an 83 year old woman who is on a psychiatric ward. Before seeing the interview, students state what they expect Ms. Smith to be like based on a case description, and pose questions they have about her. This exchange forces an investment of student interest in the session while revealing their prior knowledge, interests, and habits of thinking. The teacher uses student responses to coordinate the ensuing activity to "be within the range of capacity of the students" (Dewey 1963, p. 79). At the same time, the students are seeking to coordinate their purposes in the session with the teacher and each other within the classroom transaction. Video segments are interspersed with teacher-facilitated discussion for shared inquiry and problem solving.

The first video clip is a brief introduction between the interviewer and Ms. Smith. Students describe what they observed and why they noticed these particular things. Exploring their impulses or habits of attending to aspects of the person and situation, brings awareness to those habits of perception. Some students take a clinical posture of identifying impairments in Ms. Smith, others note her mood or her body functions and structures, still others focus on how they feel about her. Some make assumptions about Ms. Smith's past, her diagnoses, or about what she is thinking or feeling. This discussion stretches and also disciplines students' observations, giving opportunities to distinguish between observations and inferences. It is also an opportune time to contrast an occupational perspective on Ms. Smith as it differs from the viewpoint of a physician, physical therapist or psychologist.

Although Ms. Smith is malnourished and has Parkinsonism as well as bipolar disorder, she is surprisingly youthful in appearance and an engaging conversationalist. This unexpected presentation rouses curiosity about Ms. Smith as well as concern that diagnostic labels bias their views of clients. Dewey argued that emotions play a central role in attention and learning (Dewey 1958). The quality of the learning session thus far is relative to the extent to which students are interested in learning more about Ms. Smith's situation and what they need to know as occupational therapists. The subsequent interview segments allow students to pose questions and to some degree test their assumptions about Ms. Smith.

Ms. Smith appears to have lived her life as a strong willed and independent person, yet she describes herself as "very compliant." They wonder if she actually participates in the activities she claims to do. Is the interview itself a meaningful occupation? Is she covering-up for cognitive deficits through leading the conversation? Why does she become animated when discussing her daughter? Why does she avoid talking about her deceased husband? Are her hand motions religious gestures? The teacher orchestrates the learning experience while also learning from students' insights and interpretations. With each segment of the video there is more information to discuss and organize as the group co-constructs an image of Ms. Smith and her life context. The co-construction of shared concerns and knowledge deepens the peer-learning community within the class. The transaction should in and of itself be enjoyed (Dewey 1963). Principles of democracy are embedded in the process of valuing individuals' views and acknowledging that the collective discoveries of the group are superior to that of any individual. Carrying these values into clinical settings prepares students for teamwork and client centered care.

Within the transaction, the teacher strategically draws attention to select information and problems. As problems are posed, the class engages in an explicit *deliberation* process. Openly deliberating as a group brings awareness of internal ways of responding to situations, and allows the teacher to build students' habits of inquiry through the experience. For example when Ms. Smith becomes tearful, the interviewer is faced with the problem of how to respond to her tears. The students hypothesize about why she is tearful. They generate options for the interviewer's action, such as changing the subject, asking more probing questions, using reflective listening or sitting quietly. Using the Deweyan concept of *dramatic rehearsal* (Fesmire 2003), the students use their *imagination* to consider each option and play out each scenario and its consequences to determine the best choice of action for the interviewer. Collaboratively deliberating this problematic moment, and putting themselves in the role of the interviewer who weighs the moral elements of action, students have a structured and supported experience of clinical reasoning. That reasoning is comprised of the Deweyan components of self-control, deliberation, setting purposes, and carrying out the best action toward those purposes.

In subsequent video segments with Ms. Smith new problems arise—there are things that do not seem to add up. Ms. Smith expresses false beliefs about medications, leading the students to deem her unreliable, and students become doubtful and less interested in what she has to say. Later, Ms. Smith attempts to explain a problem she has in swallowing that does not seem to make medical or physiologic sense. The class sees this problem as another example of her being a poor historian or lacking insight. The teacher does not refute the class's dismissal of Ms. Smith's statements, to intensify a later revelation. At the end of the interview it is revealed that the swallowing problem she described was factual information about a rare condition. The unexpected validity of Ms. Smith's statements challenges the habit of distrusting information from clients who are labeled unreliable, or who are stigmatized as not having insight based upon their diagnosis. The moral dimension of intelligent inquiry is apparent when the students revise their judgment about Ms. Smith in light of new information.

Creativity is a component of deliberation (Joas 1996; Cutchin et al. 2008), and an essential element of occupational therapy clinical reasoning. Imagination, as part of reasoning, is "the capacity to concretely perceive what is before us in light of what could be" (Fesmire 2003, p. 65). The final portion of the session involves explicit use of *creativity*. Students generate ideas to address the problem of finding and adapting meaningful occupations in Ms. Smith's life context. Imagination and creativity are necessary to generate occupation-centered recommendations, in particular to consider Ms. Smith's occupations upon discharge from the hospital. It is difficult to form a picture of her real life circumstances from what she reveals. Yet the students, like practicing therapists, must work with what they know, and draw from their powers of observation and inquiry. The value of collaboration at this juncture becomes apparent, when the co-constructed plan of the group is always better than any individual's.

Students' learning deepens as they reflect upon the lessons from Ms. Smith. Dewey (1963) argues that thoughtful *reflection* on learning experience is essential to build continuity and reasoning. Schön's (1983) concept of professional *reflection-in-action and -on-action* is based in Dewey's theory of inquiry. Accordingly, students generate learning points and new questions. What can endure from the experience of Ms. Smith are students' habits of mind that foster growth and satisfaction in their future as learner-practitioners.

The case of Ms. Smith elicits students' attention and engagement when their existing habits of thinking are not adequate to solve the problems posed. Her story serves as a moral call for action about stigmatizing clients that particularly resonates with students who are pursuing a career of advocacy and service to others. Discourse is meaningful and therefore enjoyed when it is a just-right challenge for students' capabilities and also produces growth toward their purposes or needs. The teacher must be mindful that end-in-view for students is a shifting target, that can range from desire to appear intelligent to peers to images of themselves as leaders. The end-in-view is the next horizon which is always moving forward, it is dynamic and diverse even among students pursuing careers in OT.

16.5 Occupation as Subject Matter of the Curriculum

Dewey (1963) identified the *subject* of curriculum as the topic presented to the learner in the learning environment. He reasoned about carefully selecting meaningful subjects and having a logical progression of content. He argued for the integration of arts, literature, and sciences—an idea familiar in occupational therapy and occupational science. Yet, his overarching influence was to shift the emphasis of education from the subject itself to the learner's experience with it, while still valuing the subject matter.

Leaders in occupational therapy and occupational science contend that education should be centered on the subject of occupation (Nielson 1998; Yerxa 1998; Wood et al. 2000; Whiteford and Wilcock 2001; Hooper 2006). How occupation-centered education guides pedagogy has been less well articulated (Hooper 2006; Wood et al. 2000). Dewey's pedagogy, in tandem with his worldview of human action, holds promise to align the subject of occupation with pedagogy in occupational therapy, beyond general principles of active and self-directed learning.

Dewey's theory of experience has at its center the import of ordinary life-experiences as a basis for learning, or more specifically, the optimal learning situation. In occupation centered curricula students explore their own occupations, their meanings and contexts, so that those experiences can be understood in a fuller and more organized form. Inquiry from the discipline of occupational science, and transactionalism, can be applied in the process of doing and reflecting on occupations. Sequencing the content progressively using clinical problems of occupational participation forms habits of clinical reasoning. In Dewey's philosophy, analysis and synthesis using real-life examples are more educational, and although that assumption makes logical sense, it has not been proven through research.

In occupational science and occupational therapy, there is a remarkable association of the subject of occupation and the occupations of learning and teaching. In fact, the student experience of the learning situation is itself an occupation. Dewey's meta-theories about continuity, interaction, intelligence, control, creativity, imagination, freedom, and morality are all at play in the learning situation and in all human transactions. This cohesion has potential for profound understanding of the subject matter, with each moment having the potential for relevance to the subject of occupation. That Dewey argued for meaningful experiences rather than skill building to promote learning is a parallel to occupational therapists calling for the therapeutic power of occupation over impairment focused interventions. Thus, learning activities and evaluation of learning would be contextualized into real practice contexts as possible, a daunting task for faculty with full teaching loads. Similarly, clinicians are faced with the dilemma of creating real-life occupations for a succession of clients that change every 30 to 60 minutes. Implementation of Deweyan principles is perhaps best viewed as an aspiration.

Dewey's (1963, p. 46) statement "there is no such thing as educational value in the abstract" is a reminder to ground learning experiences in real life, but does not imply that all occupational therapy could be learned in practice situations. While on one hand Dewey argued for education to occur through evolving real life experiences and contexts, on the other he emphasizes the teacher structuring situations to optimize learning. Vygotsky (1978) offers a useful complement to Dewey to explain how that structuring occurs, and the strategies of scaffolding and fading by the teacher. The classroom is a supported place to work with theoretical concepts and reflect upon practice situations in ways that develop habits of thinking for the betterment of client experiences and outcomes. Yet, many curriculums have disconnected anatomy, neurology and psychology content, which might lead to "dispersive, disintegrated or centrifugal habits" (Dewey 1963, p. 26). Courses such as "Neurological Functions Supporting Occupation" or "Human Movement in Occupations" align with Deweyan pedagogy.

An example of a theme in an occupation centered curriculum is *occupation as a medium of change* (Wood et al. 2000). The curriculum begins with study of the evolution of human occupations, their emergence and transformations through the life span, and the relationship of geography, culture and occupation. Subsequent coursework engages students in problem based learning about how disability, displacement or other life change alters occupational patterns and possibilities. Exploring evidence and therapeutic options for individuals can evolve to population based interventions and related policies. This progression with a spiral model of learning revisits concepts in new ways for a more robust understanding of the subject. There are other ways to sequence the subject matter as long as it is well considered, and can allow for improvisation within the intentional experience.

Deweyan educational philosophy calls for a curriculum around core themes that frame *progressive organization of subject matter* (Dewey 1963, p. 73). Faculty knowledge of the curriculum as a whole gives structure and efficiency to curriculum planning (Wood et al. 2000). Shared themes and a spiral curriculum allow what Hooper (2006) termed essential *linking opportunities* between learning moments and the overall curriculum. Students evaluate the curriculum not just by the subject matter but through the lens of their experience of continuity in the subject matter. Using principles from Dewey, faculty can revisit their vision for future practice, curricular outcomes, and pedagogy, to change aspects of the curriculum which no longer fit, are not essential, or are missing (Wood et al. 2000). The quality of curriculum will reflect the collective purposes and needs of the faculty.

16.6 Conclusion

> But the easy and the simple are not identical. To discover what is really simple and act on the discovery is an exceedingly difficult task (p. 30).

John Dewey's ideal for education based on a sound theory of experience "represents the goal toward which education should continuously move" (1963, p. 83). His core beliefs about progressive education, extended by other theorists, are found in modern pedagogy. Dewey guides us to see education as a social transaction, whether on the internet or in a classroom. For Dewey (1963), education has no end or beginning. He viewed situations of learning like other situations in the stream of time, as inseparable from the past and future, but existing only in the moment. Dewey's transactional theory about human action, when aligned with a philosophy of education, underpins a coherent approach to pedagogy in occupational science and occupational therapy curriculums.

Exploration of Deweyan philosophy of education can guide a self-reflective process for faculty to analyze assumptions, habits, and use of imagination to enhance the student experience of learning. We are informed about how to teach in the practice of teaching, through being inquisitive and open to learning about teaching. We teach by co-constructing knowledge, working logically with the subject matter, and adapting to dynamic ends-in-view. An examined philosophy of experience offers a beacon for satisfaction in teaching, built from connections with students and the subject matter of occupation, along with the realization that education creates opportunity for more learning.

References

American Occupational Therapy Association. (2010). Telerehabilitation. *American Journal of Occupational Therapy, 64*(Suppl), S92–S102.

Cochran, M. (2002). Deweyan pragmatism and post-positivist social science in international relations. *Millennium - Journal of International Studies, 31*, 525.

Cunningham, C. A. (2009). Transforming schooling through technology: Twenty-first-century approaches to participatory learning. In A. D. Rud, J. Garrison, & L. Stone (Eds.), *John Dewey at 150: Reflections for a new century* (pp. 40–49). W.Lafayette: Purdue University Press.

Cutchin, M. P. (2007). From society to self (and back) through place: Habit in transactional context. *OTJR: Occupation, Participation, and Health, 27*, 50S–59S.

Cutchin, M. P., Aldrich, R., Bailliard, A., & Coppola, S. (2008). Action theories for occupational science: The contributions of Dewey and Bourdieu. *Journal of Occupational Science, 15*, 157–165.

Dewey, J. (1897). *My pedagogic creed. School Journal, 54*, 77–80.

Dewey, J. (1929). *The quest for certainty: A study of the relation of knowledge and action.* New York: Minton, Balch & Co.

Dewey, J. (1958). *Art as experience.* New York: Capricorn Books (Original work published in 1934).

Dewey, J. (1963). *Experience and education.* New York: Collier Books (Original work published in 1938).

Dewey, J. (1998). The place of habit in conduct (from *Human nature and conduct*). In L. Hickman & T. Alexander (Eds.), *The essential Dewey* (Vol. 2, pp. 24–49). Bloomington: Indiana University Press (Original work published in 1922).

Dewey, J. (2004). *Democracy and education.* Mineola/New York: Dover Publications/Macmillan (Original work published in 1916).

Fenstermacher, G. D. (2006). Rediscovering the student in Democracy and Education. In D. T. Hansen (Ed.), *John Dewey and our educational prospect. A critical engagement with Dewey's Democracy and Education* (pp. 97–112). Albany: SUNY Press.

Fesmire, S. (2003). *John Dewey and moral imagination: Pragmatism in ethics.* Bloomington: Indiana University Press.

Fishman, S. M., & McCarthy, L. P. (1998). *John Dewey and the challenge of classroom practice.* New York: Teachers College Press, Columbia University.

Fishman, S. M., & McCarthy, L. (2007). *John Dewey and the philosophy and practice of hope.* Champaign: University of Illinois Press.

Garrison, J. (1997). *Dewey and eros: Wisdom and desire in the art of teaching.* New York: Teacher's College Press.

Garrison, J. (2009). Dewey and the education of eros. In L. Hickman & G. Spadafora (Eds.), *John Dewey's educational philosophy in international perspective: A new democracy for the twenty-first century* (pp. 22–35). Carbondale: Southern Illinois University Press.

Hansen, D. (2006). Introduction to reading Democracy and Education. In D. T. Hansen (Ed.), *John Dewey and our educational prospect. A critical engagement with Dewey's Democracy and Education* (pp. 1–22). Albany: SUNY Press.

Hickman, L. (2011). Scientific concepts in Dewey's pedagogy. In L. A. Hickman, M. C. Flamm, K. P. Skowro Ski, & R. A. Rea (Eds.), *The continuing relevance of John Dewey: Reflections on aesthetics, morality, science, and society* (pp. 193–204). Amsterdam: Rodopi.

Hooper, B. (2006). Beyond active learning: A case study of teaching practices in an occupation-centered curriculum. *American Journal of Occupational Therapy, 60*, 551–562.

Hooper, B. (2008). Stories we teach by: Intersections among faculty biography, student formation, and instructional processes. *American Journal of Occupational Therapy, 62*, 228–241.

James, W. (1890). Habit: Chapter IV. *The principles of psychology.* http://psychclassics.yorku.ca/James/Principles/prin4.htm Accessed: 25 July 2011.

Jenlink, P. M. (2009). Dewey's legacy for democratic education and leadership. In P. M. Jenlink (Ed.), *Dewey's democracy and education revisited* (pp. 21–51). Lanham: Roman and Littlefield.

Joas, H. (1996). *The creativity of action.* Chicago: University of Chicago Press.

Jones, T. B. (2009). John Dewey: Still ahead of his time. In P. M. Jenlink (Ed.), *Dewey's democracy and education revisited* (pp. 137–154). Lanham: Roman and Littlefield.

Kestenbaum, V. (1977). *The phenomenological sense of John Dewey: Habit and meaning.* Atlantic Highlands: Humanities Press.

King, L. J. (1978). Toward a science of adaptive responses. *Eleanor Clark Slagle Lecture. American Journal of Occupational Therapy, 32*, 429–437.
Lave, J. (1988). *Cognition in Practice: Mind, mathematics, and culture in everyday life*. Cambridge: Cambridge University Press.
Lave, J., & Wenger, E. W. (1996). *Situated learning: Legitimate peripheral participation*. Cambridge: Cambridge University Press.
Nielson, C. (1998). The issue is—How can the academic culture move toward occupation centered education? *American Journal of Occupational Therapy, 53*, 386–387.
Oblinger, D. G., & Oblinger, J. L. (2005). *Educating the net generation*. Resource Document. Educause. http://net.educause.edu/ir/library/pdf/PUB7101.pdf
Schell, B. A., & Schell, J. W. (2008). Communities of practice: A curricular model that promotes professional reasoning. In B. A. Schell & J. W. Schell (Eds.), *Clinical and Professional Reasoning in Occupational Therapy* (pp. 289–310). Baltimore: Lippincott, Williams and Wilkins.
Schön, D. (1983). *The reflective practitioner: How professionals think in action*. New York: Basic Books.
Spadafora, G. (2009). The problem of a science of education in John Dewey's thought. In L. Hickman & G. Spadafora (Eds.), *John Dewey's educational philosophy in international perspective: A new democracy for the twenty-first century* (pp. 48–58). Carbondale: Southern Illinois University Press.
Vygotsky, L. S. (1978). *Mind and society: The development of higher mental processes*. Cambridge, MA: Harvard University Press.
Wenger, E. W. (1999). *Communities of practice: Learning, meaning, and identity*. Cambridge: Cambridge University Press.
Wenger, E.W. (2006). *Communities of practice: A brief introduction. Essay*. http://www.ewenger.com/theory/. Accessed 23 July 2011.
Whiteford, G. E., & Wilcock, A. A. (2001). Centralizing occupation in occupational therapy curricula: Imperative of the new millennium. *Occupational Therapy International, 8*, 81–85.
Wood, W., Nielson, C., Humphry, R., Coppola, S., Baranek, G., & Rourk, J. (2000). A curricular renaissance: Graduate education centered on occupation. *American Journal of Occupational Therapy, 54*, 586–597.
Yerxa, E. (1998). Occupation: The keystone for a curriculum for a self-defined profession. *American Journal of Occupational Therapy, 52*, 365–372.

Chapter 17
Educational Implications of Taking a Transactional Perspective of Occupation in Practice

Ruth Humphry and Linn Wakeford

17.1 Introduction

The challenge we address in this chapter is the education of professional students to enact a practice specifically informed by a transactional perspective on occupation (Humphry 2009; Humphry and Womack, submitted). We believe that many of the educational dilemmas and methods we discuss below are relevant to preparation in other professions, where an alternative to the assumed dichotomy between the individual and context/environment could be helpful. This chapter draws on our experiences educating graduate students about occupational therapy with children and focuses on that content area. Students typically come into the program with ideas about the roles of occupational therapists with schools and families and with previous education in human development. A transactional perspective often confronts those prior understandings.

A number of epistemological challenges arise in preparing future therapists to work from a transactional perspective. Key among these is the dominance of individualism, particularly in many Western cultures and their scientific communities (Dickie et al. 2006; Bishop 2007). For instance, several human sciences, such as physiology, neurology and psychology, are viewed as foundational bodies of knowledge in the education of health professionals. This content draws on literature that locates "what needs to be known" about the body's function and people's behavior within the individual, with only modest acknowledgement of the environment. This focus on the individual is further embedded when discussing children, because there is a tradition of understanding development as a universal, biological process that takes place within the individual child (Woodhead 1999; Wyness 2006). Finally, the singular focus on the *person* is reinforced by an implicit way of thinking that locates

R. Humphry (✉) • L. Wakeford
Department of Allied Health Sciences, Division of Occupational Science and Occupational Therapy, University of North Carolina at Chapel Hill, Chapel Hill, NC, USA
e-mail: Ruth_Humphry@med.unc.edu

M.P. Cutchin and V.A. Dickie (eds.), *Transactional Perspectives on Occupation*,
DOI 10.1007/978-94-007-4429-5_17, © Springer Science+Business Media B.V. 2013

disability as a problem within the individual (see Chap. 8). Taken together, these ways of understanding function and behavior, child development, and disability, may have the effect of communicating to future occupational therapists that knowledge about what people can and cannot do in their daily activities is best obtained by studying the individual's abilities (and disabilities) and that contexts are secondary and separate.

A transactional perspective serves as a metatheory and reflects a different view of how children act in the world and what is important to know about that action. It realigns our focus away from the individual and onto the relationships among elements of life situations. It requires a holistic perspective that locates people and their development as part of an overall system (Lerner and Overton 2008). Engaging with activities brings people into changing relationships with different elements of that system. These elements of the situation are inseparable; they mutually shape and define each other, such as how culture and identity or families and neighborhoods co-exist (Mistry and Wu 2010). From this perspective, the concern of the practitioner shifts from the individual to the activity and to how the elements of the situation relate to one another as the action unfolds.

In order to employ transactional perspectives, we ask students to adopt an epistemology that frames occupational therapy for children as working with the interdependent contextual elements related to the children's occupation rather than focusing on individual children. The following illustration of children engaged with occupation demonstrates how a transactional perspective allows one to view the situation as a functional whole. In the section following the illustration, we discuss how a transactional perspective leads to a practice that utilizes the relational elements of situations. We offer a contrast between this transactional perspective and the models of practice that foreground the child's inherent capacities to act. We conclude with a discussion of several educational strategies, not as formulas but rather as potential means for supporting growth, insight, and problem solving in future therapists.

17.2 Transactions in the Preschool Classroom

The class observed in this study was a state supported program to help disadvantaged 4 year-olds become familiar with classroom practices that they will need the following year when starting school. This study of childhood occupations was conducted by the first author[1] and targeted what is called "circle time" because large group instruction challenges preschoolers' participation more than other forms of class activity (Powell et al. 2008). The calendar is an example of a common tool with which children learn to engage in preschool classrooms, and it is often used as a circle time activity. In this classroom, the routine was referred to as "doing the calendar."

> Ms. Alston, the teacher, was asked to meet a delivery man in the yard and needed to leave the class with a new substitute teaching assistant. Before she left Ms. Alston called a

[1] Observations and fieldnotes made by Emily Furgang, research assistant.

student, Jason, to the front of the class to help the substitute with circle time. He led them in finishing a song, "Rise and Shine," and was prompted by one of his classmates that the next thing to do was the calendar. Jason called for Destiny, the designated calendar helper. She and the students did a funky cheer spelling out February. When that finished the substitute asks "Now what?" Jason replied "I forgot" and Destiny said they needed to count the numbers. She put the pointer on 1 and said "Ready? Go." With the pointer and the support of the substitute, Destiny led the students in counting the days of the month up to that day's date. When asked "What next?" She said "We hold up the day and call on someone." Destiny held up the Wednesday sign and called, "Benito!" Jason said "But we need to do today first." Destiny did not respond to him and started to prompt Benito by saying, "wa, wa, wa, wa." The substitute stepped in and said, "But today is not Wednesday." She handed Destiny the Thursday sign and Destiny called on Benito again. She prompted saying, "Th, th, th." and he answered "Thursday." In a similar manner Destiny called on other students to give yesterday's and tomorrow's names.[2, 3]

This example of childhood occupation contrasts with taking an individualistic perspective of performance, where "knowing what to do" comes from within the person. The understanding used to do the calendar is *distributed* in this classroom situation. Physical features, like the calendar and pointer, had shared meaning for the students and these objects oriented their counting of the days. Destiny remembered the sequence of events and how to prompt a response to the sign she was holding up. However, Jason and the substitute needed to help her start with the correct day of the week. Benito and other classmates may or may not have known the name of the day, but they were given the prompts to participate. In this way the class went forward successfully with the routine.

Within this example, the inseparability of elements is clear. By "doing the calendar," each child is simultaneously an individual and part of the class. In essence, the substitute and students co-construct one another's participation, and their actions reflect their interpretive representations of the classroom practice (Corsaro and Molinari 2008). They did not simply imitate or enact "doing the calendar" by rote, but rather reflected on and adapted the routine in subtle ways (e.g., Destiny took the teacher's role of asking questions). In addition, a transactional perspective of occupation presents the classroom routine of "doing the calendar" as interconnected with a larger societal agenda, i.e., to rear educated children. It also situates the activity and people in the classroom in a cultural and historic location by reflecting the educational practice of asking students to learn information by engaging in adult created activities and answering questions (Morelli et al. 2003).

17.3 Enacting a Transactional Point of View in Practice

The essence of therapy from a transactional perspective of occupation starts with an understanding of the elements that bring people, through their engagement in activities, into relationship with life situations. However, this practice is not followed by

[2] Names used are pseudonyms.

[3] Fieldnotes were edited for comprehension and verb tense.

all occupational therapists, and many may work from an individualistic perspective that locates the sources of action and any performance problems within the child. Such individualistic models of practice reflect two problematic perspectives: (1) a biomedical perspective that focuses on minimizing the effects of disabilities, and (2) a focus on acquisition of new skills (following the sequence reflected in the literature on development). These two broad approaches focus on the remediation of problems, such as sensory integration disorder or the practice of performance components, such as fine motor skills. Both are thought to be foundational to occupational performance (Case-Smith 2010; Rodger 2010) and situated within the child.

Occupational therapy practice from a transactional perspective requires patience and keen attention in order to observe, collect information, analyze, synthesize and hypothesize both before and during the planning and enacting of intervention. It also requires a commitment to enacting intervention in a manner that is congruent with daily life. These two requirements acknowledge that in order to design and implement a successful intervention, the therapist must have a good understanding of the elements of the situation itself, including the child, and then be willing to act *within* that situation. We approach the occupational therapy process as entering into circumstances that are ongoing and "messy," such as the circle time example illustrated above. Our role is to create change in the relationship of the elements in the situation, but to do so in a way that will allow the benefits of that change to persist, even as we withdraw from that situation.

The challenges for occupational therapists in adopting a transactional perspective of occupation include: (1) long-standing relationships with the fields of medicine and psychology, which have created expectations about the domains and process of our practice, (2) the resulting "popular," but not always evidence-based, practices that are enacted in a number of settings, and (3) in the U.S., a national system of healthcare and reimbursement that are largely aligned with traditional Western medical practices. These realities in our current practice environments are acknowledged, but none of these challenges preclude therapists from engaging in practice from a transactional perspective.

17.3.1 The Practice Process

In order to describe the use of a transactional perspective in the process of assessment and intervention with children, two new terms are necessary: *conversation* and *occupational situation*. In addition, although the needs of an individual child may serve as the initial reason for a referral to occupational therapy services, the actual client typically includes a family, classroom, team, or other "community" of people. Clients may also be groups of children and the adults associated with them, as opposed to an individual child.

Use of the word *conversation* reflects a change in conceptualization and terminology that may be important to practice from a transactional perspective. That is, *conversation*, as used here, refers to a reciprocal dialogue and exchange of information that differs from *therapist directed* interview and intervention planning. Conversation is the essence of relevant, day-to-day, situational understandings of how children are participating in various contexts, and is a key component of transactional practice. Results of conversation allow the therapist a better understanding of how others view the child, what others know about the child, and the concerns they have, as well as an understanding of who the people are that are currently a part of the child's life. Conversation with the child (i.e., reciprocal exchange of information) is an absolute necessity, although that conversation may occur largely non-verbally in the context of a shared activity. Conversation also contributes to the development of rapport, which is perhaps among the most crucial of its outcomes. Future transactions, including intervention, will be influenced by the rapport, respect, and trust that exists among all players in the therapeutic process, and conversation contributes significantly to those aspects of the therapeutic relationship.

The term *occupational situation* as used here is meant to convey a whole, comprised of multiple interpenetrating elements, including the client, the occupation, and temporal, cultural, social and physical contexts; but the situation is also more than the sum of those parts. The continuity among elements (child, occupation, other children, etc.) is an important dimension of the occupational situation. Applying the concept of *occupational situation* to working with children allows the therapist, for instance, to consider outdoor play as an occupational situation that provides multiple opportunities for engagement and participation. Those opportunities vary minute by minute in terms of social, physical, temporal, and cultural demands, as well as variations in interest, meaning, affect, self-efficacy, and satisfaction available to any participant. In addition, the variations in any one of the aspects of this situation influence all others. We then see the ebb and flow of occupation among all participants, both individually and as a group, and can also see how the engagement of one or more specific children fits in and evolves. We have then completed an initial aspect of the assessment process. Following the observation of this situation as a whole, we may enter it, not to exert control, but rather to participate in it. The insertion of the therapist into the occupational situation is intended to allow that therapist to learn about the child from the child, and to understand better how that child is actually participating. How is this particular outdoor play situation being constructed by this child, and how does that compare with how others are constructing it? Is it similar to or different from how this child constructs other outdoor play situations? What is the transaction that is occurring here and how is that transaction contributing to the success and satisfaction of that child or group of children on the playground? These are the types of questions that the therapist must ask as a part of both the assessment and intervention aspects of the therapeutic process and provide information to share with others in order to collaborate in the ongoing design and revision of intervention.

Using a transactional perspective, intervention is implemented with the understanding that a change in any aspect of the occupational situation will result in change in all other aspects and in how all aspects relate to one another. The therapist works within the occupational situation, engaging spontaneously and often concurrently in observation, problem-solving, and participation. Conversation also continues to be a significant contributor to the process, especially as the therapist will not always be the person intervening, and the others involved may need coaching, models, or other methods of learning to implement the intervention. The need for observation, problem-solving, conversation, and participation is true regardless of the role being taken by the therapist, e.g., whether he or she is providing parent education, modeling a strategy, changing some aspect of the environment, or interacting directly with the child in the context of an activity.

The essence of intervention from a transactional perspective lies in providing opportunities for the child to engage in occupation in a new way that is also meaningful to him or her. This requires that the therapist share control of the situation with the child and others, rather than using predetermined ideas about the opportunity that should be provided, and how the child should respond to it, as illustrated in the following example.

> Claire was a 4-year-old with mild to moderate motor impairments. Her therapists believed that her desire to ride a tricycle would best be facilitated by the use of an adapted "trike." This solution provides the riding opportunity in a single way, closing off the potential for shared control of the situation by Claire. As her therapist worked one-on-one with her, teaching her to ride the adapted trike, Claire met with some success, but tired of the activity fairly quickly and moved on to other playground activities. However, on a day when her teachers and therapists were busy with other children, Claire approached an occupational therapy (OT) student who did not know about the current intervention plan and said she wanted to ride the trike. The student pointed out where several trikes were parked on the playground and asked Claire which one she wanted to ride. Claire chose one of the newer, larger trikes, and the student helped her get positioned on it at Claire's request. Claire had to exert significant effort but pedaled away, along with several peers, slowly covering the entire distance of the bike path, with supervision for safety by the OT student. Claire's teachers and therapists looked on in amazement, as this performance was much more sophisticated and successful than any they had observed when Claire was on the adapted trike interacting with an adult. The OT student presented an opportunity that allowed Claire to choose what had most meaning to her, which resulted in a different form of social engagement and successful performance.

The provision of opportunities that will entice and support the mutual occupational and social engagement of the child emerges from the ongoing relationship among occupational situations, the child, and the therapist, and is not an exact science nor does it occur according to any standard protocol. Regardless of the therapist's knowledge, reasoning skills, or experience, there are times when he or she uses a strategy to create an opportunity for child engagement that does not work. From a transactional perspective, this is not seen as a "failure," but rather as a source of additional knowledge and understanding that can be articulated and discussed in order to create opportunity in a manner that the child *can* use. This presents a contrast to what may occur when strategies emerging from biomedical or developmental models fail to produce the specific desired results. Using those models, the therapist and the child are the primary players, so the reason for the failure must lie within one of them, e.g., the child could not hold the pencil correctly, or the therapist did not facilitate movement in the right way. Subsequent intervention strategies are likely to be limited to a continued emphasis on "within person" change. As a result, more meaningful opportunities (which may or may not have anything to do with writing his name) that are embedded in an occupational situation are lost.

In summary, occupational therapy practice with children from a transactional perspective largely consists of seeking to understand and then working *within* occupational situations to create opportunities for children to engage occupationally and socially. This creative process requires embracing a holistic perspective, sharing control, being flexible, collaborating, and being willing to take on a variety of roles. It occurs as a result of a constant intermingling of observation, conversation, participation, and reasoning, and cannot be reduced to a standard or prescriptive method. Therapists who practice this way are comfortable with an understanding of the complex and emergent occupational situation.

17.4 Educating Therapists in a Transactional Perspective of Occupation

The remainder of this chapter addresses the ways in which we educate future occupational therapists to enact a transactional perspective in practice with children. The foundations and common themes that are embedded across the curriculum ground the students in transactional thinking. Upon that grounding, we seek to build the application of that thinking to children and childhood and then to practice with children in coursework in the students' second year.

Our professional education coursework is an integrated curriculum where the faculty members share a vision of practice that focuses on using occupations that are relevant to clients as the medium of change and supports greater participation in life situations. The transactional perspective is applied in a variety of different ways, introduced in the first semester and then re-visited again in more depth during subsequent courses. This spiraling process allows students to explore the broader concepts of a transactional point of view, applied to both practice in general and to particular practice settings, e.g., how institutional policies and reimbursement are interconnected with service provision. In courses where assessment and intervention content is taught, students explore a number of perspectives, from individualistic to transactional, by applying and analyzing those perspectives in the assessment and intervention process for the diverse populations occupational therapists serve. Discussions of the links among personal histories, family histories, and cultural considerations prepare students to recognize that intervention protocols must be embedded in a larger, more multifaceted understanding of the specific client and occupational situation. As a result of these experiences in the first year, when second year students participate in courses about childhood occupations and practice with children, they are comfortable with the transactional perspective of occupation. The challenge then is to get students to apply this perspective specifically to work with children. Three means of meeting this challenge are explicated below: the first two are initiated in a fall semester course and the third in the following semester.

17.4.1 Problematizing the Popular View of Childhood

A transactional perspective of occupation differs from what is often expressed in the child development literature. This in turn affects teaching strategies. A major objective in the first course is to confront students with the weaknesses of the taken for granted perspectives on children and what they do (Humphry 2005, 2009). Students often enter our program with the understanding that psychology is "… the study of the mind and … the understanding of behavior," (American Psychological Association 2011) and/or believe in a common-sense folk psychology that explains people's action as caused by internal beliefs and desires (Rosenberg 2008). Students are given readings by critical theorists in psychology (Woodhead 1999) and other disciplines that drew on developmental psychology as the authority about child development (Roer-Strier 2005; Ryan and Grieshaber 2005; Wyness 2006).

Another exercise directed at problematizing popular views of childhood is to ask students to consider how ideas about children and what they do changes as a result of historic events such as the industrial revolution, child labor laws, and the availability of public education (Hendrick 1997). Early child studies used "scientific methods" employed in the physical sciences presumed development was relatively "universal" as it was a biological process. Thus, normative studies were carried out with relatively few children and biased toward white middle-class children. The results of these studies then were used as benchmarks to illustrate how children with different childhoods could be found precocious or deficient. The students read how even the most basic abilities have shown cultural variations (Hickey et al. 2000). Though test makers have become increasingly adept at using a more representative sample, universalism still appears in texts that speak of "the child" as if there is only one model. Students are encouraged to discuss how this presents a significant problem, particularly for those working with a growing number of ethnically and culturally diverse children.

The work of Super and Harkness (2003) provides another means of calling attention to assumptions about development. Students are introduced to the concept of "world views" as a means of understanding how parents and health professionals interpret and give meaning to children's behaviors. Readings and clinical stories are used to illustrate times when parents or professionals act on different world views they can violate the normative expectations of other people. In facilitated discussions students consider ethical challenges in collaborating with others who do not share the same assumptions about children's actions. The class reflects on the disconnect between their current understanding of childhood occupation and others' assumptions about children.

Finally with an appreciation of the social construction of childhood, students are asked to read different chapters about practice guidelines and consider how childhood is approached in occupational therapy. This discussion includes the concept of "developmentally appropriate" practice and the "developmental approach" which reifies the hierarchical sequences found in charts and tables of what skills and abilities a child is should display and at what age. A sample of this work is in Table 17.1. The left two

Table 17.1 Implications for practice of alternative assumptions about development, the child, dysfunction, and resulting model of practice

Assumptions about	Biological maturation	Skills and developmental milestones	Individual and occupations	Contextual/Person & situation integrated
What drives changes in occupational performance?	Neuro-maturation brought about by stimulation & challenges that occur through interactions with the environment This is thought to unfold naturally unless damaged	Practice in developmental sequence with emphasis on most immature skills & following the pattern of change. Needs to learn particular habits of action or skills like grip on pencil or sequence of putting a shirt on	Child's motivations to explore & master knowledge or performance challenges are key to acquisition of new occupations (Reflected by the general models of practice discussed earlier)	Societal influences, occupational opportunities, interpersonal interactions & intentions to engage shape emergent occupations
Defining the child	Childhood is a period of natural immature so the child need support in becoming mature	Child is a collection of developing skills & abilities which impact occupational performance	The child creates development through discovery of how to do things	The child is part of a coordinated system that leads to occupation
Dysfunction & practice focus	Issues are related to intrinsic immaturity & developmental readiness. Intervention is experiential stimulation to remediate delays & promote maturation of selected capacities	Asynchronous development is expected so a therapist teaches or creates challenges to missing or delayed skills. Practice with graded activities that draw out the targeted skills at the next developmental stage	Addresses the child's preferred or expected occupation thru adaptation, modification, & environmental supports to enable engagement	Focus on the occupation, nature of meaning & child's experiences in natural settings. Support engagement, scaffold & talk about doing the activity
Ideal models of practice	Neuro Developmental Treatment, practice movement for movement sake, sensory integration to target specific sensory systems	Contrived activities used to practice specific skills, developmental approaches to address the foundation(s)	Cognitive approaches that focus on doing occupation. CO-OP (Palatajko and Mandich 2004)	Coach parents, teachers & child in the natural environment. Use of peers, social stories, & models

columns reflect different assumed explanations for changes in occupational performance but both rest on assumptions that what is known about development is factual and universal. Overall, problematizing conventional concepts about child development and childhood occupations opens the students to other perspectives and heightens their abilities to analyze and sift through multiple sources of information about childhood occupations.

Because this section of the course is about ideas and ways of thinking about the interconnected, transactional processes that shape children's engagement (Humphry 2009; Humphry and Wakeford 2008) students are asked to maintain a reflective journal in which they react to readings, reflect on past observations of occupational therapy with children, and imagine the implications for children with diverse backgrounds, including the presence of a disability. The emphasis is on exploring examples from their own experiences and from contemporary literature in which the narrative is about child development.

17.4.2 Explicating Context

The remainder of the fall semester course is informed by research into the development of childhood occupation (Humphry 2005), and how that occurs in different situations. It draws heavily from cultural-historical activity theory about children that rests on the earlier work of Vygotsky and his followers (Hedegaard 2009; Rogoff 2003), as well as from sociology literature about childhood (Corsaro 2005). This work accepts a relational perspective of mutually interpenetrating person and context, where the relationship becomes the unit of analysis (Lerner and Overton 2008).

To contextualize occupations, the course simultaneously locates activities in a socio-cultural context and the different social institutions where children live their lives. Socio-cultural context is addressed through discussion of the interplay of social divisions that place children and families in different categories based on resources and occupational situations. Three of these categories, ethnicity, socio-economic status, and ability/disability (Payne 2006) are selected for discussion Social institutions are introduced as structured places that take the forms of the family home, child care programs, and schools (Hedegaard 2009). Students are asked to think of these institutions as forming functional systems, where children navigate the varying forms of activities, values, and expectations.

17.4.3 Scaffolding Transaction in Application to Practice

Just as the theoretical and philosophical understanding of a transactional perspective is introduced and re-visited in various learning experiences within the curriculum, the enactment of practice from that perspective also must be scaffolded. Scaffolding, which also may be known as guided practice, is a method of facilitating learning based on the Vygotskian notion that learning takes place in a social context (Vygotsky 1978). When used in professional education, scaffolding occurs through the combination of knowledge and collaboration (social interaction) between faculty and students (Tilley et al. 2007). Scaffolding includes both modeling and the structuring of assignments to move students from the simple to the complex, and is documented as a teaching strategy in practice professions as a way to develop reasoning skills (e.g., Hersh and Cruice 2010; Dickieson et al. 2008) and physical (technical) skills (e.g., Tilley et al. 2007; Weddle and Hollan 2010).

We see a need for scaffolding transactional thinking because of the difficulty and relative lack of experience of students in translating theory to practice. The students' ability to view occupational situations as complex, relational, and constantly evolving, as well as their willingness to view children and childhood in a "non-conventional" manner, provides them with ways to *think* about enacting practice with children. Yet they then struggle with the question of what to *do*. This is often a point at which they may wish to move away from a transactional perspective, and resort to more structured theoretical models that appear to make "what to do" easier to determine. For instance, the translation from thinking to doing from a developmental model can seem relatively clear, e.g., if the child cannot yet hold a pencil correctly, a developmental model would suggest that intervention must first address that issue, and then begin to work on writing one's name. When students are attracted to linear models and ways of thinking (such as developmental models), the challenge educationally is to help them see that they can: (1) generate notions of "what to do" from transactional thinking, (2) do so in a way that they begin to trust, and (3) internalize the process. This challenge is met in several ways within the design of learning experiences and includes the use of a transactional approach to the teaching process itself.

Story-telling is one means for modeling the use of transactional thinking, while keeping students engaged. Stories, photos, and videos related to the instructor's and other therapists' personal experiences in practice, presented with clearly articulated intersections of thinking and doing, give the students examples of the application of a transactional perspective. In addition, this type of story-telling generates further questions, comments, and stories from the students themselves that then lead to further discussion and further explication of transaction *as lived*. Similar results can occur when students are assigned various research articles related to intervention strategies or techniques and then examine those from the standpoint of their usefulness in practice, depending on one's theoretical perspective, including transaction.

Scaffolding student learning about applying transactional perspectives to practice also occurs in the structure and content of assignments. Case-based group and fieldwork assignments offer clear opportunities for applied learning, and the structure of these assignments is used to guide thinking along transactional lines. For example, the first question in each case-based assignment is "Who is this child?" The expectation is clear that the answer is to be holistic, including likes/dislikes, key contexts, and key relationships, with less emphasis on diagnosis. Assignments also include sections that require a synthesized description of the situation, followed by articulated reasoning and justification for the assessment and/or intervention decisions made by the student. A section for reflective statements is included, in which the student is asked to critique her/his own ideas and actions. Feedback from the instructor typically targets the synthesis, reasoning, and reflective sections, as these are where the students' understanding of and ability to apply a transactional perspective are most evident. Expectations of student performance increase with each assignment, particularly in terms of integrating all elements of the therapeutic situation and reflecting on one's own role within that situation.

The core elements of occupational therapy practice with children from a transactional perspective are observation, conversation/collaboration and working within an occupational situation to create meaningful, shared opportunities for children to participate socially and occupationally in new or different ways. However, it is often difficult for students and new therapists to enact the shared control, willingness to critique one's own thinking and actions, flexibility, and spontaneity that generally are required in this kind of practice, and to trust the transactional process and their ability to work within in it. Therefore, scaffolding their ability to translate, if not fully synthesize, transactional *thinking* into *doing* is a key feature of creating practitioners who can utilize this transactional perspective in providing occupational therapy for children.

17.5 Conclusion

In this chapter, we articulated a number of theoretical, epistemological and practical challenges that may arise in educating future occupational therapy practitioners to adopt and use a transactional perspective in their practice with children. We also shared both general and specific approaches we have taken to meet those challenges. These approaches include embedding the exploration of transactional perspectives throughout the entire curriculum, encouraging students to question assumptions and conventional perspectives on children and childhood occupations, clearly explicating concepts related to context and to the relationships of persons and situations, and the scaffolding of translating transactional thinking to practice, via modeling, story-telling, and the structure and content of case-based assignments.

References

American Psychological Association. (2011). Available at http://www.apa.org/support/about/apa/psychology.aspx#answer

Bishop, R. C. (2007). *The philosophy of social sciences*. New York: Continuum International.

Case-Smith, J. (2010). An overview of occupational therapy for children. In J. Case-Smith & J. C. O'Brien (Eds.), *Occupational therapy for children* (6th ed., pp. 1–21). Maryland Heights: Mosby/Elsevier.

Corsaro, W. (2005). *The sociology of childhood*. Thousand Oaks: Pine Forge Press.

Corsaro, W. A., & Molinari, L. (2008). Entering and observing in children's worlds: A reflection on a longitudinal ethnography of early education in Italy. In P. Christensen & A. James (Eds.), *Entering and observing in children's worlds* (2nd ed., pp. 239–259). New York: Routledge.

Dickie, V., Cutchin, M. P., & Humphry, R. (2006). Occupation as transactional experience: A critique of individualism in occupational science. *Journal of Occupational Science, 13*, 83–93.

Dickieson, P., Carter, L. M., & Walsh, M. (2008). Integrative thinking and learning in undergraduate nursing education: Three strategies. *International Journal of Nursing Education Scholarship, 5*, 1–15.

Hedegaard, M. (2009). Children's development from a cultural-historical approach. *Mind, Culture, and Activity, 16*, 64–81.

Hendrick, H. (1997). Constructions and reconstructions of British childhood: An interpretive survey, 1800 to present. In A. James & A. Prout (Eds.), *Constructing and reconstructing childhood: Contemporary issues in the sociological study of childhood*. London: Falmer Press.

Hersh, D., & Cruice, M. (2010). Beginning to teach the end: The importance of including discharge from aphasia therapy in the curriculum. *International Journal of Language & Communication Disorders, 45*, 263–274.

Hickey, A., Froude, E., Williams, A., Hart, T., & Summers, J. (2000). Performance of Australian children on the Miller assessment for preschoolers compared with USA norms. *Australian Occupational Therapy Journal, 47*, 86–94.

Humphry, R. (2005). Model of processes transforming occupations: Exploring societal and social influences. *Journal of Occupational Science, 12*, 36–41.

Humphry, R. (2009). Occupation and development: A contextual perspective. In E. B. Creapeau, E. S. Cohn, & B. A. B. Schell (Eds.), *Willard & Spackman's occupational therapy* (11th ed., pp. 22–32). Baltimore: Lippincott Williams & Wilkins.

Humphry, R., & Womack, J. (submitted). Transformations of occupations: A life course perspective. In B. A. B. Schell, G. Gillen, & M. Scaffa (Eds.), *Willard & Spackman's occupational therapy* (12th ed.). Baltimore: Lippincott Williams & Wilkins.

Humphry, R., & Wakeford, L. (2008). Development of everyday activities: A model for occupation-centered therapy. *Infants & Young Children. An Interdisciplinary Journal of Special Care Practices, 21*, 230–240.

Lerner, R. M., & Overton, W. F. (2008). Exemplifying the integration of the relational developmental system: Synthesizing theory, research and application to promote positive development and social justice. *Journal of Adolescent Research, 23*, 245–255.

Mistry, J., & Wu, J. (2010). Navigating cultural worlds and negotiating identities: A conceptual model. *Human Development, 53*, 5–25.

Morelli, G. A., Rogoff, B., & Angelillo, C. (2003). Cultural variation in young children's access to work or involvement in specialized child-focused activities. *International Journal of Behavioral Development, 27*, 264–274.

Polatajko, H., & Mandich, A. (2004). Enabling occupation in children: The Cognitive Orientation to daily Occupational Performance (CO-OP) approach. Ottawa, ON: CAOT Publications ACE.

Payne, G. (2006). *Social divisions* (2nd ed.). New York: Palgrave Macmillian.

Powell, D., Burchinal, M. R., File, N., & Kontos, S. (2008). An eco-behavioral analysis of children's engagement in urban public school preschool classrooms. *Early Childhood Research Quarterly, 23*, 108–123.

Rodger, S. (2010). Becoming more occupation-centered when working with children. In S. Rodger (Ed.), *Occupation-centered practice with children: A practical guide for occupational therapist* (pp. 21–44). Oxford: Wiley.

Roer-Strier, D. (2005). Human development education for social workers in multicultural societies. *Social Work Education, 24*, 311–326.

Rogoff, B. (2003). *The cultural nature of human development*. New York: Oxford University Press.

Rosenberg, A. (2008). *Philosophy of social science* (3rd ed.). Boulder: Westview.
Ryan, S., & Grieshaber, S. (2005). Shifting from developmental to postmodern practices in early childhood teacher education. *Journal of Teacher Education, 56*, 34–45.
Super, C. M., & Harkness, S. (2003). The metaphors of development. *Human Development, 46*, 3–23.
Tilley, D. S., Allen, P., Collins, C., Bridges, R. A., Francis, P., & Green, A. (2007). Promoting clinical competence: Using scaffolded instruction for practice-based learning. *Journal of Professional Nursing, 23*, 285–289.
Vygotsky, L. (1978). *Mind in society: The development of higher psychological processes*. Cambridge: Harvard University Press.
Weddle, A. B., & Hollan, J. D. (2010). Profession perception and expert action: Scaffolding embodied practices in professional education. *Mind, Culture, and Activity, 17*, 119–148.
Woodhead, M. (1999). Reconstructing developmental psychology – Some first steps. *Children and Society, 13*, 3–19.
Wyness, M. (2006). *Childhood and society: An introduction to the sociology of childhood*. New York: Palgrave Macmillan.

Chapter 18
Twenty-First Century Pragmatism and Social Justice: Problematic Situations and Occupational Reconstructions in Post-Civil War Guatemala

Gelya Frank

18.1 Introduction

Pragmatist philosopher John Dewey (1958) elaborated upon his concept of occupations as the means by which people confront and solve problematic situations in their lives. A *situation* in Dewey's view is a problematic matter that unsettles one's view of truth and requires reformulation or solution through experience. The resulting change comes by doing something—that is, through reflective action. Dewey's uniquely specialized definition of the term *occupation* refers to this mindful activity or embodied engagement in problem-solving. No matter how slight or provisional, the solution or change that occurs is transactional and has effects both individually and socially. Dewey's perspective on the relationship between situations and occupations has immediate relevance to the way that non-governmental organizations (NGOs) work for human rights and social justice on the ground. Throughout the world, including in Guatemala, an occupational lens helps to understand how social change can and actually does take place in certain complex situations such as the aftermath of wars (Thibeault 2011).

Dewey's political thinking tended away from a focus on state power toward, instead, an organic model of social democracy based on citizen participation (Westbrook 1991). This is an approach to politics that arguably must be supplemented by political theories that address state power and by post structural theories of governance. Relatively recently, however, American historian Robert Putnam (1993, 2000) has provoked a new consideration of democratic politics scaled to the level of face-to-face relations (Lichterman 1996, 2005; Eliasoph 1998). This scale lends itself to examining transactional relationships between *situations*—which by definition are *problematic situations*—and *occupations* among non-state collective actors.

G. Frank (✉)
Division of Occupational Science and Occupational Therapy,
University of Southern California, Los Angeles, CA, USA
e-mail: gfrank@usc.edu

M.P. Cutchin and V.A. Dickie (eds.), *Transactional Perspectives on Occupation*,
DOI 10.1007/978-94-007-4429-5_18, © Springer Science+Business Media B.V. 2013

At the same time, we must also consider globalization and transnational activism as a relevant part of contemporary contexts (Keck and Sikkink 1998).

In the case of post-civil war Guatemala, for example, social justice efforts are driven less by government than by non-governmental organizations (NGOs) that are organized by or for Guatemalan citizens. The bulk of funding, volunteer labor, professional expertise, and other resources comes from abroad. Many traditional-style charities on this NGO model dispense goods and services without any other kind of participation from the recipients of such direct aid. But there are also many projects to reduce disparities in health care, education, employment, housing, law enforcement and justice that depend integrally on occupational engagement. Such projects typically attempt to build capacities and capabilities to achieve an effect both for individuals and the social situations of which they are a part (Sen 1999; Nussbaum 2011).

This chapter presents a brief description and analysis of three NGOs currently working in Guatemala. Parallels are discussed with pragmatist reform approaches during the progressive era in the United States, circa 1890–1920, while contemporary features and innovations are also noted. From large to small, these NGOs and their projects—Common Hope, located just outside Antigua; Long Way Home, in San Juan Comalapa; and the KIDS Restaurant, in San Gaspar Vivar—use occupations as a model for social transformation (Frank and Zemke 2009). Such NGOs can be analyzed and evaluated using the following framework of inquiry:

- What is the situation that this NGO addresses? *How is the situation understood or framed? What kinds of projects does the NGO sponsor to achieve its aims? Who determines what aspects of the situation need to be addressed? How does the NGO determine, reflect on, and revise what needs to be done? How is occupation facilitated or considered as a vehicle for social change?*
- What occupations go into ameliorating the situation? *How does the NGO actualize what needs to be done? Who does what? How engaging are the occupations in a Deweyan sense? How are the occupational capacities of individuals and the population developed that can further ameliorate their situation?*

18.2 Pragmatist Reformism, Globalization, and NGOs

American philosophers in the pragmatist tradition have taken the stance that social progress is possible and have affirmed evidence of positive changes in certain broad social situations (cf. Rorty 1998). Such affirmations of what Rorty (2000) calls "social hope" reflect an ameliorative orientation in stark contrast to Continental philosophies. As Cutchin and Dickie (2012) noted, twentieth century pragmatism placed a strong emphasis on theorizing action that relates to the improvement of human lives. "The concern for what works, i.e., how to create a better world," Cutchin and Dickie wrote, "is logically connected to needing to know how action occurs. If scientists and theoreticians want to *make* a better place for themselves and others, they need to know how the previous process of making erred and improve upon it (2012, p. 23)."

John Dewey has been viewed as having most fully articulated the democratic philosophy guiding the progressive era reforms associated with the settlement movement (Pettegrew 2000; see also Seigfried 1999). Democracy, in Dewey's view, is "an ethical ideal [which] calls upon men and women to build communities in which the necessary opportunities and resources are available for every individual to realize fully his or her particular capacities and powers through participation in political, social, and cultural life" (Westbrook 1991, p. xv). Working in this vein, progressive era reformers offered opportunities funded by philanthropy (funding from major donors to develop programs) rather than charity (direct aid to individuals of cash or goods). Further, the opportunities and benefits of social work were transactional between social workers and the populations served.

The "objective side" of social work, wrote settlement leader Jane Addams (1893a), addressed the situation of the urban poor directly. Hull House Settlement, which Addams cofounded with Ellen Gates Starr in 1889, offered well-baby clinics and kindergartens, arts and crafts programs for older children and adults, gymnasium and sports programs, afterschool programs, summer camps, visiting nurse services, public health education, groups for immigrant women to discuss issues and share experiences in their native language, labor organizing, a labor museum, adult classes in English, preparation for citizenship and participation in political campaigns. The "subjective side," wrote Addams (1893b), concerned the situation of the predominantly female settlement workers who were well-educated but expected to devote their lives to domesticity. Settlement work met their need to contribute to a larger purpose in the public sector and provided the opportunity to learn about life from direct experience by encountering the people they served.

Now, at the start of the twenty-first century, there are many parallels with the situation faced by the pragmatist reformers a century ago, but there are also new challenges. On what Addams called "the objective side," globalization and neoliberal economic policies have created new distributions of wealth and poverty based on reduction of taxes, deregulation, and government austerity (Sassen 2006). International development marked by rapid flows of information and capital produces uneven results (Inda and Rosaldo 2008). Uneven growth creates disparities (Harvey 1989; Escobar 1999; Sen 1999). Digital networking permits information and resources to produce new networks and forms of community across national borders (Latour 2007; Castells 2009). Populations are in flux due to wars and genocides, economic displacements, diasporas, and asylum seeking, but also travel and tourism associated with abundant and relatively inexpensive transportation.

On what Addams might have called the subjective side, the voluntary engagement by citizens concerned with globalized issues, there has been a sharp rise since the 1980s in transnational social movements and in the number and types of NGOs that advocate for social justice and human rights (Keck and Sikkink 1998). This fact serves as evidence that a heightened sense of global interconnectedness has emerged. This sensibility has been whetted, in part, by the damage done by trade agreements such as NAFTA (North American Trade Agreement) and disasters such as hurricanes and tsunamis, nuclear accidents, and global warming that appear to be related to corporate and political irresponsibility. As information becomes swiftly and abundantly available through digital sources, as well as standard news media, many people feel the need to channel their compassion and their outrage into action.

NGOs are not a panacea for the world's problems. They are hard to sustain, their targets are selective, their reach is limited, and their efforts are often duplicative and wasteful of resources that might be used more effectively if combined or coordinated (Provan and Milward 2001). Also, like other collective actors such as businesses (firms or corporations) they have interests of their own that hamper their ability to "do good" or "do the right thing" in given situations (Fisher 1997; Prakash and Gugerty 2010). In some situations, however, such as in Guatemala today, NGOs are a crucial source of advocacy, services, and opportunities for social goods that the government fails to provide.

The rapid increase in the number of NGOs worldwide since the 1980s is a response to wide-ranging neoliberal policies launched by governments of the United States and United Kingdom (Sassen 2006; Keck and Sikkink 1998). Clearly, today global citizens feel that they cannot rely on governments alone to resolve poverty and other forms of social injustice. This is especially the case because governments are often among the worst perpetrators of abuses (Hajjar 2004). Guatemala's civil war is a prime example, with covert and overt repression of the majority indigenous Maya population and military operations aided by the United States. The situations of inequality that NGOs address in Guatemala are structural and are not likely to diminish without positive intervention. The nature and magnitude of these complex problematic situations are suggested by such terms as *structural violence* (Farmer 2004), *functional apartheid* (Heggenhougen 1995), *occupational injustice* (Wilcock and Townsend 2000), and *occupational apartheid* (Kronenberg and Pollard 2004).

18.3 Problematic Situations and Occupational Reconstructions

Cutchin and Dickie (2012) proposed that John Dewey's pragmatist approach to philosophy is "particularly relevant to an occupational science that is concerned with issues that speak to making a better world, such as social justice, inclusion, and participation" (p. 24) Concerning Dewey's book *Experience and Nature*, Cutchin (2008) emphasized that Dewey's pragmatism is transactional. Following Dewey's approach, the concept of an *occupation* cannot really stand alone without specifying its relationship within a given context. *Situation* is the missing relational or transactional concept with which occupation might, and— to assess the impact of occupations in social transformation—ought to be paired. I suggest that Dewey's theorization of the relationship between *occupations* and *situations* deserves special attention from among occupational scientists (Frank 2011). So how did Dewey conceive of the concepts of occupation and situations? And how did he characterize the relationship between them?

Dewey defined a *situation* as a problem that interrupts an otherwise habitual and customary flow of experience (Cutchin 2008). Philosopher James Campbell (1995) noted that Dewey considered *situations* (which Dewey also sometimes referred to as *problematic situations*) to be indeterminate, hence emotionally troubling. If a problematic situation is confronted rather than avoided, reflection is required, leading to an action that offers at least a provisional resolution. It is true that Dewey (1916) used the term *occupation* in many ways, some of them extremely commonplace and general—e.g. a form of employment, such as teaching or farming (p. 124), or an everyday habitual activity, such as writing with a typewriter (p. 154).

But in other contexts, Dewey meant something more specific and more theoretically powerful, as we can see in his essay on the psychology of occupations. Dewey (1915/1990, pp. 132–133) explained: "The fundamental point in the psychology of an occupation is that it maintains a balance between the intellectual and the practical phases of experience. As an occupation it is active or motor; it finds expression through the physical organs—the eyes, hands, etc." An occupation, he continued, "also involves continual observation of materials, and continual planning and reflection, in order that the practical or executive side may be successfully carried on." Dewey concluded: "Occupation as thus conceived must, therefore, be carefully distinguished from work which educates primarily for a trade. It differs because its end is in itself; in the growth that comes from the continual interplay of ideas and their embodiment in action, not in external utility."

Thus it seems clear that Dewey conceived of occupations in a special sense, as not so much the routine activities of daily life, but activities that are transformative because of the manner in which they engage mind and body. Occupations, in this Deweyan sense, are specifically those activities that engage reflective processes in the course of remedial and/or creative actions. Occupations, in this definition, reconstruct the individual's experience and environment. Dewey has been quoted to say: "Ideas are worthless except as they pass into actions which rearrange and reconstruct in some way, be it little or large, the world in which we live" (Campbell 1995, p. 56). Occupations are actions that rearrange and reconstruct the world in which we live. It is conceptually consistent with Dewey's framework to regard an *occupation* as an action in the specialized and precise sense of providing a resolution to some problematic situation.

As Dickie et al. (2006) point out, from a transactional viewpoint, occupations are never only individual and personal, but also are collective and social. Dewey's focus on the psychology of occupations, for example, was not meant solely to improve the learning of individual students. Rather, his entire approach to education by doing was intended as an experiment in social democracy (Westbrook 1991). Dewey rejected rote learning in favor of engaging students' natural curiosity by offering them things to do. But his program carefully framed the meaning of occupations in terms of their historical origins and social value, not just their intrinsic interest to the individual.

While it is not possible to go into the implications of philosophy's linguistic turn for a contemporary pragmatist approach to social justice (Brandom 2000), we should at least expect to take language into account when framing what counts as a situation. Dewey had a very specific concept of *occupation* that I recommend we should retain as definitive, but his concept of *situation* is nonspecific. This combination of definitional features—the specificity of what we mean by occupation and the nonspecificity of what could be meant by "the situation"—actually turns out to be favorable pairing of terms for a real-world application. This pairing opens a wide range of possibilities for changing the world—or, to paraphrase Dewey, for rearranging and reconstructing the world in some way, be it little or large.

18.4 The Situation in PostCivil War Guatemala

The word *situation* appears in everyday usage and scholarly literature to refer to problematic experiences of a complex nature. Regarding the chronic state of fear experienced by Maya women in a Guatemalan village in the 1980s during the civil war due to surveillance, intimidation, sexual violation, disappearance, torture, and mass murder, an anthropologist asked: "Might survival itself depend on panoply of responses to a seemingly intractable *situation*?" (Green 1994, p. 227, emphasis added). Similarly, Guatemala's truth and reconciliation commission's report referred to "situaciones *que fueron formándose a lo largo del tiempo y cuyos efectos influyen de una forma acumulativa en la conducta humana y en la práctica social de esta sociedad*" (http://shr.aaas.org/guatemala/ceh/mds/spanish/cap1/chist.html, emphasis added). To translate, these were "situations that were formed over time and whose cumulative effects influence human conduct and the social practices of this society."

The current situation in Guatemala, a country of 13 million people, includes deleterious effects of the 36-year civil war on state institutions and civil society. In 1951, when Jacabo Arbenz took office as president of Guatemala, 2% of landowners owned 70% of the arable land. Arbenz implemented a liberal agrarian reform law to break up the large estates and foster individually owned small farms. The land reform program involved redistribution of 160,000 acres of uncultivated land owned by the United Fruit Company. United Fruit was compensated for its land. But in 1954, the Eisenhower Administration carried out a covert operation that overthrew Arbenz's government and supported a succession of military dictatorships (Schlesinger et al. 2005). These US-backed governments were ultimately responsible for an estimated 160,000 deaths and 40,000 disappearances during the civil war that broke out in 1960 and ensued for 30 years, according to the final report of Guatemala's truth and reconciliation commission, the Commission for Historical Clarification (CEH 1999).

Indigenous Maya groups speaking 22 distinct languages comprise about half of Guatemala's population and are concentrated in the western highlands. Maya accounted for 83% of the Guatemalan government's victims (CEH 1999). The CEH reported also that 93% of the atrocities committed during the conflict had been the work of the armed forces. The situation of state-sponsored violence ended officially in 1996, yet indigenous and ladino (non-indigenous) Guatemalans continue to suffer the effects not only of the war, but other abuses. The civil war was fought over inadequate land, but the sad irony is that there has been a failure of the national government in the post-civil war period to adequately address the basic problem of land distribution and economic injustice.

The government is universally said to be "*débil*" (weak), hampered by an electoral system that includes dozens of political parties that fragment the vote, the absence of a civil service system, and a complete change in government every 4 years. Corruption is universally believed to be rampant, such as in the current election cycle in which it is widely speculated that candidates are beholden for campaign funds to anonymous donors engaged in narcotic drug trafficking. The absence of adequate law enforcement and justice is so severe as to entail monitoring by the United Nations Special International Commission Against Impunity in Guatemala (Comisión Internacional contra la Impunidad en Guatemala or CICIG). Moreover the civil war was responsible for ruptures in the social fabric that are difficult to repair as the result of genocide and disappearances (particularly of men ages 15–35), destruction of entire villages and displacement of populations, refugeeism and migration, food insecurity, inadequate housing, unclean water and lack of sewage, and lack of educational opportunities (CEH 1999).

Since the 1996 Peace Accords (United Nations 1996), Guatemalan government programs to increase health and education access have been undermined by inadequate funding. The Center for Economic and Social Rights has gathered useful data about the situation. Although Guatemala has the largest economy in Central America, half the Guatemalan population lives in poverty (≤ U.S. $2/day or $800/year) and 15% in extreme poverty (≤U.S. $1/day or $400/year) (CESR 2008). The Peace Accords entailed commitments to expand the tax base in order to generate the additional resources needed to increase social spending. But CESR reports that "Guatemala still has one of the lowest tax bases in the region and among the most generous tax exemptions and fiscal incentives for business. Guatemala's tax base of 12% was below the Central American average of 16% in 2006" (CESR 2008, http://www.cesr.org/section.php?id=33).

CESR noted the following stark disparities: "The richest 10% of the population accounts for 43% of the country's income. Three quarters of Guatemala's indigenous population is poor, double the proportion of non-indigenous poor. Land concentration is among the most unequal in the region. Large commercial farms make up less than 2% of Guatemalan farms, but occupy 57% of the land. And although subsistence farmers make up the vast majority of all farms in Guatemala, they only occupy one-fifth of agricultural land." (Ibid.). While Guatemala achieved some "modest improvement" in terms of inequality and poverty between 2000 and 2006, the improvements did not benefit the poorest but those in the middle range of distribution. Most of the changes occurred due to markets, not investments by the Guatemalan state.

The United States and other large bilateral donors such as Spain, Germany, Norway, and Sweden have invested millions of dollars to help meet the goals of the Peace Accords (Peace Accords http://www.usaid.gov/pubs/cbj2002/lac/gt/, accessed 9/3/11). Major multi-national donors include the International Development Bank, the World Bank, Central American Bank for Economic Integration, United Nations agencies, and the European Union. The problem remains how to transfer power and build capacity among the majority of the population, that is, the sector of the Guatemalan people that is mainly rural and indigenous, and that is most marginalized and least empowered. Into this breach has come a flood of NGOs, large and small, implementing direct person-to-person projects built with funds from abroad and making use of occupations as points of entry into complex situations.

18.5 Transnational NGOs and Occupational Reconstructions in Guatemala

Common Hope (www.commonhope.org), Long Way Home (www.longwayhomeinc.org) and KIDS Restaurant (www.kidsrestaurant.org) offer three models of transnational NGOs and projects that aim to ameliorate the situation of Guatemalans and that can be analyzed and evaluated occupationally. The observations reported here were made by the faculty and students of the NAPA-OT Field School in Antigua, Guatemala www.napaotguatemala.org during visits in 2009, 2010, and 2011. The NAPA-OT Field School offers an interdisciplinary program that draws from occupational therapy and occupational science, anthropology, and other disciplines.

The field school operates through partnerships with existing non-governmental organizations (NGOs) that provide direct and indirect services in Guatemala. The field school's primary affiliation is with Common Hope.

At least 10,000 NGOs operate in Guatemala, ranging from well-established, complex organizations to small-scale start-up organizations, as well as any number of groups that lack a formal structure and fly below the radar of accountability (PAHO 2007). Guatemala's NGOs thus vary widely on a number of important criteria such as their focus on advocacy and/or direct services; mission and scope; institutional structure and decision making; fiscal model with respect to sources of revenue; legal status in Guatemala and abroad; positions of Guatemalan and transnational actors within the organization; accountability to stakeholders such as donors and the populations served; scope and type of projects; and relationship to Guatemalan public, tax-supported agencies and government policies (cf. Prakash and Gugerty 2010).

Further, NGOs can be evaluated with regard to how they engage populations by means of occupations. An overarching concept of *occupational capacity* will be useful here, defined as the ability or potential ability to do things that would improve a particular situation through engagement in occupations. In the analysis below, occupational capacity is considered in terms of *occupational reconstructions, points*

Table 18.1 Terms to define and analyze occupational capacity

Term	Definition
Occupational capacity	The ability or potential ability of an organization, project, population, or individual to do things that would improve a situation by means of engaging in occupations
Occupational reconstruction	The use of occupations by a collective actor such as an NGO to restore or reconstruct a problematic situation
Point of entry	The starting point and pathway by which a collective actor such as an NGO introduces change into a situation by means of engaging individuals in occupations (e.g. by providing funds for a child to go to school, starting an indigenous women's weaving cooperative, or offering the opportunity to work in a community program to allow a family to accrue "sweat equity" to earn a home)
Occupational capital[a]	The skills, capacities, and/or capabilities that an individual or population acquires as a result of the occupations in which they engage or have engaged
Occupational cascade	A sequence of occupations that are made possible or that result from introducing one or more occupations into a situation

[a]This term was proposed by Jessica Joson, M.A., OTR/L, a former student (2009) and coordinator (2010) in the NAPA-OT Field School in Antigua, Guatemala

of entry, *occupational capital*, and *occupational cascades* (see Table 18.1, Terms to Define and Analyze Occupational Capacity). A key question with regard to occupational capacity is: Can the "doing" in this situation be redefined or redistributed by the organization, project, population, or individual in a manner that could improve the situation more?

18.5.1 Common Hope

Common Hope was founded by a Catholic family from St. Paul, Minnesota in the United States who visited Guatemala and subsequently dedicated themselves to helping the country's poor. In 1986, during the difficult war years, Common Hope organized itself legally as non-profit organization registered in Guatemala and the state of Minnesota. In addition to its executive director and board in the United States, Common Hope has an active in-country Guatemala director and extensive staff that provide comprehensive education, health, and social services for 18 communities, mainly in the area around Antigua.

Until recently, Common Hope's model centered primarily on soliciting and fostering a relationship between a specific, known sponsor in the United States with a specific, known child in Guatemala through the sponsor's payment of the child's school-related expenses. In 2010, 2,696 students attended school with the help of Common Hope, with rates that exceed the Guatemalan average for advancement in grade levels and in primary school and especially high school graduation (http://www.commonhope.org/wp-content/uploads/2011/08/2010-results.png). The sponsor-a-child approach, used by NGOs such as World Vision and Save the Children, evokes compassion and humanitarian giving (Barnett 2011). It is a charity model that puts a vulnerable face on poverty while also fostering transnational, citizen-to-citizen helping relationships.

While Common Hope's main programmatic emphasis has been on the relationship between the North American adult donor and the Guatemalan child recipient, the goals are indeed occupational. Common Hope aims to enable a child's activities by keeping him or her in school, while also bettering the conditions of the child's family. Common Hope's family impact can be measured in 2010, for example, by the provision of 9,584 medical and dental consultations to participating families, and, occupationally, by 5,532 h of sweat equity worked by families through Common Hope's collaboration with Habitat for Humanity "to earn homes that are clean, safe and dry" (http://www.commonhope.org/wp-content/uploads/2011/08/2010-results.png).

Once a family commits to sending and keeping the sponsored child in school, the family itself receives regular visits from Common Hope's Guatemalan social workers and becomes eligible for a range of services: classes and workshops in parenting skills; use of the primary care clinic and pharmacy; assistance in home building through Habitat for Humanity, Construcasa, and Common Hope's own construction projects; and other forms of social support. Adult education classes in vocational skills were previously offered and are now offered through referrals. Sponsors of children receive personal letters and photos. If sponsors visit Guatemala, Common Hope can arrange for them to meet their sponsored children and families. These transnational relationships can last years or a lifetime, with deepening ties and, in some cases, abundant direct provision of gifts of toys, clothes, electronic equipment, and other goods in addition to the sponsor's fixed, regular monetary donations through the NGO.

Despite the prominence of a charity model in the sponsor-a-child approach, Common Hope also embodies the twentieth century pragmatist approach to social uplift and democratization, as seen in the settlement movement. An institution supported by philanthropy, Common Hope is a haven for families on the model of a community center. Outside its security-guarded gates is a violent and exploitative environment, while inside the appearance and atmosphere is reminiscent of an idyllic college campus. Within a compassionate if bureaucratic structure, Common Hope provides some direct services such as its clinic and pharmacy. But the main focus conceptually and practically is to create opportunities. Further, as in the twentieth century settlement model, many of these opportunities apply to the non-Guatemalans who provide resources for the program (Addams 1893b). North American volunteers come into the "neighborhood" either for short-term projects (such as contributing labor to construct housing) or on a residential basis as long-term staff. Occupations of the more than 515 volunteers in Guatemala and the United States included 8,274 volunteer hours in 2010 (http://www.commonhope.org/wp-content/uploads/2011/08/2010-results.png).

Common Hope's newest educational project moves beyond the sponsor-a-child model to capacitate schools to raise achievement through placing the schools' most effective teachers in the first three grades and providing coaches for principals and teachers (Tamalyn Gutierrez, Guatemala Director, Common Hope, August 2011, Personal communication). It can be seen as employing the same kind of transactional model that is proposed by Frank and Zemke (2009), using occupations that capacitate individuals (principals and teachers) at the same time as capacitating social institutions (schools). Common Hope's target population remains the children who are receiving educational opportunities through its program. School attendance remains Common Hope's *point of entry* into the lives of children and their families. Education builds *occupational capital* that will allow the next generation to take advantage of opportunities that will improve their own lives and Guatemala's situation.

18.5.2 Long Way Home

Long Way Home (www.longwayhome.com), in San Juan Comalapa, a municipality in the department of Chimaltenango, was founded in the optimistic post-civil war environment by an ex-Peace Corps volunteer with activist and development-minded friends. Much smaller in scope and scale than Common Hope, this NGO launched itself in 2004 with 501(c) (3) non-profit status in the United States and initial goals of promoting youth employment and better sanitation. Comalapa's population is 95% Kaqchikel Maya and the predominant form of employment is subsistence farming. The town was a center of indigenous resistance to Guatemala's military dictatorship during the war years. Opportunities for the next generation are extremely limited and gangs of youth linked to narcotrafficking have taken hold. The town also has environmental problems that are endemic in Guatemala, including the accumulation of trash and waste, unsafe drinking water resulting in disease, and deforestation and erosion as a result of cutting wood for fuel.

Although Long Way Home solicits and accepts grants from foundations and donations from individuals in United States, it does not employ a charity model to address this situation, but a model that we are terming *occupational reconstruction*. It began by partnering with the Guatemalan organization, Chuwi Tinamit (San Juan Comalapa Development Organization), on community development projects including the building of a park for soccer and a new structure for Tecnico Maya, a school that offers bilingual and bicultural education in Spanish and Kaqchikel. The new Appropriate Technologies Vocational School will offer academic preparation along with courses in carpentry, masonry, mechanics (including bicycle repair), electrical, welding, horticulture, and training in the business and technology of alternative energy production.

The Long Way Home project sidesteps the possibly paternalistic aspects of its focus on industrial education by emphasizing community empowerment and community ownership, along with a twenty-first century emphasis on sustainability. A key aspect of the project is its "green" philosophy that relates environmental clean-up to the use of natural and recycled materials, creative design based on experiential handling of objects, and hands-on construction methods. The structures are cheap to build, provide insulation against the weather and protection against earthquakes. Outer walls are built from inexpensive, recycled tires and earth bags, covered with cob (clay mixed with sand, straw, water and earth) and a layer of stucco. Discarded colored or clear glass bottles become windows. Partitions are made from trash-filled plastic bottles within a lathe and wire frame. The structures are in the process of being built by a small team of local construction workers along with transnational volunteers, especially church groups and student interns from the United States, who pay fees to participate. Guatemalans and non-Guatemalans, working side by side, are learning new skills that build their *occupational capital*.

The project's occupational capacity—its ability to improve a situation through occupations—is exceptionally well-developed. Youth and their families now enjoy recreational occupations at the popular Chuwi Tinamit park, below a terraced slope where the Tecnico Maya school is being built. The occupation of playing soccer is the point of entry. To gain entrance to the park, each person must pay a fee either in cash or by bringing a recycled plastic bottle filled with trash. Not surprisingly, payment in trash has resulted in both a plentiful supply of green building materials and a change of local environmental consciousness and habits. Further, whenever they glance up from the soccer field, community members see the progress in construction of Technico Maya's new school, where their "park fees" (plastic bottles filled with trash) are used to build the handsome, innovative structure.

Long Way Home's website addresses the anticipated cascade effects of its occupational approach: "The most immediate way that the construction of the vocational school will contribute to the economy of Comalapa is through providing jobs for teachers. Not only will the current Tecnico Maya teachers have a more consistent source of income (from sale of green fuels and other enterprises), but the newly added vocational curriculum will require the addition of several new teachers from within the community. The long-term economic effects of the vocational school will be felt when a group of skilled young Comalapans, uniquely trained to be environmental entrepreneurs, enter the Guatemalan job market."

Long Way Home's approach is intuitively very close to Dewey's definition of occupation, particularly with regard to mind-body engagement, but also his general philosophy of education based on learning by doing things together (Dewey 1990). Green architecture is Long Way Home's point of entry into Guatemala's complex, problematic situation. Transactions that cascade from its efforts at occupational reconstruction happen simultaneously and in multiple arenas: among local individuals, families and community agencies in Comalapa; between the community and the natural environment; and between locals and transnational partners.

18.5.3 KIDS Restaurant

KIDS Restaurant is project of T.E.S.S. Unlimited (http://www.tessunlimited.nl/English), a small NGO founded in The Netherlands in 2008 by a young Dutch woman living in Guatemala. Although T.E.S.S. Unlimited is small enough to be considered a micro-NGO, its energetic founder has launched several ongoing local projects that are well-regarded: an educational program in the village of San Gaspar Vivar, a milk program for undernourished children, a surgical referral program for babies with cleft palate, and, now, the KIDS Restaurant. Located in a rented house, the project is staffed by volunteers who during the week teach a small team of local children the skills needed to run a restaurant. On weekends the restaurant caters to a fixed-menu, reservations-only dinner clientele comprised mainly of tourists who can afford to pay 75Q (about $10) per meal. These dinner guests learn about the project through local advertising and are shuttled by a T.E.S.S. Unlimited van to the out-lying location from Antigua's Parque Central.

Working in a restaurant is the occupational point of entry for this cohort of children, but the program builds their occupational capital in innumerable ways. The children are a team in which girls and boys work in pairs and rotate roles, 1 week as chef, 1 week as wait staff, and so forth. Each week the menu takes on a different international cuisine as its theme, which involves a lesson in geography and culture. These activities build the children's occupational *capital.* Since the clientele is English-speaking, the children are given English language lessons so that they can comfortably speak to the guests and attend to their needs. The children also learn mathematics, measurement, accounting, and computer skills. Not incidentally, they become familiar and comfortable with interacting with a powerful class of socially conscious, transnational clientele. They gain a persona as distinctive individuals who are doing something important and admirable. As with Long Way Home, an *occupational cascade* is embedded in the numerous interrelated activities of running a restaurant and in the vision of possibilities for the children's future employment.

18.6 Conclusion

Theorizing about occupations and social justice is arguably one the most important areas to which occupational science can make a timely, relevant, and useful contribution (Frank 2012). Land reform, better health, good jobs, higher levels of education, and a well-functioning and fair justice system still elude most indigenous and urban Guatemalans despite 36 years of civil war to attain social justice and human rights. Although Guatemala's government is weak and civil society worsening in some ways, Guatemalan NGOs work actively and optimistically to reconstruct the situation through occupations with transnational partners and resources. The situation is reminiscent of the pragmatist reforms in the United States during the progressive era. Building on the twentieth century pragmatist legacy of social reform, this chapter proposes that Dewey's thinking about problematic situations and occupational solutions offers a transactional framework for description, analysis, research, and evaluation of complex processes of social transformation in our own time.

References

Addams, J. (1893a). The objective necessity of social settlement. In *Philanthropy and social progress* (pp. 27–56). New York: Thomas Y. Crowell & Co.

Addams, J. (1893b). The subjective necessity of social settlement. In *Philanthropy & social progress* (pp. 1–26). New York: Thomas Y. Crowell & Co.

Barnett, M. (2011). *Empire of humanity: A history of humanitarianism*. Ithaca/London: Cornell University Press.

Brandom, R. B. (Ed.). (2000). *Rorty and his critics*. Malden: Blackwell Publishers.

Campbell, J. (1995). *Understanding John Dewey: Nature and cooperative intelligence*. Chicago: Open Court Publishing.

Castells, M. (2009). The rise of the network society: The information age. In *Economy, society, and culture* (2nd ed., Vol. I). Malden: Blackwell-Wiley.

CEH. (1999). *Guatemala: Memoria del Silencio*. Comisión para el Esclarecimiento Histórico. http://shr.aaas.org/guatemala/ceh/mds/spanish/toc.html

CESR. (2008). *Guatemala fact sheet*. Center for Economic and Social Rights. http://www.cesr.org/section.php?id=33

Cutchin, M. P. (2008). John Dewey's metaphysical ground-map and its implications for geographical inquiry. *Geoforum, 39*, 1555–1569.

Cutchin, M. P., & Dickie, V. A. (2012). Transactionalism: Occupational science and the pragmatic attitude. In G. Whiteford & C. Hocking (Eds.), *Critical perspectives on occupational science: Society, inclusion, participation* (pp. 23–37). London: Wiley.

Dewey, J. (1958). *Experience and nature*. New York: Dover Edition (Original work published in 1925).

Dewey, J. (1990). The psychology of occupations. In *The school and society* (pp. 131–137). Chicago: University of Chicago Press (Original work published in 1915).

Dewey, J. (1916). *Democracy and education: An introduction to the philosophy of education*. New York: The Macmillan Co.

Dickie, V. A., Cutchin, M. P., & Humphry, R. (2006). Occupation as transactional experience: A critique of individualism in occupational science. *Journal of Occupational Science, 13*, 83–93.

Eliasoph, N. (1998). *Avoiding politics: How Americans produce apathy in everyday life*. Cambridge: Cambridge University Press.

Escobar, A. (1999). The invention of development. *Current History, 631*, 382–396.

Farmer, P. (2004). Anthropology of structural violence. *Current Anthropology, 35*, 305–325.

Fisher, W. F. (1997). Doing good? The politics and antipolitics of NGO practices. *Annual Review of Anthropology, 26*, 439–464.

Frank, G. (2011). The transactional relationship between occupation and place: Indigenous cultures in the American Southwest. *Journal of Occupational Science, 18*, 3–20.

Frank, G. (2012). Occupational therapy/occupational science/occupational justice: Moral commitments and global assemblages. The 2010 Ruth Zemke lecture in occupational science. *Journal of Occupational Science*, early online.

Frank, G., & Zemke, R. (2009). Occupational therapy foundations for political engagements and social transformation. In N. Pollard, D. Sakellariou, & F. Kronenberg (Eds.), *A political practice of occupational therapy* (pp. 111–136). Edinburgh: Elsevier/Churchill Livingston.

Green, L. (1994). Fear as a way of life. *Cultural Anthropology, 9*, 227–256.

Hajjar, L. (2004). Human rights. In A. Sarat (Ed.), *The Blackwell companion to law and society* (pp. 589–604). Oxford: Blackwell Publishers.

Harvey, D. (1989). *The condition of postmodernity*. Oxford: Blackwell Publishers.

Heggenhougen, K. (1995). The epidemiology of functional apartheid and human rights abuses. *Social Science & Medicine, 40*, 281–284.

Inda, J. X., & Rosaldo, R. (Eds.). (2008). *The anthropology of globalization: A reader* (2nd ed.). Malden: Blackwell Publishing.

Keck, M. E., & Sikkink, K. (1998). *Activists beyond borders*. Ithaca: Cornell University Press.
Kronenberg, F., & Pollard, N. (2004). Overcoming occupational apartheid: A preliminary exploration of the political nature of occupational therapy. In F. Kronenberg, S. Simo Algado, & N. Pollard (Eds.), *Occupational therapy without borders: Learning from the spirit of survivors* (pp. 58–86). Oxford: Elsevier.
Latour, B. (2007). *Reassembling the social: An introduction to Actor-Network-Theory*. New York: Oxford University Press.
Lichterman, P. (1996). *The search for political community: American activists reinventing commitment*. Cambridge: Cambridge University Press.
Lichterman, P. (2005). *Elusive togetherness: Church groups trying to bridge America's divisions*. Princeton: Princeton University Press.
Nussbaum, M. C. (2011). *Creating capabilities: The human development approach*. Cambridge: Harvard University Press.
PAHO. (2007). *Health system profile – Guatemala*. Guatemala: Pan American Health Organization, Washington, DC.
Pettegrew, J. (2000). *A pragmatist's progress?: Richard Rorty and American intellectual history*. Lanham: Roman & Littlefield.
Prakash, A., & Gugerty, M. K. (2010). *Advocacy organizations and collective action*. Cambridge: Cambridge University Press.
Provan, K. G., & Milward, H. B. (2001). Do networks really work? A framework for evaluating public-sector organizational networks. *Public Administration Review, 61*, 414–423.
Putnam, R. (1993). *Making democracy work*. Princeton: Princeton University Press.
Putnam, R. (2000). *Bowling alone: The collapse and revival of American community*. New York: Simon and Schuster.
Rorty, R. (1998). *Achieving our country: Leftist thought in twentieth-century America*. Cambridge: Harvard University Press.
Rorty, R. (2000). *Philosophy and social hope*. New York: Penguin.
Sassen, S. (2006). *Territory, authority, rights: From medieval to global assemblages* (updated ed.). Princeton and London: Princeton University Press.
Schlesinger, S., Kinzer, S., & Coatsworth, J. H. (2005). *Bitter fruit: The story of the American coup in Guatemala, revised and expanded* (David Rockefeller Center Series on Latin American Studies). Cambridge: Harvard University Press.
Seigfried, C. H. (1999). Socializing democracy: Jane Addams and John Dewey. *Philosophy of the Social Sciences, 29*, 207–230.
Sen, A. (1999). *Development as freedom*. New York: Anchor Books.
Thibeault, R. (2011). Rebuilding lives and societies through occupation in post-conflict areas and highly marginalized settings. In Frank Kronenberg, Nick Pollard, & Dikaios Sakellariou (Eds.), *Occupational therapies without borders, Vol. 2: Towards an ecology of occupation-based practice* (pp. 155–161). Edinburgh: Churchill Livingstone/Elsevier.
United Nations. (1996). Agreement on a firm and lasting peace, December 29, 1996 UN ref. no. A/51/796-S/1997/114, Annex II.
Westbrook, R. B. (1991). *John Dewey and American democracy*. Ithaca: Cornell University Press.
Wilcock, A., & Townsend, E. (2000). Occupational justice interactive dialogue: Occupational terminology. *Journal of Occupational Science, 7*, 84–86.

Chapter 19
Occupational Justice's Intents and Impacts: From Personal Choices to Community Consequences

Rachel Thibeault

> Occupational justice (entails) four occupational rights: to experience meaning and enrichment in one's occupations; to participate in a range of occupations for health and social inclusion; to make choices and share decision-making power in daily life; and to receive equal privileges for diverse participation in occupations (Townsend and Wilcock 2004, p.75).

The foreign students are ebullient: they are leaving the country, proud of what they have accomplished in their two months in Nicaragua. They have managed to distribute every single one of the nearly 100 old wheelchairs they had collected at home and brought with them. Like they do every year, they have also helped build a school, a clinic, and part of a bridge. They learned some Spanish and readily ate local fare. Their supervisors are pleased with their adaptability and a special reception awaits them at their North American university to celebrate their contribution to the Nicaraguan village, an event, always well covered by the media, which often translates into increased enrollment.... As the students pack up their bags, poor women living by the half-built school undertake their own informal post-mortem. Like every year, they were laid off by their employers to make way for the free manpower provided by the students. Their children were already starving before the foreigners came; now, their toddlers show signs of irreversible brain damage associated with malnutrition. At the Association of People with Disabilities, morale is also at its lowest point. By flooding the market with used, poorly fitted wheelchairs, the students have indirectly caused several cases of potentially fatal pressure sores among their members and destroyed the Association's small business. For the past several years, the Association of People with Disabilities has run a very successful workshop that produces good quality wheelchairs adapted to local conditions and that can be repaired locally when needed. The workshop offers valued employment to people with disabilities who otherwise would have to resort to begging. If shipping is entered into the equation, the used wheelchairs came at a high financial and environmental cost. And now, they will last just long enough to put the Association members all into bankruptcy. (Excerpts from Rachel Thibeault's journal, participatory-action research project on post-conflict social inequalities, Nicaragua, 2003.)

R. Thibeault (✉)
School of Rehabilitation Sciences, University of Ottawa, Ottawa, ON, Canada
e-mail: rthibeau@uottawa.ca

M.P. Cutchin and V.A. Dickie (eds.), *Transactional Perspectives on Occupation*,
DOI 10.1007/978-94-007-4429-5_19, © Springer Science+Business Media B.V. 2013

19.1 Introduction

On the road to occupational justice I have often noticed that obstacles are of a systemic nature, the fruit of either corporate greed or ill-informed social policies. Governments and multinationals are portrayed as Goliaths attempting to crush grassroots Davids, those well-intentioned social actors who, we think, could do no harm. Caught in this polarized view, we observe the power play between protagonists and fail to understand the more subtle underpinnings of occupational justice. We overlook the fact that a community's occupational landscape is usually the end product of a vast array of influences, both positive and negative, that encompasses way more than the Grassroots vs. System issue. Although understandable, this dualism leads to a skewed perspective that does not capture the situation's complexity and may yield damaging outcomes. The occupational scene thus needs to be analyzed objectively, above and beyond entrenched personal opinions and political leanings. Reflecting the dominant discourse, some of the current writings on occupational justice focus chiefly on this single political tension, inadvertently feeding a narrow and antagonistic stance. For example, the indiscriminate use of the term "occupational apartheid" may polarize debate and trigger conflict where mediation would have been possible had inflammatory language been avoided. Occupational apartheid is defined as:

> …the segregation of groups of people through the restriction or denial of access to dignified and meaningful participation in occupations of daily life on the basis of race, color, disability, national origin, age, gender, sexual preference, religion, political beliefs, status in society, or other characteristics. Occasioned by political forces, its systematic and pervasive social, cultural, and economic consequences jeopardize health and wellbeing as experienced by individuals, communities and societies (Kronenberg and Pollard 2005, p.67).

Since its coining, the term occupational apartheid has been used in contexts where there was no willful, legal exclusion of people with disabilities but simply ignorance on the part of the powers in place. Consequently, by immediately casting potential employers as apartheid supporters, all hopes of establishing a congenial collaboration beneficial to all were lost. As was demonstrated in Nicaragua, adhering to cleaved views may in the end jeopardize the very rights we intend to promote.

If we use the reductionist Grassroots vs. System lens to look at that example, we stop where the students have stopped, at a syllogism that prevents further analysis: We are the generous, grassroots guys. We mean well. Therefore all subsequent action stemming from our good intentions will be positive. True, none of the students or supervisors depicted above meant to wreak havoc on the locals. In fact, some even defined themselves as change agents for greater social justice and were quite vocal in the defense of the rights of people with disabilities. Yet, their passage in Nicaragua translated into occupational deprivation for the most vulnerable members of the host community. Again, this kind of negative impact is usually associated with corporate or government practices, but experience has shown that it is also quite common when individuals working on behalf of the grassroots are involved.

Individuals, as much as agencies, tend to ignore the necessity of closely examining their motivations and conceptual tenets along with the context in which they will intervene. Without prior reflection, they often launch into action, fueled by good will and cultural biases that may prove highly detrimental. It is thus one thing to accompany vulnerable communities towards greater autonomy or wellbeing, and it is quite another to approach the endeavor in the appropriate manner. For the past 25 years, I have been engaged in community-based rehabilitation with many different populations. From the High Arctic to South Africa by way of South East Asia, Central America, and the Middle East, I have partnered with groups faced with HIV/AIDS, war, leprosy, landmines, and extreme violence. These experiences have taught me some valuable lessons regarding community development and empowerment, the first being that proper scrutiny and spirit count as much if not more than action. Successful implementation and protection of occupational rights rely obviously on the awareness and recognition of such rights, but they also depend on a vision that goes beyond the purely political into the realms of the philosophical and the ethical.

My sentiment and argument are very much in line with the transactional perspective and its larger field of vision, the pragmatic attitude (Cutchin and Dickie 2012). As Cutchin and Dickie explain, John Dewey's philosophy was not just about transaction. He was focused on how criticism could be intelligently (reflectively) brought to bear on problematic situations. His vision was for individuals to be informed by and engaged with communities, and for all action, including those that are based in reconstructing situations, to be based in responsibility. The argument to follow consistently echoes the Deweyan approach as reflected in the emerging literature on transactional perspectives on occupation.

19.2 Occupational Rights and Their Violation

If we come back to the Nicaragua experience, we quickly conclude that, despite the best of motives, the students violated three of the four core occupational rights. This example clearly illustrates how a process supposedly designed to benefit and empower local populations introduces instead occupational imbalance of life-threatening magnitude. A closer look can help us understand how these rights were violated so we can then explore ways of preventing or mitigating future damage.

19.2.1 Right 1: Participation in a Range of Occupations for Health and Social Inclusion

Unknowingly, the placement offered an exotic academic experience to the detriment of the local residents' right to participate in occupations necessary for income, health and social inclusion. Students got to bask superficially in local culture while not only missing deeper social realities but also endangering the very people they had come to help. Not only did the poorest women lose their life-sustaining, income-generating occupations, but they lost them at a time that was pivotal for their children's development. By disregarding the community's occupational web, this placement implicitly perpetuated the colonialist mentality of exploitation, this time, pedagogical and occupational in nature. The message to students was that they could appropriate local occupations if it contributed to their learning despite disruptions to long-established, vital local occupational patterns.

This example is no exception to the general rule: the vast majority of agencies active in community development, be it in high-income or low-income countries, tend to disregard the communities' occupational webs and pay little attention to fair occupational participation for all members. I have been reviewing grant applications for major donor agencies for over 15 years and not once have I encountered one concerned about the potential impacts of proposed programs on the greater occupational web of the target community. Just as in the example, projects are designed according to the agency's (and not the community's) needs and/or around perceived community needs. A Western template is generally imposed which mostly includes the provision, by external actors, of goods and services (building schools, clinics, offering food programs, etc.) in a way that is divorced from local occupational realities. Who will teach in the school? Who will work at the clinic? Who will grow and prepare the food given out through external agencies? And if staff or workers are brought in from outside, what will be the occupational impact on the community members? None of these questions are widely raised nor answered prior to project implementation.

19.2.2 Right 2: Making Choices and Sharing Decision-Making Power in Daily Life

At no point in the process were the Nicaraguans involved in defining their needs and goals. Decisions were made in North America with minimal input from the locals, again a common occurrence and an approach found most typically with three types of seemingly very different social agencies: government bodies mandated to design policies and with limited access to real-life, field-related data; non-governmental organizations (NGO) that vigorously embrace Western-style social activism; and faith-based organizations working from a charitable angle. These three types of agencies, "archetypes" of sorts in community development, rarely get clustered together since they often embody opposing political positions. Yet, in spite of their widely divergent views, they may, on the ground, produce similarly unfortunate outcomes, namely short-lived projects that do not respect local priorities or culture for lack of sharing power with local stakeholders.

Government bodies often adopt policies that make the act of knowing their own target populations arduous. For example, for safety or health reasons, official procedure may prohibit employees from collecting information in slums or other less-than-stable areas, forcing agencies to rely on dubious secondary data. The resulting expert reports constitute weak and incomplete evidence on which to build policies and projects while the concerned communities are left out of the equation, without mechanisms to rectify inaccuracies or fill in the gaps. Ironically, in terms of decision-making, the target group remains peripheral, both as the key knowledge provider and stakeholder. With NGOs, the process differs but may still lead to comparable results. Emboldened by models of Western activism, foreign workers are sometimes seen taking it upon themselves to own and fight local battles and may pose as fiery, righteous leaders. This appropriation of power, together with an imperfect understanding of local ways and traditions, usually triggers disempowerment in local participants and rising antagonism in local authorities. No true consultation is held at the local level: blinded by their own idealism and a deep-seated belief in the infallibility of their morals, foreign workers often see no point in the exercise. The process frequently ends with broken communities ostracized in their own milieu and foreign enablers blaming local conditions for the project's collapse as they themselves disengage swiftly. They then go home, a luxury denied the communities they have contributed to weaken.

With faith-based organizations working from a charitable perspective, the purpose is evidently to improve local conditions, but the very focus on charity, rather than on the building of local competence and capacity, defeats that purpose. Several organizations make heavy use of the imagery of poverty and dejection to raise funds, concealing the strengths of the local community. The message conveyed revolves around children with big bellies and babies covered in dirt and flies, giving the community an entirely negative, distorted image of itself, a false sense of its own inability to cope. Unwittingly, these agencies erode local leadership and foster powerlessness through very narrow occupational choices: potential leaders keen on developing greater autonomy and willing to participate in decision-making quickly get reduced to the role of aid recipient. Stripped of its power and valued social roles, the community then slowly descends into passivity and learned helplessness.

In the three situations (government, NGO, and faith-based organization programs), the community is robbed of its power and dignity through well-intentioned people and policies: the discourse is conducive to development but the attitudes run contrary to it. With professed goals such as eradicating poverty, providing health care or fighting for social justice, the agencies still undermine the communities they are meant to serve through exerting control over their decision-making process, keeping local stakeholders away from the driver's seat.

19.2.3 Right 3: To Experience Meaning and Enrichment in One's Occupations

Resource-poor, marginalized communities are especially vulnerable to learned helplessness (Fisher 2008). When instilled and left unchecked, as happened in Nicaragua, such helplessness greatly reduces the community's occupational span: convinced of their uselessness, unaware of their potential, community members dream rather small if they dare dream at all. Stifling natural drives for meaning and enrichment, they merely settle for means of survival to the detriment of all other forms of occupations. Occupational justice here rests with the tactful collective exploring of possibilities and the enabling of an occupational scope that truly respects local talents, tastes and culture. To achieve this scope, charity-leaning tendencies, narcissistic motivations, righteousness, and failure of the imagination must first be recognized and addressed.

19.2.4 Right No. 4: To Receive Equal Privileges for Diverse Participation in Occupations

Although it does not appear in the Nicaragua example, this occupational right is also violated regularly, frequently with regards to gender issues. Across a very broad range of cultures and in an oft-repeated scenario, women's occupations receive negligible recognition or compensation when compared to those of men. The occupational schedule of a typical woman in rural Burkina Faso, for example, reveals a disproportionate amount of hard work while the men's schedules include just as disproportionate an amount of leisure time (Barrett 1997; Carr and Hartl 2010). But marked discrepancies are not the unique lot of low-income countries: they are also found in the industrialized world, where women cumulate multiple roles much more often than men.

19.3 Principles to Protect Occupational Rights

The Nicaragua example vividly highlights the popular saying that the road to hell is paved with good intentions. The students and their supervisors meant well and yet, the host community ended up the poorer for it. How, then, can we work with communities while respecting and promoting the four rights embedded within occupational justice? I have derived three principles and an occupation-based, community-building process for greater occupational justice from reflection and past experience.

19.3.1 First Principle: Examine Personal Values, Motives and Attitudes

My experience has shown that traditional occupational therapy values of client-centeredness, social justice, empowerment, and enablement yield more long-term, positive outcomes when applied in a spirit of equality and solidarity. Working from that perspective, a project's goals and strategies reflect local needs, knowledge, networks, and culture thus maximizing chances of success. A close preliminary examination of personal values and motives seems necessary to do so and prevent the unintentional imposition of one's biases unto the host community. Development enablers perform best when they act as collaborators rather than leaders and when they are as willing to be transformed as to transform. If they succeed in shedding their expert label and look for and excise any savior complex that may be lurking under the surface, they will notice a substantial qualitative difference in the rapport they maintain with their host country partners. Perceived as safe, respectful team players, they will find their natural place within the organization and the development process.

19.3.2 Second Principle: Adopt an Occupational Lens

Frequently, community consultation gets reduced to its sole monetary aspects and becomes an exercise in economic ills and issues. The resulting profile, a glorified spreadsheet, does not capture the true identity of the community nor its aspirations. Key features such as meaning, interdependence, and community-building are ignored since they rarely translate into direct financial terms. An occupational lens brings into focus a picture of the community that is much sharper. And this can be achieved through a series of questions firmly anchored in a transactional perspective: What is the community's current web of occupations? How are they actively interrelated? What occupations are deemed the most important by the community? What are the cultural, spiritual, religious and social occupations that the community wishes to maintain despite their economic cost? What would be the likely consequences of modifying specific links in the occupational chain?

Issues of power are then also addressed: Are there instances of occupational deprivation, alienation or exploitation (Polatajko et al. 2007)? And what are the main threats to that community's occupational equilibrium? Occupational justice from a transactional perspective rests on the answers to these questions and on explicit democratic mechanisms that protect equitable social participation and the occupational equilibrium of all individuals involved.

19.3.3 Third Principle: Establish Fair and Sustainable Partnerships with Communities

To establish fair partnerships with communities, the community enabler must ensure that all planning is carried out with and by communities and organizations, in accordance with their needs and without displacing local people or creating unsustainable programs. The occupational opportunities offered should be financially accessible and feasible for all participants across gender, class, race, ability and sexual orientation. To ensure that all voices are heard and that the process will be fair, participative methodologies are key. In 2007, I came across the Social Analysis System (SAS^2),

> …an international initiative supporting learning and dialogue grounded in action. Through a community of practice, website, and publications, the initiative provides access to an integrated collection of practical tools and strategies for collaborative inquiry, planning and evaluation in complex settings involving multiple stakeholders. The tools and strategies are theoretically informed, fully participatory, flexible and relevant to many sectors and fields of study (SAS² website 2011).

They have been part of my community-building toolbox ever since, allowing me to better understand my partners and allowing us, together, to tailor more comprehensive solutions.

19.4 An Occupation-Based, Community-Building Process for Greater Occupational Justice

An attempt at embodying the three principles above, the occupation-based, community-building process I have jointly developed over the years with my local partners could be broken down into myriads of strategies and decisions, but it can also be easily summarized into seven steps that usually unfold over a period of 7–10 years.

Step 1 is quite simple: it requires me to befriend the community I am working with and for. Without some form of closeness and commitment, collaborations cannot blossom. Befriending the community means participating in events and celebrations that are meaningful and transformative for my partners. Through my joining in, these same events and celebrations end up transforming me as well. Participation offers shared occupations, a common ground on which to cultivate relationships, and collective memories that instill a sense of belonging. It may take many shapes: going caribou hunting with Inuit partners, planting trees in Ethiopia, playing wheelchair basketball in Zambia, or preparing berbere (a local, highly sophisticated blend of spices) with women in Ethiopia. Skill does not matter and the foreigners' clumsiness may often contribute to some added lighthearted bonds.

Step 2 has to do with discovery and communication. To develop a sound community spirit, there must be a safe space for all to meet and get to know each other. To do so, my partners and I resort to three main means. The first of these are non-threatening, collective occupations to promote increased informal contact within the community. This could be preparing a pot luck dinner, playing sports, or going on an outing together. Second, we establish what we call a Communication Charter. This Charter gets designed through interactive tools for analyzing social dynamics, role playing, or any other culturally appropriate strategies. The goal is to explicitly acknowledge the communication breakdowns most likely to occur, identify solutions before we get into crisis mode, and pledge to adhere to the principles jointly agreed upon. For example, working at the epicenter in post-earthquake Haiti with farming communities struggling with Post-Traumatic Shock Disorder, issues of gender equality and fair distribution of workloads and resources were to be expected. A community meeting was called to address these concerns and, together, local men and women charted their preferred course of action should conflict arise.

Throughout this process, we also get to assess the community's implicit power differentials and collect information that is crucial to the planning of interventions that will not jeopardize further the most vulnerable partners.

The purpose of the third step is to uncover core values. Instead of turning to conventional interviews and questionnaires to do so, my partners and I opt for an interactive, home-based, occupation-focused approach. We go to homes or work sites to collect narratives about daily life as we watch it unfold. We see and appreciate what community members do, providing them with direct validation which, in turn, yields even richer communication and insights.

Step 4 deals with promoting dignity and equality. It relies on an occupational analysis of the community in terms of social status. The key questions are: Which occupations carry the highest status? Are they consistently performed by most community members or just an elite few? Can we gently redistribute power along occupational lines to enhance autonomy and respect for the weaker members? For example, for ex-child soldiers in Sierra Leone who were being demobilized, it was an honor to accompany and serve blind elders throughout the day. Since the extent of trauma made it impossible for the ex-soldiers to go back to the life of a child, such a task, imbued with a deep sense of responsibility and trust normally associated with maturity, allowed for the rebuilding of their status and self-esteem. At step four, we also look at the occupational burden put on specific groups such as women or people with disabilities. Traditionally, these two subgroups end up caring for the sick, the orphans, and older people with disabilities, thus taxing considerably their already meager resources. We then try to gradually and gently modify local habits and promote teamwork around the more labor-intensive occupations.

To change mentalities, strong and positive leaders are required. At Step 5, we attempt to identify and support such leaders. Again, the focus is occupational: the selection is not based on discourse, politician-style, but on hard evidence of what the aspiring leader has done for the community. The objective is to promote individuals truly devoted to the collective good. Moreover, leaders should be closely related to the communities they wish to represent, socially and occupationally. Candidates without lived experience of the occupational and social realities of their community rarely make efficient advocates. This is observed even more acutely when working with people living with disabilities; if the chosen leader has no disability and no understanding of the occupational ramifications of disability, not only does advocacy suffer, but gains for the group also tend to be associated with the fact that the leader has no disabilities, further entrenching disempowerment.

Step 6 calls for the strengthening of networks. Here, the nature of collective occupations starts to shift subtly. At Step 2, the objective was to create a safe, informal space for the community to grow closer. At Step 6, we aim to enhance cohesiveness and solidarity and increase political influence. At this point, the community begins to develop an identity of its own and to see itself as a specific group. Community-building occupations at Step 6 could be divided into three categories: solidarity-building, identity-building, and network-building. Solidarity-building occupations revolve around giving back to the community, for example, adapting the local playground for children with disabilities, doing a cleaning bee for an older couple, or creating a community garden. Acting together to give back to the entire community mobilizes goodwill and sets the tone for future projects. Identity-building occupations require that the community reaches out of its immediate boundaries as a single, distinct entity since a community is any group with a sense of shared identity. An ethnic neighborhood could have a kiosk at a fair to promote its culinary heritage. A community of people living with disabilities could march together for a cause that resonates with their ideals. An informal youth group could write a brief on access to school loans and bursaries to their MP. Once the community perceives itself as a cohesive, unified body, individual members can tap into their respective networks for the benefit of the whole. Network-building activities could include social events that will facilitate connections with similar groups (inviting outsiders to community meals or artistic performances) or more formal partnerships in projects leading to common goals.

By Step 7, the community has usually developed its strengths and only requires discreet enablement towards the realization of set goals or projects. The community has learned not only to discuss issues, but also to do things together, with the direct impact of stimulating cohesiveness. So, Step 7 is about sustainability. Before withdrawing, some more questions need to be asked: Have we promoted occupations that have a future within the community's context? Have we raised expectations we could not fulfill? And, if so, how will we rectify the situation? Is there adequate follow-up? Have we evaluated the process, outcomes and impacts? And with the right interactive, culturally appropriate tools?

So, we now end up with an occupational process that spans the whole continuum, from needs assessments and mobilization to community monitoring and maintenance, with carefully selected occupations fostering dignity, self-discovery, solidarity, leadership building and collective inquiry. At pivotal moments, occupations can also contribute to the lessening of power differentials and the galvanizing of vulnerable groups. Throughout, these occupations weave a stronger social fabric that will sustain the community in the long run.

19.5 Conclusion

Community development has not been a traditional venue for occupational therapists, and this is puzzling given the fact we bring to it not only the power of occupation, but also a robust client-centered approach. Our holistic vision and our focus on social justice and what is truly meaningful for a community positions us remarkably well in the field. Be it with individuals or communities, our key roles subsist. Working from a strength-based perspective we first enable—accompanying the community group in its quest for meaning and helping give it shape. We open new occupational horizons, revealing unexplored avenues. We act as connectors, creating or strengthening networks that will embolden vulnerable communities. We put our power in the service of the community, an additional lever towards autonomy and dignity. Community development is in fact the perfect arena for expressing our traditional roles: the client is plural, but the methods and principles so fundamental to occupational therapy stay unchanged.

19.5.1 The Last, Silent Step

Finally, we reach the last silent step: reflecting on our involvement with the community. It is tempting to ask ourselves the wrong question: How will we be remembered? It is far more challenging to ask the right question: Have we learned and grown enough with this community to give more and better to the next one? In my experience, if we truly enable communities without taking center stage, people quickly forget our contribution, as it should be. It is the community and its local, positive leaders who over time put in the efforts despite drudgery and obstacles. They deserve the credit. They deserve the limelight. We should remain in the background, observing how the community comes of age and controls its own destiny. Our work is done and the relationship gradually morphs into something akin to friendship. With some communities, connections are closely maintained. With others, when life brings us back into their fold, it is as if we had never left: we get the warm welcome they bestow unto a friend, but not on a hero, which we were never meant to be in the first place.

Before embarking on the shared journey of community-building, we need to ponder what our motivations and expectations are: the savior complex, this need to own the community's destiny rather than simply enabling it, has endangered many a community and cultivating modest sources of gratification appears to be the healthier choice. Rachel Naomi Remen's words best capture a simple, safe and sound reason for doing community building: "It's about touching the lives that touch mine in a way that makes a difference" (Remen 2000, p.274). Nothing more. Nothing less.

References

Barrett, H. R. (1997). Women, occupation and health in rural Africa: Adaptation to a changing socioeconomic climate. *Journal of Occupational Science: Australia, 4*, 5–16.

Carr, M., & Hartl, M. (2010). *Lightening the load*. London: International Fund for Agricultural Development (IFAD)/Practical Action Publishing Ltd.

Cutchin, M. P., & Dickie, V. A. (2012). Transactionalism: Occupational science and the pragmatic attitude. In G. Whiteford & C. Hocking (Eds.), *Critical perspectives on occupational science: Society, inclusion, participation* (pp. 23–37). London: Wiley.

Fisher, G. (2008). A model of occupational empowerment for marginalized populations in community environments. *Occupational Therapy in Health Care, 22*, 55–71.

Kronenberg, F., & Pollard, N. (2005). Overcoming occupational apartheid: A preliminary exploration of the political nature of occupational therapy. In F. Kronenberg, S. Algado, & N. Pollard (Eds.), *Occupational therapy without borders: Learning from the spirit of survivors* (pp. 58–86). Edinburgh: Elsevier/Churchill Livingstone.

Polatajko, H. J., Milke, D., Baptiste, S., Doble, S., Caron-Santha, J., Kirsh, B., et al. (2007). Occupational science: Imperatives for occupational therapy. In E. Townsend & H. Polatajko (Eds.), *Enabling occupation 2007* (pp. 63–86). Ottawa: CAOT Publication ACE.

Remen, R. N. (2000). *My grandfather's blessings*. New York: Rivermead Books.

SAS² website. (2011). *From community-based research, organizational learning, project planning and evaluation to public engagement*. Accessed 4 Aug 2011 at http://www.sas2.net/

Townsend, E., & Wilcock, A. (2004). Occupational justice and client-centered practice: A dialogue in progress. *Canadian Journal of Occupational Therapy, 71*, 75–87.

Chapter 20
Transactional Perspectives on Occupation: Main Points of Contribution in This Volume

Virginia A. Dickie and Malcolm P. Cutchin

20.1 Introduction

Can a theoretical and philosophical tradition from the late nineteenth and early twentieth century America be relevant to diverse twenty-first century intellectual challenges across the globe? We set out to edit this book knowing that a transactional perspective on occupation and its grounding in the pragmatism of John Dewey had served us well in our own scholarship and believing that this perspective had the potential to inform the global discourse on occupation that has developed in recent years. The chapters in this volume support our assumptions that a transactional perspective can provide a common ground for a wide range of scholarship ranging from understanding occupation with an individual focus to informing population-based studies. Among other contributions, the chapters herein offer substantive use and explanation of key concepts in the transactional perspective, such as embodiment, growth, habits, the situation, sociality, and place integration.

The work in this book supports development of knowledge and theory concerning occupation in a number of ways, including the following:

- It positions occupation as the functional coordination of problematic situations, not as a link between the dualism of person and environment.
- It situates the study of occupation across a continuum from individual meanings to issues of social justice.
- It demonstrates the manner in which a transactional perspective can add to and work with other theoretical perspectives.

V.A. Dickie (✉) • M.P. Cutchin
Department of Allied Health Sciences, Division of Occupational Science and Occupational Therapy, University of North Carolina at Chapel Hill, Chapel Hill, NC, USA
e-mail: virginia_dickie@med.unc.edu

M.P. Cutchin and V.A. Dickie (eds.), *Transactional Perspectives on Occupation*,
DOI 10.1007/978-94-007-4429-5_20, © Springer Science+Business Media B.V. 2013

- It presents a number of research methods and approaches that are useful in examining occupation with a transactional vantage.
- It provides examples in which the construct of transaction can be used to understand complex occupational wholes.

Each of these will be discussed in the following sections.

20.2 Occupation as the Functional Coordination of Problematic Situations

The transactional perspective is funded by core concepts of Deweyan philosophy. Among those is the problematic (indeterminate) situation. Problematic situations are those when change occurs and individual or social habits of thought and behavior prove to be inadequate or ineffective. These may happen when policy changes, as in the practice of school-based occupational and physical therapy (Chap. 11); in immigration circumstances (Chaps. 6, 13); in the classroom (Chaps. 16, 17), in times when life and occupations are disrupted (Chaps. 3, 9); or when societies are disrupted by war or natural disasters (Chaps. 18, 19). The point here is that the necessity for creativity and action is generated within situations of all types and scopes. Such problematic situations include all aspects of the environment/context. In the same way that people exist within situations through occupation, they respond to these situations with occupation. The effect is to re-coordinate the situation with influences that may or may not have benefit for others or the environment. Among other insights, the works in this book suggest that transactional perspectives force one to look beyond the individual action and to the relationship of occupation to society and environment through this process.

20.3 The Study and Understanding of Occupation from Individual to Societal Levels

The chapters in this book demonstrate how a transactional perspective can be used to examine any dimension of occupation from individual experience to community development efforts. While we critiqued the dominant focus on individual experience in earlier publications on this perspective, we never claimed that individual experience was unimportant (Cutchin 2004; Dickie et al. 2006; Cutchin et al. 2006) and the range of topics here extends our position. For example, an immigrant experiences life in her own unique way, as does her daughter (Chap. 6), but these experiences are part of a complex situation of coexisting, but not always compatible, cultures and the immigration experiences of both. In a similar vein, Stone (Chap. 8) explains how individual experience of disability can only be understood in the social, situated context in which it occurs.

While individual experience may be a focus of study, such experience never occurs in isolation: the individual is always in a context. "Dewey (1962) characterized individuality as a product of the associated living that characterizes human experience" (Aldrich and Cutchin Chap. 2), and such embodied associations include other humans and the vast non-human world in which they dwell and transact. Further, population-level concerns about issues such as social justice have become increasingly prominent in the occupational science discourse, and a transactional perspective provides the framework to incorporate that work into the canon.

20.4 Compatibility of Transactional and Other Theoretical Perspectives

A number of authors who responded to the invitation to submit chapters to this book took on the challenge of weaving Deweyan pragmatism into work that was grounded in other theoretical traditions. Heidegger, Bourdieu, Ricoeur, and Foucault all figure in these works (Chaps. 3, 4, 5, 6), and we are excited about the dialogue generated when pragmatism is brought into play. An interesting commonality among those chapters is that although the theoretical viewpoints have important differences, they are able to find useful points of complementarity. Going a step further, we suggest that a transactional perspective is certainly not compatible with every theory of human behavior (for example, the classical or operant conditioning in behaviorism), but there are certainly many (and other) theoretical perspectives with which it can have a conversation. The analyses provided in this book should serve additional explorations and syntheses of transactional and other perspectives on occupation. Those using transactional perspectives can serve as teachers and students in such efforts.

20.5 Varied Research Methods for a Transactional Perspective on Occupation

A transactional perspective does not prescribe a research methodology. Relevant data may be found in many sources and accessed in many ways. In part, methods are chosen based on the questions of concern and the scale of the study. The transactional perspective on occupation is holistic and acknowledges complexity and uncertainty, but research is necessarily bounded by topic and time. Thus investigators will define a scope for their inquiry and determine the best methods for achieving their research goals. As in any research, attention to methods is critical and research results must clearly present the methods and the rationale for their use.

The contributions of authors who took up the issue of methods in this book (Chaps. 12, 13, 14, 15) provide an intriguing diversity of arguments that pertain to what transactional perspectives imply for methodological options. While the skew is toward qualitative methods, Heatwole Shank (Chap. 15) offers an argument for mixed methods that also moves beyond existing literature on the topic. That innovation is echoed in Chaps. 12 and 13 where the transactional unit of analysis and the transactional nature of ethnography are examined in novel ways. Rudman (Chap. 14) suggests critical discourse analysis as a way to remain true to the situational focus of transactional perspectives but add an important critical/power component. Contributors have built important new bridges between transactional theory and methods. These contributions were badly needed in the literature on transactional perspectives on occupation.

20.6 Complex Occupational Wholes Viewed as Transactions

A transactional perspective can encapsulate occupations and situations at any level. For example, from a transactional vantage, examination of therapeutic practice may focus on the therapist-client relationship and treatment activities, but it could also look at practice in a broader perspective to include institutional structures, policies, and productivity expectations. The men's shed in Wicks' account (Chap. 10) is understood to include church decisions about property, types of work done in the shed, properties of the work such as saw dust, local needs for manufactured products, internal politics, conditions of being retired from the work force, and so forth. Likewise, home modification experiences are examined in Chap. 9 as integrative processes that entail older adults, landlords, apartments, providers, and policy makers. Chapters 18 and 19 offer an even broader view of the complex situations that organizations and individuals enter in order to support occupation. Assuming a transactional perspective gives one the option of larger or smaller scale understanding of occupation.

20.7 Conclusion

In the introductory chapter to this volume we expressed our discomfort with the notion of a transactional perspective as transactional*ism*, a position we assert again here. We have found the notion of transaction to be extremely helpful for addressing the complexity of occupation, not so much as a rigid philosophical and theoretical basis, but rather as a way to more perceptively and creatively view the phenomena that are variously labeled *occupation*. Dewey suggested that ideas were "proleptic" (anticipatory in function; suggesting possibilities) and to be used as tools for inquiry into worldly affairs, not as pre-figured answers to problems (Boisvert 1998). There is much to digest in the work of John Dewey, and much of his version of pragmatism may be fruitful for occupational science, but it is the usefulness of this work that we applaud, rather than seeing it as setting forth any sort of dogma to be followed. Thus, we urge readers to think about the implications of a transactional perspective on the way they view occupation, the manner in which it is studied, and the extent to which it captures the whole of occupation rather than looking for it as an explicit guide for their scholarship.

This book has taken shape in ways that we could not have predicted. We started with an ends-in-view to edit a scholarly book that extended the arguments we began in earlier work introducing and developing our ideas of transaction (Cutchin 2004; Dickie et al. 2006; Cutchin et al. 2008). The authors who responded to our call for proposals did just that—many building on work conceptualized and completed from different theoretical traditions—and in doing so demonstrating the potential for the transactional perspective. We hope this book will be an inspiration to continue this project, building the body of knowledge on situated occupation and applying that knowledge to the good of our planet and those who inhabit it.

References

Boisvert, R. D. (1998). *John Dewey: Rethinking our time*. Albany: State University of New York.

Cutchin, M. P. (2004). Using Deweyan philosophy to rename and reframe adaptation-to-environment. *American Journal of Occupational Therapy, 58*, 303–312.

Cutchin, M. P., Dickie, V., & Humphry, R. (2006). Transaction versus interpretation, or transaction and interpretation? A response to Michael Barber. *Journal of Occupational Science, 13*, 97–99.

Cutchin, M. P., Aldrich, R. M., Bailliard, A., & Coppola, S. (2008). Action theories for occupational science: The contributions of Dewey and Bourdieu. *Journal of Occupational Science, 15*, 157–165.

Dickie, V., Cutchin, M. P., & Humphry, R. (2006). Occupation as transactional experience: A critique of individualism in occupational science. *Journal of Occupational Science, 13*, 83–93.

Index

M.P. Cutchin and V.A. Dickie (eds.), *Transactional Perspectives on Occupation*,
DOI 10.1007/978-94-007-4429-5_7, © Springer Science+Business Media B.V. 2013

The manufacturer's authorised representative in the EU is Springer Nature Customer Service Centre GmbH, Europaplatz 3, 69115 Heidelberg, Germany. If you have any concerns regarding our products, please contact ProductSafety@springernature.com

Printed and bound by CPI Group (UK) Ltd, Croydon, CR0 4YY
30/09/2026
02225505-0009